G.F. HANDEL

GARLAND COMPOSER
RESOURCE MANUALS
(VOL. 19)

GARLAND REFERENCE LIBRARY
OF THE HUMANITIES
(VOL. 717)

GARLAND COMPOSER RESOURCE MANUALS

General Editor: Guy A. Marco

1. *Heinrich Schutz: A Guide to Research* by Allen B. Skei
2. *Josquin Des Prez: A Guide to Research* by Sydney Robinson Charles
3. *Sergei Vasil'evich Rachmaninoff: A Guide to Research* by Robert Palmieri
4. *Manuel de Falla: A Bibliography and Research Guide* by Gilbert Chase and Andrew Budwig
5. *Adolphe Adam and Leo Delibes: A Guide to Research* by William E. Studwell
6. *Carl Nielsen: A Guide to Research* by Mina F. Miller
7. *William Byrd: A Guide to Research* by Richard Turbet
8. *Christoph Willibald Gluck: A Guide to Research* by Patricia Howard
9. *Girolamo Frescobaldi: A Guide to Research* by Frederick Hammond
10. *Stephen Collins Foster: A Guide to Research* by Galvin Elliker
11. *Bela Bartok: A Guide to Research* by Elliott Antokeletz
12. *Antonio Vivaldi: A Guide to Research* by Michael Talbot
13. *Johannes Ockeghem and Jacob Obrecht: A Guide to Research* by Martin Picker
14. *Ernest Bloch: A Guide to Research* by David Z. Kushner
15. *Hugo Wolf: A Guide to Research* by David Ossenkop
16. *Wolfgang Amadeus Mozart: A Guide to Research* by Baird Hastings
17. *Nikolai Andreevich Rimsky-Korsakov: A Guide to Research* by Gerald R. Seaman
18. *Henry Purcell (1658/9–1695): A Guide to Research* by Franklin B. Zimmerman

G.F. Handel
A Guide to Research

Mary Ann Parker-Hale

GARLAND PUBLISHING, INC. • NEW YORK & LONDON
1988

© 1988 Mary Ann Parker-Hale
All rights reserved

Library of Congress Cataloging-in-Publication Data

Parker-Hale, Mary Ann, 1951–.
   G.F. Handel : a guide to research / Mary Ann Parker-Hale.
     p. cm. — (Garland composer resource manuals ; vol. 19)
(Garland reference library of the humanities ; vol. 717)
   Includes index.
   ISBN 0-8240-8452-7 (alk. paper)
   1. Handel, George Frideric, 1685–1759—Bibliography. I. Title.
II. Series. III. Series: Garland composer resource manuals ; v. 19.
ML134.H16P37   1988
780'.92'4—dc19   88-27472
                                                                CIP
                                                                 MN

Printed on acid-free, 250-year-life paper
Manufactured in the United States of America

Portrait of Handel by Balthasar Denner.
Courtesy National Portrait Gallery, London

Garland Composer Resource Manuals

In response to the growing need for bibliographic guidance to the vast literature on significant composers, Garland is publishing an extensive series of research guides. The series, which will most likely appear over a five-year period, encompasses almost 50 composers; they represent Western musical tradition from the Renaissance to the present century.

Each research guide offers a selective, annotated list of writings, in all European languages, about one or more composers. There are also lists of works by the composers, unless these are available elsewhere. Biographical sketches and guides to library resources, organizations, and specialists are presented. As appropriate to the individual composers, there are maps, photographs, or other illustrative matters, and glossaries and indexes.

CONTENTS

Preface xi

Acknowledgments xiii

Abbreviations xv

I. Background 3

    1. General History 3
    2. Music of the Period 6
    3. Aesthetics, Art, Literature, and Musical Thought 9
    4. Music and Cultural Life in England 17
    5. Music and Cultural Life in Germany 25
    6. Music and Cultural Life in Italy 28

II. Handel's Life and His Works in General 31

    1. Eighteenth-Century Handel Biographies 31
    2. Biographies, Comprehensive Studies, and Collections of Essays 38
    3. Studies of Particular Biographical Issues 48

III. Sources 67

    1. Catalogues 68
    2. General Studies on Sources 71
    3. Special Studies of the Sources 74
    4. Compositional Method and Borrowings 88

IV.	List of Handel's Works	103
	1. Works-Lists, Catalogues, and Collected Editions	103
	2. Vocal Music	
	Operas	107
	Oratorios	111
	Odes and Serenatas	112
	English Pastorals, Masques, Music Dramas, and Theater Music	112
	Chamber Cantatas	113
	Songs and Arias	117
	Latin and Italian Sacred Music	117
	German Church Music	118
	English Church Music	118
	3. Instrumental Music	
	Orchestral Concertos	120
	Solo Concertos	121
	Sonatas for Solo Instrument with Continuo	121
	Trio Sonatas	122
	Overtures, Sinfonias, and Suites	123
	Keyboard Music	123
	Music for Musical Clock	125
V.	Studies of Handel's Music	127
	1. General Studies of the Music	127
	2. Operas	131
	3. Oratorios	155
	4. Odes and Serenatas	170
	5. English Pastorals, Masques, Music Dramas, and Theater Music	173
	6. Vocal Chamber Music	178
	7. Church Music	185
	8. Instrumental Music	195

Contents

VI. Performance Practice and the Performance Tradition	211
1. Performance Practice	211
2. Modern Performances	232
3. The Handel Tradition: Reputation and Practice	239
Bibliographies and Bibliographic Essays	263
Discographies	265
Handel Societies	267
Handel Archive	267
Newsletters and Journals	269
Reviews of Hallische Händel-Ausgabe *Editions*	271
Index of Handel's Works	275
Index of Names	281
Index of Authors	287

PREFACE

Preparing a guide to the vast literature on George Frideric Handel (1685–1759) seems a daunting task. Even during his lifetime he was scrutinized in print in his native Germany, and the English Handel literature, beginning in earnest only one year after his death, has flourished virtually continuously until the present day. And yet, a survey of the general picture of Handel research over the past two centuries reveals a clear pattern; except for the magnificent accomplishments of Friedrich Chrysander (1826–1901) and the nineteenth-century biographies of Victor Schoelcher and a few others, most of the significant achievements have been made during the past three decades. Doubtless there are many reasons for this anomaly, among them the fact that German musicologists of the late nineteenth and early twentieth centuries seemed more interested in Johann Sebastian Bach than his more cosmopolitan contemporary. And it may also be that scholars were inspired by the pioneering works of Otto Erich Deutsch, whose documentary biography appeared in 1955, and Winton Dean, whose comprehensive study of the dramatic oratorios and masques was issued in 1959.

In any case, the items in the present volume reflect a significant emphasis on recent writings. Publications that appeared after 1985 are not included, except for a very few particularly important items. The author emphasizes that the listings are selective, rather than comprehensive. Program notes, speeches and books or articles of a popular nature are rarely included. Apologies must be made in advance for the inevitable cases where scholarly works have been overlooked, in spite of best efforts to find everything. In a few cases, items have not been examined, but have been included with a note to that effect.

In the annotations themselves, the author has tried to indicate which items are indispensable, which come to questionable conclusions, which have been disputed, etc. Because the first chapter covers a wide variety of subjects, not all of which are among the author's specialties, its annotations are somewhat less detailed than those of the remaining chapters.

Certain portions of this book, for example the works-list, are offered as convenient check-lists. The list of reviews of HHA volumes provides a unique guide to these concise and revealing sources of information.

Because a number of recent books and essays have summarized the latest discoveries in Handel biography, it seemed unnecessary to provide a biographical introduction. Most of the individual chapters contain brief introductions to the literature discussed therein.

For definitions, studies of genres, and information on composers and other musical personalities, the reader is advised to consult the twenty-volume *New Grove Dictionary of Music and Musicians*, edited by Stanley Sadie (London: Macmillan Publishers Ltd., 1980).

Mary Ann Parker-Hale

Toronto

October, 1987

ACKNOWLEDGMENTS

It is a pleasure to acknowledge the assistance of numerous friends and colleagues. The staff of the Edward Johnson Music Library, and in particular Suzanne Meyers Sawa, Kathleen McMorrow and Lawrence Beckwith, were tireless in their efforts to locate materials and answer pesky questions. The people at the University of Toronto Inter-Library Loan Department, and especially Jane Lynch, were unfailingly helpful. Bryan Martin assisted energetically with a few aspects of the research. The Humanities and Social Sciences Committee of the University of Toronto Research Board provided financial support. William R. Bowen's technical and scholarly expertise was crucial to the preparation of the manuscript. Most of all, the author wishes to thank Alfred Mann for his guidance and moral support.

ABBREVIATIONS

HG	*G.F. Händels Werke: Ausgabe der Deutschen Händelgesellschaft.* Vols. 1–48; 50–96; suppl. 1–6. Ed. Friedrich Chrysander. Leipzig: Breitkopf und Härtel; Bergedorf bei Hamburg: by the editor, 1858–94, 1902; reprint ed., 1965.
HHA	*Hallische Händel-Ausgabe im Auftrage der Georg Friedrich Händel-Gesellschaft.* In progress. Ed. Max Schneider, Rudolf Steglich, Walther Siegmund-Schultze and others. Kassel: Bärenreiter, 1955–.
Konferenzbericht Halle (Saale) 1977	*G.F. Händel als Wegbereiter der Wiener Klassik: Bericht über die wissenschaftliche Konferenz zu den 27. Händelfestspielen der DDR in Halle (Saale) am 24. und 25. Juni 1977.* Wissenschaftliche Beiträge 1977/39, G4. Halle (Saale): Martin Luther Universität, 1977.
Konferenzbericht Halle (Saale) 1979	*G.F. Händel und seine Italienischen Zeitgenossen: Bericht über die wissenschaftliche Konferenz zu den 27. Händel festspielen der DDR in Halle (Saale) am 5. und 6. Juni 1978.* Wissenschaftliche Beiträge 1979/8, G5. Halle (Saale): Martin Luther Universität, 1979.

ABBREVIATIONS

Konferenzbericht
Halle (Saale) 1980

Fragen der Aufführungspraxis und Interpretation Händelscher Werke in Vergangenheit und Gegenwart: Bericht über die wissenschaftliche Konferenz zu den 28. Händelfestspielen am 11. und 12. Juni 1979. Wissenschaftliche Beiträge 1980/7, G6. Halle (Saale): Martin Luther Universität, 1980.

Konferenzbericht
Halle (Saale) 1981

Anthem, Ode, Oratorium—ihre Ausprägung bei G.F. Händel: Bericht über die wissenschaftliche Konferenz zu den 29. Händelfestspielen der DDR am 16. und 17. Juni 1980. Wissenschaftliche Beiträge 1981/14, G7. Halle (Saale): Martin Luther Universität, 1981.

Konferenzbericht
Halle (Saale) 1982

Probleme der Händelschen Oper (insbesondere am Beispiel "Poro"): Bericht über die wissenschaftliche Konferenz zu den 30. Händelfestspielen der DDR am 15. und 16. Juni 1981. Wissenschaftliche Beiträge 1982/21, G8. Halle (Saale): Martin Luther Universität, 1982.

Konferenzbericht
Halle (Saale) 1983

Thematik und Ideenwelt der Antike bei Georg Friedrich Händel: Bericht über die wissenschaftliche Konferenz zu den 31. Händelfestspielen der DDR am 14. und 15. Juni 1982. Wissenschaftliche Beiträge 1983/24, G10. Halle (Saale): Martin Luther Universität, 1983.

Konferenzbericht
Halle (Saale) 1984

Georg Friedrich Händel im Verständnis des 19. Jahrhundert: Bericht über die wissenschaftliche Konferenz zu den 32. Händelfestspielen der DDR am 13. und 14. Juni 1983. Wissenschaftliche Beiträge 1984/38, G11. Halle (Saale): Martin Luther Universität, 1984.

Abbreviations

RILM *Répertoire internationale de littérature musicale.* v. 1–. 1967–. ISSN 0033-6955.

G.F. HANDEL

APPENDIX

I

BACKGROUND

1. General History

1. Andrieux, Maurice. *Daily Life in Papal Rome in the Eighteenth Century*. Trans. Mary Fitton. London: George Allen and Unwin, 1968. 223p. DG 814 A513.

   Appeared originally in 1962 as *La vie quotidienne dans la Rome pontificale*. Readable account giving general background for Handel's early stay in Rome. Plates, index, bibliography.

2. Carswell, John. *From Revolution to Revolution: England 1688–1776*. London: Routledge & Kegan Paul, 1973. 204p. DA 48 C29. ISBN 0-7100-7608-8.

   Published in the series *The Development of English Society*, it reveals much about the social and political *milieu* in which Handel found himself in England. Chronological Table, index, suggestions for further reading.

3. *Dizionario biografico degli italiani*. vol. 1–. Rome: Instituto della enciclopedia italiano, 1960–. DG 463 D5.

   Offers detailed biographical articles on Italian personalities. Lists sources and bibliographic references. Volume 32, published in 1986, is still at the beginning of letter "D."

3

BACKGROUND

4. Erdmannsdörffer, Bernhard. *Deutsche Geschichte vom westfälischen Frieden bis zum Regierungsantritt Friedrichs des Großen 1648–1740*. 2 vols. Berlin: G. Grote, 1892–93. Repr. Darmstadt: Wissenschaftliche Buchgesellschaft, 1974. 690, 472p. DD 190 E7. ISBN 3-534-01155-4.

The classic work on the subject. Dense, without index. Published in Fraktur.

5. Fauchier-Magnan, Adrien. *The Small German Courts in the Eighteenth Century*. Trans. Mervyn Savill. London: Methuen, 1958. 292p. DD 193 F313.

First published in 1947 as *Les petite cours d'Allemagne au XVIIIème siècle*, it features a general first section entitled "Germany after the Peace of Westphalia" and then focuses on the Duchy of Württemberg. Index, bibliography, plates.

6. Holborn, Hajo. *A History of Modern Germany*, vol. 2. New York: Knopf, 1964. 557p. DD 175 H62 v. 2.

This second volume deals with the period 1648–1840, giving a general historical background and including a chapter entitled "Religious, Intellectual, and Artistic Life in the Age of the Baroque." Index, maps.

7. Owen, John B. *The Eighteenth Century 1714–1815*. A History of England, 6. London: Thomas Nelson and Sons, 1974. 365p. DA 480 09 1974. ISBN 0-17-711050-3.

Emphasizes political and economic developments. Index, suggestions for further reading.

8. Plumb, John H. *The First Four Georges*. London: Hamlyn Publishing Group, 1974. 208p. DA 480 P55 1974. ISBN 0-600-38702-X.

The text was originally published as an unassuming monograph in 1956. The current edition is lavishly illustrated in the manner of a "coffee-table book." Gives a strong feeling of the eighteenth-century English *milieu*. Index, bibliography.

General History 5

9. Quazza, Guido. "L'Italia e l'Europa durante le guerre di successione." In *Storia d'Italia*, vol. 2, pp. 779–931. 2nd ed. Turin: Unione Tipografico, 1965. DG 467 S76.

   Gives background on early eighteenth-century Italy. Plates, maps, bibliographic note.

10. Schumann, Reinhold. *Italy in the Last Fifteen Hundred Years: A Concise History*. Lanham, Maryland: University Press of America, 1986. 397p. DG 467 S38. ISBN 0–8191–5628–0.

    Accessible summary of background history. Chapter 12 is of particular interest for Handelians. Chronology, reading lists, index.

11. Scott, Arthur Finlay. *The Early Hanoverian Age, 1714–60*. London: Croom Helm, 1980. 175p. DA 485 S35. ISBN 0–7099–0145–3.

    Collects contemporary commentary on a variety of issues from royalty, sports, religion, social life, etc., to the arts. Plates.

12. Sinclair-Stevenson, Christopher. *Blood Royal: The Illustrious House of Hanover*. London: Jonathan Cape, 1979. 227p. DA 480 S675. ISBN 0–224–01477–3.

    Exuberant and readable history. Plates, index.

13. Turberville, A.S., ed. *Johnson's England: An Account of the Life and Manners of His Age*. 2 vols. Oxford: Clarendon Press, 1933. Repr. 1952, 1965. 405, 404p. DA 485 T77.

    Assemblage of essays by experts on numerous aspects of life in eighteenth-century England, including travel, London, poverty, costume, taste, music, etc. Index, plates.

14. Vaussard, Maurice. *Daily Life in Eighteenth-Century Italy*. Trans. Michael Heron. London: George Allen & Unwin, 1962. 218p. DG 447 V313.

    First appeared in 1959 as *La vie quotidienne en Italie au XVIIIe siècle*. General background under the headings "The Background," "Society, Morals and Manners," "Holidays and

Entertainments," and "Economic Life." Plates, bibliography, index.

2. Music of the Period

15. Abraham, Gerald, ed. *Concert Music 1630–1750.* New Oxford History of Music, 6. London: Oxford University Press, 1986. 786p. ML 160 N44 v. 6. ISBN 0–19–316306–3.

    Packed with information about Handel and his contemporaries, including long sections on ode and oratorio in England (Rosamond McGuinnes, Anthony Hicks, Gerald Abraham) and on solo song and vocal duet (especially the Italy and Germany sections by Hans Joachim Marx). The various instrumental genres are covered in detail. Musical examples, bibliography, index.

16. Braun, Werner. *Die Musik des 17. Jahrhunderts.* Neues Handbuch der Musikwissenschaft, 4. Wiesbaden: Akademische Verlagsgesellschaft Athenaion, 1981. 385p. ML 160 B684. ISBN 3–7997–0746–8.

    Offers a clear, up-to-date summary of seventeenth-century music by a top-notch scholar. Well organized and indexed. Lavishly illustrated. Glossary. Reading list after each chapter.

17. Bukofzer, Manfred F. *Music in the Baroque Era, from Monteverdi to Bach.* New York: Norton, 1947. 489p. ML 193 B8.

    Much of the historical information has been superseded, but it is still worth reading. Offers a revealing discussion of Handel's choral style. Survey, followed by chapters on Form, Musical Thought, and Sociology of Baroque music. Musical examples, index, bibliography, "Checklist of Baroque Books on Music," plates.

18. Dahlhaus, Carl, ed. *Die Musik des 18. Jahrhunderts.* Neues Handbuch der Musikwissenschaft, 5. Laaber: Laaber-

Music of the Period 7

Verlag, 1985. 434p. ML 195 M97 1985. ISBN 3-89007-035-5.

Prepared in collaboration with Sigrid Wiesmann, Ludwig Finscher and others, this volume is one of the most up-to-date treatments of eighteenth-century music. Provides a survey from about 1720 to about 1814, in which Handel's music is examined free from the strait-jackets of "Baroque" and "Classic." Reading lists at ends of chapters, examples, illustrations, indexes, glossary.

19. Fuller Maitland, J.A. *The Age of Bach and Handel.* The Oxford History of Music, 4. Oxford: Clarendon Press, 1902. 362p. ML 160 088 1901 v. 4.

Of course the information is outdated, but it is worth reading for the special insights of the author. The chapter on Latin Church Music, for example, is informed by his knowledge of many still unpublished Italian works in British libraries. Musical examples, index.

20. Heriot, Angus. *The Castrati in Opera.* London: Secker & Warburg, 1956. Repr. New York: Da Capo, 1974. 243p. ML 400 H47. ISBN 0-306-70650-4.

Chapter on the theatrical conditions concentrates on Italy, but gives a colorful impression of Italian opera everywhere in the eighteenth century. Biographical information on many of Handel's singers. Bibliography, general index.

21. Lewis, Anthony and Nigel Fortune, eds. *Opera and Church Music 1630-1750.* New Oxford History of Music, 5. London: Oxford University Press, 1975. 869p. ML 160 N44 v. 5. ISBN 0-19-316305-5.

Extensive essays, densely packed with useful information, by various experts. Especially useful in this volume are the chapters on Italian opera 1700-1750 (Hellmuth Christian Wolff) and opera in England and Germany (Jack A. Westrup). Chapters on church music in England, Germany and Italy are also germane. Generous musical examples, plates, bibliography, index.

22. Lindgren, Lowell. "The Baroque Era." In *Schirmer History of Music*, pp. 299–456. New York: Schirmer, 1982. ML 160 S32. ISBN 0–02–872190–X.

    Offers a clear, informed survey directed to beginners. Many illustrations and examples. Bibliographic notes and lists of scores at the end of each section. Index.

23. Montagu, Jeremy. *The World of Baroque and Classical Musical Instruments*. London: David & Charles, 1979. 136p. ML 465 M65. ISBN 0–7153–7593–8.

    Lucid text, 101 plates, bibliography, index.

24. Palisca, Claude. *Baroque Music*. 2nd edition. Englewood Cliffs, New Jersey: Prentice-Hall, 1981. 300p. ML 193 P34 1981. ISBN 0–13–055954–7.

    The best modern treatment. Surveys the period, displaying an especially fine understanding of Italian music. Generous musical examples, including a few entire pieces. "Bibliographic Notes" at the end of each chapter. Index.

25. Strohm, Reinhard. "Italienische Opernarien des frühen Settecento." *Analecta Musicologica* 16 (1976): 1–268, 1–342.

    Offers a monumental study of Italian opera arias in the crucial decade of the 1720's. Part One begins with examinations of individual arias by such composers as Francesco Gasparini, Johann Adolph Hasse, Nicola Porpora, Alessandro Scarlatti and Leonardo Vinci, and continues with detailed studies of text, accompaniment, parody procedures, etc. Part Two contains 114 musical examples, many of complete arias, as well as comprehensive detailed catalogues of the operatic works of 31 composers. Includes catalogue of pasticcios, overview of opera repertoire in Naples and Rome from 1707 to 1734, bibliography and indexes.

26. Talbot, Michael. "The Concerto Allegro in the Early Eighteenth Century." *Music and Letters* 52 (1971): 8–18, 159–72.

Aesthetics

Investigates with revealing results the structure of concerto fast movements, dealing with Albinoni and Corelli in the first part, and Torelli and Vivaldi in the second.

3. Aesthetics, Art, Literature, and Musical Thought

27. Artz, Frederick B. *From the Renaissance to Romanticism: Trends in Style in Art, Literature and Music, 1300–1830.* Chicago: University of Chicago Press, 1962. 311p. N 6350 A7.

   Attempts to relate the arts in a historical framework. The section on Baroque art is weakened by the lack of illustrations, and the music section betrays a lack of understanding in some areas. The essay on Baroque literature provides useful background. Bibliography, index of names.

28. Bate, Walter Jackson. *From Classic to Romantic: Premises of Taste in Eighteenth-Century England.* Cambridge: Harvard University Press, 1946. Repr. New York: Harper, 1961. 197p. BH 221 G7 B36.

   Originally presented as the Lowell Lectures in 1945. Readable account of the growth of rationalistic philosophy in the seventeenth and eighteenth century and the subsequent advance of empiricism. Theories of poetry can be applied to Handel's English librettos. English taste begins to favour "original genius" by the 1740s.

29. Blunt, Anthony, ed. *Baroque and Rococo Architecture and Decoration.* London: Paul Elek, 1978. 352p. NA 590 B37 1978. ISBN 0-236-40062-2.

   Offers the dimensions of a "coffee-table book" with informed commentary. Glossary, 429 plates, bibliography, index.

30. Buelow, George J. "Johann Mattheson and the Invention of the *Affektenlehre.*" In *New Mattheson Studies,* pp. 393–407. Ed. George J. Buelow and Hans Joachim Marx. Cambridge:

Cambridge University Press, 1983. ML 55 M327 N5 1983. ISBN 0-521-25115-X.

Rejects the notion that there was a comprehensive "system" called the Doctrine of the Affections in the Baroque period. Offers an informed and objective summary of what Mattheson actually said on the subject.

31. _____. "Music, Rhetoric and the Concept of the Affections: A Selective Bibliography." *Notes* 30 (1973-74): 250-59.

Lists primary and secondary sources that contain significant material on rhetorical principles in music. Includes sections designed to introduce students of music to non-musical works on rhetoric and oratory.

32. _____. "Rhetoric and Music." *New Grove Dictionary of Music and Musicians*. Ed. Stanley Sadie. London: Macmillan, 1980. Vol. 15, pp. 793-803. ML 100 G8863. ISBN 0-333-23111-2.

Presents an extensive discussion, including background on interrelationships between music and the spoken arts, theoretical discussions, musical examples showing musical figures, and a sensible discussion of the Affections.

33. Burt, Nathaniel. "Opera in Arcadia." *Musical Quarterly* 41 (1955): 145-70.

Investigates the origins of Metastasian opera reform. Plates.

34. Dammann, Rolf. *Der Musikbegriff in deutschen Barock*. Cologne: Arno Volk, 1987. 523p. ML 275.3 D34.

Treats theoretical and philosophical concepts of music in the Baroque era, with an emphasis on German sources. Plates, muusical examples, bibliography.

35. Darenberg, Karlheinz. *Studien zur englischen Musikaesthetik des 18. Jahrhunderts*. Hamburg: Cram, de Gruyter & Co., 1960. 130p. ML 286.3 D37.

Aesthetics 11

In the first part, presents excerpts from thirty-four English writers on aesthetics, and particularly the theory of imitation, in music. The discussion in the second part deals occasionally with Handel in particular (pp. 63–67). Bibliography.

36. Dobrée, Bonamy. *English Literature in the Early Eighteenth Century, 1700–1740.* Oxford: Clarendon Press, 1959. 701p. PR 445 D62.

    Contains chapters on "Critics and Aestheticians" and "The Drama", as well as poetry, novels, etc. Index, bibliography, chronological table.

37. Fassini, Serto. "Paolo Rolli contro il Voltaire." *Giornale storico della letteratura italiana* 49 (1907): 83–99.

    Discusses Rolli's response to Voltaire's *Essay upon the Epic Poetry of All the European Nations from Homer down to Milton* (1727).

38. Foss, Michael. *The Age of Patronage: The Arts in Society 1660–1750.* London: Hamish Hamilton, 1971. 234p. NX 705.5 G7 F6. ISBN 241-01971-0.

    Provocative and informed look at the arts and society in England during Handel's period, and especially at the fundamental changes in which he played a significant role. Illustrations, index.

39. Gay, Peter. *The Enlightenment: An Interpretation.* New York: W.W. Norton, 1977. 555p. B 802 G3 1977. ISBN 0-393-00870-3.

    Supplies background for the philosophical thought of the eighteenth century. Last part is an extended bibliographical essay. First published in 1966. Index, bibliography.

40. Hagstrum, Jean. *The Sister Arts: The Tradition of Literary Pictorialism and English Poetry from Dryden to Gray.* Chicago: University of Chicago Press, 1958. 337p. PR 445 H3.

Offers profound ideas on English poetry which may well be related to the style of Handel's settings. Index, plates.

41. Harris, John. *The Palladians.* London: Trefoil Books, 1981. 132p. NA 1123 P2 H36. ISBN 0-86294-001-X.

    Reproduces drawings from the Royal Institute of British Architects collection. Shows English buildings created in imitation of Andrea Palladio between about 1615 to 1750. Introduction, index.

42. Hazard, Paul. *The European Mind (1680–1715).* Trans. J. Lewis May. London: Hollis & Carter, 1953. 454p. D 273.5 H32.

    Originally published in 1935 as *La crise de la conscience européenne (1680–1715)* (3 vols.). Offers a revealing survey of European thought during the period in which Handel's own ideas were formed. Includes a chapter entitled "Laughter and Tears: Opera Triumphant." Index.

43. _____. *European Thought in the Eighteenth Century.* Trans. J. Lewis May. Cleveland: Meridian, 1963. 490p. B 802 H313.

    Includes chapters on "The World of Letters and Ideas," "Sentiment" and "The Feelings." Index. Originally published in 1946 as *La pensée européene au XVIIIème siècle* (3 vols.).

44. Hempel, Eberhard. *Baroque Art and Architecture in Central Europe.* Trans. Elisabeth Hempel and Marguerite Kay. Harmondsworth: Penguin Books, 1965. 370p. N 6410 H453.

    Gives an idea of Handel's surroundings in Germany, with chapters on painting, sculpture and architecture. Plates, maps, index, bibliography.

45. Hollander, John. *The Untuning of the Sky: Ideas of Music in English Poetry, 1500–1700.* Princeton: Princeton University Press, 1961. 467p. ML 3849 H54.

Aesthetics

Includes discussions of Dryden's 1687 St. Cecilia's Day odes and *Alexander's Feast*, both set by Handel. Index, bibliography.

46. Jensen, H. James. *The Muses' Concord*. Bloomington: Indiana University Press, 1976. 255p. NX 451.5 B3 J46 1976. ISBN 0-253-33945-6.

    Discusses aesthetic theories and especially frames of reference common to all the arts during the Baroque period. Particularly useful are the two chapters on rhetorical theory and one entitled "Passions, Rhetoric and Characterization." Illustrations. Index of names. Useful bibliographic references.

47. Le Huray, Peter and James Day, eds. *Music and Aesthetics in the Eighteenth and Early Nineteenth Centuries*. Cambridge: Cambridge University Press, 1981. 597p. ML 3845 M97. ISBN 0-521-23426-3.

    Presents very short excerpts in English translation from a wide variety of original sources. Each is introduced with a few concise paragraphs of background material. Contains Harris' *Three Treatises* (1744) and Avison's *Essay* (1752), but the excerpts are much shorter than in item 49. There are a number of other passages relevant to Handel; see the detailed index. Bibliography.

48. Lipking, Lawrence. *The Ordering of the Arts in Eighteenth-Century England*. Princeton: Princeton University Press, 1970. 503p. NX 543 L56. ISBN 0-691-06177-7.

    Focuses on painting, music, and poetry, with good sections on English music criticism. Plates.

49. Lippman, Edward, ed. *Musical Aesthetics: A Historical Reader*, vol. 1. Aesthetics in Music, 4. New York: Pendragon, 1986. 430p. ML 3845 M975 1986. ISBN 0-918728-41-X (v. 1).

    Presents excerpts in English from writings on musical aesthetics from antiquity to 1800. Of special interest is the section from Avison's *Essay on Musical Expression* (1752), which discusses several Handel examples. Annotated list of authors; index. Short bibliography after each section.

50. Lonsdale, Roger, ed. *Dryden to Johnson.* History of Literature in the English Language, 4. London: Barrie & Jenkins, 1971. 445p. PR 437 L6. ISBN 0-214-65148-7.

   Includes essays by various scholars on Dryden, Pope, Poetry 1700-40, Drama from 1710 to 1780, Fielding and Smollett, etc. Index, bibliography.

51. Mann, Alfred. *The Study of Fugue.* New York: W.W. Norton and Company, 1965. 339p. ML 448 M25.

   First published in 1958, it presents a history of fugal theory, emphasizing the vitality of Baroque ideas on fugue. Offers substantial excerpts in translation from four eighteenth-century treatises. Musical examples, index, bibliography.

52. Paulson, Ronald. *Hogarth: His Life, Art and Times.* 2 vols. New Haven: Yale University Press, 1971. 558, 557p. ND 497 H7 P38. ISBN 0-300-01388-4.

   Comprehensive critical biography of the artist, loaded with beautiful plates. Reveals much about Handel's English surroundings. Index.

53. Raynor, Henry. *A Social History of Music from the Middle Ages to Beethoven.* London: Barrie and Jenkins, 1972. 373p. ML 3795 R4. ISBN 0-214-65783-3.

   Offers an interesting chapter on England during the seventeenth and eighteenth century, but the Handel chapter is little more than biographical. Useful "Note on currencies." Index, bibliography.

54. Rogerson, Brewster. "The Art of Painting the Passions." *Journal of the History of Ideas* 14 (1953): 68-94.

   Offers a survey of the arts in the eighteenth century, showing how the idea of the Affections related to poetry, drama, music, and the visual arts.

* Rudolph, Johanna. "Meine Seele hört im Sehen." *Händel-Jahrbuch* 7-8 (1961-62): 35-67.

Cited below as item 604.

55. Segel, Harold B. *The Baroque Poem.* New York: Dutton, 1974. 328p. PN 1221 S4. ISBN 0-525-06118-5.

   An anthology of Baroque poetry from various countries, preceded by a discussion of Baroque literature, poetic theory and style. Bibliography, index.

56. Siegmund-Schultze, Dorothea. "Zur Rezeption der Antike im England der Händelzeit." In *Konferenzbericht Halle (Saale) 1983*, pp. 37-50.

   Marxist interpretation of classical antiquity's influence on English thought. Illuminating comments on Milton, Dryden, Pope, and the Earl of Shaftesbury.

* Smith, Ruth. "Intellectual Contexts of Handel's English Oratorios." In *Music in Eighteenth-Century England: Essays in Memory of Charles Cudworth*, pp. 115-33. Ed. Christopher Hogwood and Richard Luckett. Cambridge: Cambridge University Press, 1983. ML 55 C85. ISBN 0-521-23525-1.

   Cited below as item 536.

57. Summerson, John. *Georgian London.* 3rd ed. London: Barrie & Jenkins, 1978. 349p. NA 970 S86. ISBN 0-214-20460-X.

   First published in 1945, it offers an examination of architecture in eighteenth-century London. Some of the buildings Handel worked in are described. Plates, floor plans, index.

58. Tapié, Victor-Lucien. *The Age of Grandeur: Baroque and Classicism in Europe.* London: Weidenfeld and Nicolson, 1957. 305p. N 6410 T313.

   Originally published in 1957 as *Baroque et classicisme.* Accessible summary of Baroque architecture. Numerous plates, including illustrations of London buildings of Handel's time. Index, bibliography.

59. Wittenkower, Rudolf. *Art and Architecture in Italy 1600 to 1750.* Harmondsworth: Penguin Books, 1980. 664p. N 6916 W5 1980. ISBN 0-14-056116-1.

   First published in 1958, it offers a comprehensive chronological survey, generously illustrated. Bibliography, index.

60. Wolff, Hellmuth Christian. "Die Bedeutung der Bilddokumente für die Geschichte der Oper." *Hudební veda* 10/2 (1973): 151-59.

   Discusses the aims of the *Répertoire iconographie de l'opéra*. Shows how pictorial documents can answer questions about an opera, suggesting that manneristic painting influenced the texts and stage scenery of Baroque opera, including Handel's. Not examined.

61. Young, Percy. "Zur Bedeutung von Barock und Rokoko im England des 18. Jahrhunderts." *Händel-Jahrbuch* 17 (1971): 43-48.

   Describes the unique situation in eighteenth-century England vis-à-vis a distinction between Baroque and Rococo styles.

62. _____. "John Dryden: Klassiche Literatur und neue Musik." In *Konferenzbericht Halle (Saale) 1983*, pp. 51-59.

   Shows that Dryden united Classical and Christian ideals and exerted a lasting influence on the intellectual world of Handel's era. Gives a lively account of the poet and his times, then reviews the Handel connections, with references to Milton.

63. Zauft, Karin. "Einige Anmerkungen zur Problematik des Einflußes der englischen Aufklärung auf die musikalische Dramaturgie der Händel-Oper." *Händel-Jahrbuch* 29 (1983): 25-31.

   Demonstrates using examples from *Poro* that Handel moved from the aristocratically based *opera seria* towards the more realistic bourgeois concepts of musical drama favored by Mozart and Beethoven.

64. Zottos, Ion P. "The Completest Concert, or Augustan Critics of Opera: A Documentary and Critical Study in English Aesthetics." Ph.D. dissertation. University of Pennsylvania, 1977. 338p.

    Part I deals with attempts to introduce Italian opera to London, with special reference to Handel's *Rinaldo*. Not examined.

4. Music and Cultural Life in England

65. Baker, C.H. Collins and Muriel I. *The Life and Circumstances of James Brydges, First Duke of Chandos, Patron of the Liberal Arts*. Oxford: Clarendon Press, 1949. 493p. DA 483 C5 B3.

    Provides detailed background to Handel's Cannons period. Plates, index.

66. Bartlett, Ian. "Boyce and Early English Oratorio I." *Musical Times* 120 (1979): 293–97.

    Discusses English oratorios by Maurice Greene, Willem De Fesch and William Boyce, emphasizing Boyce's *David's Lamentation over Saul and Jonathan*. Musical examples.

67. Burnett, Henry. "The Sacred Music of Maurice Greene (1696–1755): A Study of the Problems Confronting the Composer of English Church Music during the Early Eighteenth Century." Ph.D. dissertation. City University of New York, 1978. 566p.

    Traces the decline of English church music after Purcell. Examines Greene's church music. Includes a discussion of Greene's relationship, biographically and musically, to Handel. Not examined.

68. Chapman, Clive. "'Sir, it will not do!' John Rich and Covent Garden's Early Years." *Musical Times* 123 (1982): 831–35.

Discusses the career of the impresario and actor John Rich, the role of incidental music in plays at Covent Garden, and the early seasons there. Plate.

69. Cibber, Colley. *An Apology for the Life of Mr. Colley Cibber, Written by Himself.* 2 vols. Ed. Robert W. Lowe. London: Nimmo, 1889. 337, 416p. PR 3347 A8 1889.

This edition has plates and introductory material, as well as an index. Spirited autobiography tells of London theater life in the early eighteenth century.

70. Daub, Peggy. "Music at the Court of George II (r. 1727–1760)." Ph.D. dissertation. Cornell University, 1985. 398p.

Not examined.

71. Dearnley, Christopher. *English Church Music 1650–1750.* London: Barrie & Jenkins, 1970. 308p. ML 3131 D4. ISBN 257–65787–8.

Offers a readable historical background, discussing conditions in the Chapel Royal, the cathedrals and, to a limited extent, the parishes. Provides a list of composers, including Handel, each with a short biographical note and list of church compositions. Examples, plates, index.

72. Delany, Mary. *Autobiography and Correspondence of Mary Granville, Mrs. Delany.* 6 vols. Ed. *Lady* Llanover. London: Richard Bentley, 1861–62.

Contains a wealth of information on English society and letters fron the correspondence of a great admirer and acquaintance of Handel. Index at the end of the last volume—"Volume 3, second series."

73. Dorris, George. *Paulo Rolli and the Italian Circle in London.* The Hague: Mouton and Co., 1967. 310p. PQ 4731 R2 Z63.

Gives background on Italian literature and literary circles during the early eighteenth century. Offers an entertaining and

England   19

beautifully written survey of Italian opera in England. Includes a critical biography of Rolli, as well as accounts of Antonio Conti, Scipione Maffei, and Antonio Cocchi. Appendix is a checklist of operas produced in London during 1705–44. Bibliography, index.

74. Downes, John. *Roscius Anglicanus, or an Historical Review of the Stage.* London, 1708. Ed. Judith Milhous and Robert D. Hume. London: Society for Theatre Research, 1987. 164p. PN 2592 D6. ISBN 0–85430–043–0.

   This remarkable book gives an account of the London stage from 1660 until the time of writing. Newest edition has authoritative introduction and documentation. Index, bibliography.

75. Elkin, Robert. *The Old Concert-Rooms of London.* London: Edward Arnold Ltd., 1955. 167p. ML 286.8 L5 E44.

   Surveys London's concert rooms and concert halls, including the King's Theatre and the Crown and Anchor Tavern, during the eighteenth and nineteenth centuries. Plates, bibliography, index.

76. Fiske, Roger. *English Theatre Music in the Eighteenth Century.* 2nd ed. Oxford: Oxford University Press, 1986. 684p. ML 1731.3 F58 1986. ISBN 0–19–316409–4.

   From the first page, presents clearly a huge fund of invaluable information on theatres and theatrical practice in Handel's day. Places Handel's stage music in its cultural contexts. Interesting information on *Semele* (pp. 35–38) and the music for *Alceste* (p. 200). Bibliography, general index. Index of all works that survive from 1695 to 1800.

77. Gibson, Elizabeth. "Owen Swiney and the Italian Opera in London." *Musical Times* 125 (1984): 82–86.

   Discusses the Irish impresario's activities after 1713, when he left England. Summarizes his correspondence with the Duke of Richmond during the years 1724–29, when Swiney, then living in Italy, acted as an agent for the Royal Academy of Music.

78. Gooch, Bryan N. "Poetry and Music in England: A Comparison of Styles from 1660 to 1760." Ph.D. dissertation. University of Victoria, 1968. 773p.

Interdisciplinary study including chapters on meaning in music, taste in the era of Pope and Handel, and the divergence of poetry and music. Not examined.

79. Gregg, Edward. *Queen Anne*. Routledge & Kegan Paul, 1980. 483p. DA 495 G73. ISBN 0-7100-0400-1.

Sympathetic and detailed re-telling of the Queen's eventful reign. Plates, bibliography, index.

80. Halton, Ragnhild. *George I, Elector and King*. London: Thames and Hudson, 1978. 416p. DA 501 A2 H4.

Extensive background, numerous illustrations. Bibliography, index.

81. Hervey, John. *Some Materials Toward Memoirs of the Reign of King George II*. 3 vols. Ed. Romney Sedgwick. London, 1931. 1004p. (numbered throughout). DA 501 A3 H47.

Exceedingly spicy memoirs of this intimate of the royal family gives details on the family quarrel that played an important role in the rival opera companies of the 1730s. Alleges that Frederick, Prince of Wales deliberately set out to ruin Handel by supporting the Opera of the Nobility. Index.

82. Highfill, Philip H. et al. *A Biographical Dictionary of Actors, Actresses, Musicians, Dancers, Managers and Other Stage Personnel in London, 1660–1800*. Carbondale: Southern Illinois University Press, 1973–. PN 2596 L6 H57. ISBN 0-8093-0518-6.

At present, ten volumes of this valuable reference tool (up to "Nash, Robert") have appeared. Entries range from the briefest mentions of actors or other personalities to more extensive es-

England

says with pictures of characters about whom more is known. Maps, theater site plans, etc.

83. Hume, Robert D., ed. *The London Theatre World 1660–1800.* Carbondale: Southern Illinois University Press, 1980. 394p. PN 2592 L64. ISBN 0-8093-0926-2.

A collection of twelve essays on various aspects of the London theater. Includes Curtis Price's "Music As Drama," which features discussions of works by Matthew Locke, Henry Purcell, and Thomas Durfey. Musical examples, illustrations, index, bibliography.

84. _____. "Covent Garden Theatre in 1732." *Musical Times* 123 (1982): 823–26.

Describes the original Covent Garden theatre, with details on its early seasons. Plate.

85. Knapp, J. Merrill. "Eighteenth-Century Opera in London before Handel, 1705–1710." In *British Theatre and the Other Arts 1660–1800*, pp. 67–104. Ed. Shirley Strum Kenny. Washington D.C.: Associated University Presses, 1984. PN 2592 B74. ISBN 0-918016-65-7.

Shows that Italian opera was already established in London when Handel arrived. Includes a list of operas performed there between 1705 and 1710. Musical examples.

86. Larsson, Roger B. "Charles Avison's 'Stiles in Musical Expression'." *Music and Letters* 63 (1982): 261–75.

Examines Avison's categorization of expressive styles, especially as it is found in the second edition (1753) of the *Essay on Musical Expression*. Particularly interesting for its evaluation of the influence of Avison's theories.

87. Lindgren, Lowell. "Parisian Patronage of Performers from the Royal Academy of Musick (1719–28)." *Music and Letters* 58 (1977): 4–28.

Outlines plans for producing Italian opera in Paris during the early 1720s. Includes correspondence by Anastasia Robinson, Attilio Ariosti, and Paolo Rolli.

88. Lindgren, Lowell E. "A Bibliographic Scrutiny of Dramatic Works Set by Giovanni and His Brother Antonio Maria Bononcini." Ph.D. dissertation, Harvard University, 1972. 1094p.

    Surveys the Bononicinis' lives and works. Discusses Giovanni's career in London. Focuses on his opera *Il trionfo de Camilla*, including a facsimile of the Naples libretto (1696). Bibliography, works-lists, thematic catalogue. Not examined.

89. *The London Stage 1660–1800*. 11 vols., index. Carbondale: Southern Illinois University Press, 1965–68. PN 2592 L6.

    Comprehensive day-by-day listing of performers in London theatres, including operas. Casts where available. Editorial introductions. Part 2 (1700–29), in two volumes, was edited by Emmett L. Avery. Part 3 (1729–47), in two volumes, was edited by Arthur H. Scouten. Each volume has its own index, and a comprehensive index volume appeared in 1979 (ISBN 0-8093-0907-6).

90. Lord, Phillip. "The English-Italian Opera Companies 1732-3." *Music and Letters* 45 (1964): 239–51.

    Describes attempts by Thomas Arne senior and John Frederic Lampe to establish companies for the production of "English operas, set after the Italian manner." Evaluates the effects on Handel of Arne's *Acis and Galatea* production.

* McGuinness, Rosamond. *English Court Odes 1660–1820*. Oxford: Clarendon Press, 1971. 249p. ML 1631 M2.

    Cited below as item 553.

91. Milhous, Judith and Hume, Robert D. "An Annotated Guide to the Theatrical Documents in PRO LC 7/1, 7/2 and 7/3." *Theatre Notebook* 35 (1981): 25–31.

England

Presents documents from the Lord Chamberlain's records concerning theatrical orders, prohibitions and agreements, etc., especially during the years 1660–1720.

92. Milhous, Judith. *Thomas Betterton and the Management of Lincoln's Inn Fields 1695–1708.* Carbondale: Southern Illinois University Press, 1979. 287p. PN 2598 B6 M54. ISBN 0-8093-0906-8.

Presents a full account of the London theater during this period, including information on the introduction of Italian opera. Aims to show the importance of theater management policy and company history to English drama. Shows also that cut throat competition was a significant factor in the London theater world even before Handel arrived.

93. Millner, Fredrick L. "Hasse and London's Opera of the Nobility." *Music Review* 35 (1974): 240–46.

Estabishes that, although Hasse never visited London in the 1730s, as has sometimes been stated, his music was peformed there, often in pasticcios.

94. Myers, Robert Manson. "Mrs. Delaney: An Eighteenth-Century Handelian." *Musical Quarterly* 32 (1946): 12–36.

Reviews the fascinating history of Mary Granville Pendarves Delany, whose autobiography and correspondence furnish colorful details about Handel and many other aspects of musical life in London for over sixty years. Plate.

95. Nalbach, Daniel. *The King's Theatre 1704–1867.* London: The Society for Theatre Research, 1972. 164p. ML 1731.8 L72 K55. ISBN 0-85430-003-1.

Deals with architectural design, the management, and what the author calls "Artists and Audiences." Reveals details about stage machinery and sets. Index.

96. Nicoll, Allardyce. *A History of Early Eighteenth-Century Drama 1700–1750.* 2nd ed. Cambridge: Cambridge University Press, 1929. 431p. PR 711 N5.

Offers background material on the theatres as well as the dramas. Includes "Hand-list of Plays," with operas included. Index.

97. Price, Curtis. "The Critical Decade for English Music Drama, 1700–1710." *Harvard Library Bulletin* 26 (1978): 38–76.

    Discusses in detail the complex relationships between the growing influence of Italian opera on English musical theater and the power struggles in London theaters of the time.

98. Rinkel, Lawrence S. "The Forms of English Opera: Literary and Musical Responses to a Continental Genre." Ph.D. dissertation. Rutgers University, 1977. 249p.

    Surveys operatic forms in England from Milton (*Comus*) through Handel (*Saul*) to the twentieth century. Argues that English opera is most successful when parodying European conventions. Not examined.

99. Robinson, Michael F. "Porpora's Operas for London, 1733–1736." *Soundings* 2 (1971–72): 57–87.

    Reviews the five operas composed for London by Nicolo Porpora, giving details on sources and librettos, and analyzing arias, recitatives, ensembles, orchestral style and musical unity. Makes specific comparisons with Handel. Musical examples.

100. Rogers, Pat. "The Critique of Opera in Pope's *Dunciad*." *Musical Quarterly* 59 (1973): 15–30.

    Discusses Alexander Pope's allusions to opera, Handel, and his associates. Argues that Pope's awareness of the contemporary operatic scene was greater than has generally been realized.

101. Streatfield, Richard A. "Handel, Rolli and the Italian Opera in London in the Eighteenth Century." *Musical Quarterly* 3 (1917): 428–45.

    Presents material derived from a set of letters of Paolo Rolli, discovered by the author in the Biblioteca Estense at

Modena. Surveys Rolli's role in the London opera scene of Handel's day. Plate.

102. Wolff, Hellmuth Christian. "Eine englische Händel-Parodie: *The Dragon of Wantley* (1737)." *Händel-Jahrbuch* 29 (1983): 43–54.

 Describes an English operatic satire with music by John Frederic Lampe. Musical examples.

103. Young, Percy M. "Die Problematik der Oper in England während der ersten Hälfte des 18. Jahrhundert." In *Konferenzbericht Halle (Saale) 1982*, pp. 7–21.

 Discusses social background of English musical theater. Shows that attempts to reconcile an essentially "grass-roots" tradition with the styles of Italian opera were short-lived compared to that English tradition itself, which survived even in the works of Gilbert and Sullivan. Presents examples by Jeremiah Clarke, Daniel Purcell, Thomas Augustine Arne, J.C. Smith, Johann Ernst Galliard and John Frederick Lampe.

5. Music and Cultural Life in Germany

* Braun, Walter. "Beiträge zu G.F. Händels Jugendzeit in Halle (1685–1703)." *Wissenschaftliche Zeitschrift der Martin-Luther-Universität Halle-Wittenberg* VIII, 4 (1959): 851–62.

 Cited below as item 182.

104. Eckardt, Hans William. "Hamburg zur Zeit Johann Mattheson: Politik, Wirtschaft und Kultur." In *New Mattheson Studies*, pp. 15–44. Ed. George J. Buelow and Hans Joachim Marx. Cambridge: Cambridge University Press, 1983. ML 55 M327 N5. ISBN 0–521–25115–X.

 Offers a comprehensive background for Hamburg in the early eighteenth century. Illustrations.

105. Flemming, Willi. *Deutsche Kultur im Zeitalter des Barocks.* 2nd ed. Handbuch der Kulturgeschichte. Konstanz: Akademische Verlagsgesellschaft Athenaian, 1960. 440p. DD 65 F54 1960.

Lavishly illustrated cultural history of Germany in the seventeenth and early eighteenth centuries, arranged according to general topic. Index, reading lists.

106. Flummerfelt, Joseph R. "Friedrich Wilhelm Zachow: A Study of His Published Church Cantatas and Their Influence upon Handel." DMA dissertation. University of Illinois, 1971. 336p.

Offers biographical and background information on Zachow, as well as an assessment of his influence on Handel's choral style. Not examined.

107. Jaacks, Gisela. "Das öffentliche Musikleben in Hamburg um 1700." In *Händel und Hamburg: Ausstellung anläßlich des 300. Geburtstages von Georg Friedrich Händel*, pp. 11–27. Ed. Hans Joachim Marx. Hamburg: Karl Dieter Wagner, 1985. ML 410 H13 H234. ISBN 3-88979-009-7.

Describes musical institutions in Hamburg during the late seventeenth and early eighteenth centuries. Plates.

108. Marx, Hans Joachim. "Geschichte der Hamburger Barockoper. Ein Forschungsbericht." *Hamburger Jahrbuch für Musikwissenschaft* 3 (1978): 7–34.

Chronicles the history of the Hamburg opera from its founding in 1678 to its closing in 1738. Takes modern research into account. Plate. Bibliography.

* Moser, H.J. *Der junge Händel und seine Vorläufer in Halle.* Der rote Turm, 5. Halle (Saale): Gebauer Schwetschke, 1929.

Cited below as item 232.

Germany

109. Meyer, Reinhart, ed. *Die Hamburger Oper.* 4 vols. Munich: Kraus Reprint, 1980–84. 398, 574, 341, 397p. ML 48 H36. ISBN 3-601-00136-5.

   Offers fascimiles of librettos of operas performed in Hamburg during the years 1678–1730. Includes Handel's *Rinaldo*, as produced there in 1715. Fourth volume contains commentary and bibliography. Index.

110. Rathje, Jürgen. "Zur hamburgischen Gelehrtenrepublik im Zeitalter Matthesons." In *New Mattheson Studies*, pp. 101–24. Ed. George J. Buelow and Hans Joachim Marx. Cambridge: Cambridge University Press, 1983. ML 55 M327 N5 1983. ISBN 0-521-25115-X.

   Offers information on the literary circles of Hamburg, and especially on Johann Albert Fabricius (1668–1736), Johann Hübner (b. 1668), Michael Richey (1678–1761), and Barthold Heinrich Brockes (1680–1747).

111. Serauky, Walter. *Musikgeschichte der Stadt Halle.* 2 vols., suppl. Halle (Saale): Buchhandlung des Waisenhauses, 1935–42. Repr. Hildesheim: Olms, 1971. 362, 585, 650p. ML 279.8 H14 S4.

   Offers a detailed history of music in the city of Handel's birth. Volume one treats the seventeenth century. The first part of volume 2 deals with the Baroque period, while the second part goes up to the nineteenth century. Musical supplements originally published in separate volumes. Index.

112. Sittard, Josef. *Geschichte des Musik- und Concertwesens in Hamburg vom 14. Jahrhundert bis auf die Gegenwart.* Leipzig, 1890. Repr. Hildesheim: Olms, 1971. 392p. ML 283.8 H1955. ISBN 3-487-04010.

   The standard general work on music in Hamburg, but the period of Handel's stay is not covered in any detail. Index.

113. Thomas, Günter. *Friedrich Wilhelm Zachow.* Regensburg: Bosse, 1966. Kölner Beiträge zur Musikforschung, 38. 321p. ML 410 Z33 T5.

Meticulous critical biography of Handel's teacher, with notes on the sources, a catalogue of works and three newly-discovered keyboard works. Handel is mentioned frequently. Bibliography, musical examples, index.

114. Wolff, Hellmuth Christian. *Die Barockoper in Hamburg (1678–1738).* 2 vols. Wolfenbüttel: Möseler, 1957. 416, 212p. ML 1729 H3 W6.

Exhaustive study of the texts and music of operas presented in Hamburg. Bibliography, indexes, plates. Second volume consists entirely of musical examples from pieces by Theile, Franck, Kusser, Keiser, Telemann, and others. Includes Handel's *Almira* and *Ottone* in Telemann's arrangement.

6. Music and Cultural Life in Italy

115. Benzoni, Gino. "Venezia al tempo di Vivaldi." In *Antonio Vivaldi da Venezia all'Europa*, pp. 30–37. Ed. Francesco Degrada and Maria Teresa Muraro. Milan: Electa editrice, 1978. ML 410 V82 A85.

Focuses on the political, economic, and social background to music-making in Venice in the early eighteenth century. Plates.

116. Dent, Edward J. *Alessandro Scarlatti: His Life and Works.* London: Edward Arnold Ltd., 1960. 252p. ML 410 S22 D5 1960.

A reprint of the 1905 classic, with preface and additional notes by Frank Walker. Offers an excellent background to Italy and the vocal genres, enlivened by the author's incomparable insights. Musical examples, catalogue of extant works, index.

117. Goldoni, Carlo. *Memoirs of Carlo Goldoni.* Trans. John Black. New York: Knopf, 1926. 484p. PQ 4698 A6 E5.

Originally published in 1787, this autobiography reveals much about operatic life in the eighteenth century. Introduction by William A. Drake, but no index.

118. Rose, Gloria. "The Italian Cantata of the Baroque Period." In *Gattungen der Musik in Einzeldarstellungen: Gedenkschrift Leo Schrade*, vol. 1, pp. 655-77. Ed. Wulf Arlt, Ernst Lichtenhahn and Hans Oesch. Berne: Francke, 1973. ML 448 G28.

Provides an excellent capsule history of the genre, starting in the early seventeenth century. Musical examples.

119. Stefani, Gino. *Musica e religione nell'Italia barocca*. Uomo e cultura, 14. Palermo: Flaccovio, 1975. 261p. ML 3303 S73.

Offers a fascinating view of the unique place of music in Italian churches of the period. Excellent background for Handel's Latin church music. Bibliography.

120. Weaver, Robert Lamar and Norma Wright Weaver. *A Chronology of Music in the Florentine Theater 1590–1750*. Detroit Studies in Music Bibliography, 38. Detroit: Information Coordinators, 1978. 421p. ML 1733.8 F6 W4. ISBN 0–911772–83–9.

Chronicles musical productions in Florence. Concludes that *Vincer se stesso* (*Rodrigo*) was performed in the Fall of 1707. Plates, bibliography, indexes.

121. Wolff, Hellmuth Christian. *Die Venezianische Oper in der zweiten Hälfte des 17. Jahrhunderts*. Berlin: Elsner, 1937. Repr. in Bibliotheca Musica Bononiensis III, 48. Bologna: Arnaldo Forni Editore, 1975. 235p. and supplement.

Pioneering comprehensive study of Venetian opera in the second half of the seventeenth century. Musical supplement contains excerpts from works by Cavalli, Sartorio, Legrenzi, Pollaroli, Ziani and Pallavicini. Plates, musical examples, index, bibliography.

122. Zanetti, Roberto. *La musica italiana nel settecento.* 3 vols. Storia della musica italiana da Sant' Ambrogio a noi. Busto Arsizio: Bramante Editrice 1978. 1615p. (numbered throughout). ML 290.3 Z36.

Treats eighteenth-century music in Italy by genre, giving historical background, and some discussions of the music. Plates, musical examples, index, bibliography.

II

HANDEL'S LIFE AND HIS WORKS IN GENERAL

1. Eighteenth-Century Handel Biographies

Handel was the first composer to be the subject of several extended biographies in his own century. England and Germany were both fertile ground for Handel biographies, but for different reasons.

In England, Mainwaring's *Memoirs of the Life of the Late George Frederic Handel* (item 132), appearing within months of the composer's death, belonged to the newly flourishing genre of literary biography. Mainwaring seems to have been wary of being identified with the fashionable and sometimes lucrative practice of publishing biographies soon after the demise of the notorious or newsworthy. Not only did he publish the book anonymously, but he also called attention to his own restraint, stating that his only design had been "to give the Reader those parts of his character, as a Man, that any way tend to open and explain his character as an Artist" (page 142).

The other factor in the relatively large number of English Handel biographies was the composer's overriding dominance in the musical world, and also increasingly as a kind of cult figure (See Robert Manson Myers, *Handel's Messiah: A Touchstone of Taste*, item 891). His monumental choral style was especially suited to ceremonial occasions, and became closely identified with the English national personality. As Burney put it, "The English, a manly, military race, were instantly captivated by the grave, bold and nervous style of Handel, which is congenial with their manners and sentiments" (item 123, page iv). This national fervor reached its zenith in the Handel Commemorations celebrated during the late eighteenth and early nineteenth centuries at Westminster Abbey, which took on the importance of state occasions, the royal family being present. Burney's impressive account of the grand spectacle of 1784 is not without its humorous moments, as he describes elegantly dressed ladies screaming and fainting while the gentlemen tussle in a frantic effort to gain admission to the Abbey.

In Germany, where biography as a literary form developed only late in the century, Handelian biography generally took the form of short articles in musical dictionaries and translations of English works. The influence of the theorist-composer Johann Mattheson, who knew Handel and was the recognized German authority on him, was as far-reaching as Mainwaring's in England.

Up until now, most scholarly work on eighteenth-century Handel biography has concentrated on the transmission of facts and on republication of the sources. The following list deals only with extended or comprehensive accounts.

123. Burney, Charles. *An Account of the Musical Performances in Westminster Abbey and the Pantheon in Commemoration of Handel.* London: Payne & Robinson, 1785. Facs. repr. Amsterdam: Knuf, 1964. 139p. ML 410 H13 B9.

Attention to accuracy and detail, as well as a vibrant description of Handel in his later years, make this an indispensable document. "Sketch of the Life of Handel," works-list, and a lengthy account of the 1784 Handel Commemoration, with illuminating comments. Reprint has no modern introduction.

124. _____. *Dr. Karl Burney's Nachricht von Georg Friedrich Handel's Lebensumständen und der ihm zu London im Mai und Juni 1784 angestellten Gedächtnisfeier.* Trans. Johann Joachim Eschenburg. Berlin: 1785. Facs. repr. Leipzig: Deutsche Verlag für Musik, (196?). 102p. ML 410 H13 B93.

Eighteenth-Century Biographies 33

German translation of item 123. Numerous comments and corrections show that Eschenburg was familiar with all the German writings on Handel, including Reichardt's upcoming volume (item 138). Biography and "Händel's musikalische Charakter" available in item 139.

125. Coxe, William. *Anecdotes of George Frederick Handel and John Christopher Smith.* London: Bulmer, 1799. Facs. repr. New York: Da Capo, 1979. 98p. ML 410 H13 C87. ISBN 0–306–79512–4.

First published anonymously. Contains biographies of Handel and Smith (the younger) followed by a works-list for Smith with examples of his music. Preface acknowledges Mainwaring, Burney, and Hawkins, but promises "original Anecdotes." Views Handel as hero, but also tries to establish the importance of Smith, the author's stepfather. Contains a description of Handel's lost childhood notebook (p. 6). Modern introduction by Percy Young provides useful historical information.

* Cudworth, Charles. "Mythistorica Handeliana." In *Festskrift Jens Peter Larsen*, pp. 161–66. Ed. Nils Schiørring, Henrik Glahn and Carsten E. Hatting. Copenhagen: Wilhelm Hansen, 1972. ML 55 L23 F5. ISBN 87–7455–0004.

Cited below as item 190.

126. Dean, Winton. "Charles Jennens' Marginalia to Mainwaring's Life of Handel." *Music and Letters* 53 (1972): 160–64.

Describes Royal Academy of Music copy of item 132 with annotations by Handel's associate and oratorio librettist. One anecdote and a number of corrections reveal Jennens' perspicacity as well as a somewhat crusty personality. Jennens identifies the poet of the Birthday Ode as Ambrose Philips (1674–1749). Two plates.

127. Grant, Kerry S. *Dr. Burney As Critic and Historian of Music.* Studies in Musicology 62. Ann Arbor: UMI Research Press, 1983. 381p. ML 423 B9 G7 1983. ISBN 0–8357–1375–X.

Studies Burney's achievement in the most profound way. Refers frequently to his writings on Handel, concluding that his "concern over the necessity of courting the favor of the King and other powerful Handelians caused him to misrepresent his critical opinion of Handel by omission, obfuscation and improbity" (p. 287). Index, bibliography.

128. Halsband, Robert. "The 'Penury of English Biography' before Samuel Johnson." In *Biography in the 18th Century*, pp. 112–27. Ed. J.D. Browning. New York: Garland, 1980. CT 21 B47. ISBN 0-8240-4007-4.

Describes the best and worst of English biography in the late seventeenth and early eighteenth centuries. Evaluates Samuel Johnson's contributions to literary biography. About half of Johnson's *Lives of the Poets* (London, 1779) have a three-part structure (chronological relation of events, description of personality etc., critical analysis) which resembles Mainwaring's design. No specific mention of Handel biographies.

129. Hawkins, John. *A General History of the Science and Practice of Music*. Vol. 5, pp. 262–418. London: T. Payne, 1776. ML 159 H39.

Dover edition of 1963, an unabridged republication of the edition published by Alfred Novello in 1853, contains an introduction by Charles Cudworth. There is also an Akademische Druck- u. Verlagsanstalt reprint of Novello's 1875 edition (Graz, 1969). The Handel biography, interspersed with material on contemporary composers, is on pp. 856–914 of Volume 2 in both modern reprints.

One of the most informative early accounts. Adds details to the basic account of Mainwaring, particularly on lives of singers and others. Strong opinions, social commentary, considerations of general historical issues. Some eyewitness accounts, including a "quotation" from Handel about his arrival at Hanover (p. 267; 858 in repr.).

130. Kivy, Peter. "Mainwaring's *Handel*: Its Relation to English Aesthetics." *Journal of the American Musicological Society* 17 (1964): 170–78.

Eighteenth-Century Biographies 35

The critical views of Mainwaring (and Robert Price) in item 132 are entirely consistent with contemporary English aesthetics. Most notable is the notion of the sublime, with its implications of grandeur and freedom from restrictions. Explains one aspect of the immense popularity of Handel's music in the England of the late eighteenth and nineteenth centuries.

131. Longaker, Mark. *English Biography in the Eighteenth Century.* University of Pennsylvania Press, 1931. Repr. New York: Octagon Books, 1971. 519p. CT 34 G7 L6 1971.

    Contains nothing specifically about Handel biographies, but offers entertaining general background. Index; bibliography at end of each chapter.

132. Mainwaring, John. *Memoirs of the Life of the Late George Frederic Handel.* London: Dodsley, 1760. Facs. repr. New York: Da Capo, 1980. 208p. ML 410 H13 M2. ISBN 0–306–76042–8.

    The first extended composer biography. Published anonymously. Based on information derived from J.C. Smith Jr., the account of Handel's life is elegant, detailed and surprisingly objective in view of the literary style of the times. Although not all the facts are accurate, the *Memoirs* are the single most influential source of Handel biography. The "Catalogue of Works," compiled by James Harris, is followed by "Observations on the Works," the combined effort of Mainwaring and Robert Price.

    Da Capo reprint contains a fine introduction by J. Merrill Knapp.

133. _____. *Georg Friedrich Händels Lebensbeschreibung . . . übersetzet auch mit einigen Anmerkungen . . . versehen vom Legationsrat Mattheson.* Trans. Johann Mattheson. Hamburg: by the author-translator, 1761. 156p. ML 410 H13 M22.

    Mattheson translates Mainwaring (item 132) complete, adding a lengthy preface and a series of petulant corrections.

The translator's prejudices are clear, but the historical details become increasingly unclear as the reader wades through Mainwaring's footnotes and then Matheson's. Best to consult the third set of notes provided by Siegmund-Schultze in item 139, where the entire translation appears, pp. 39–140.

Annotated edition by Bernhard Paumgartner (Zürich: Atlantis-Verlag, 1947) contains an introduction as well as Mattheson's *Ehrenpforte* article (item 136) and Burney's observations on Mattheson. An edition by Hedwig and E.H. Müller von Asow (Vienna: Frisch & Perneder, 1949) has no commentary. A facsimile reprint was edited by Walther Siegmund-Schultze for the VEB Deutscher Verlag für Musik in Leipzig, 1976.

134. _____. *Memorie della vita del fu G.F. Händel con l'aggiunta di un catalogo delle sue opere e di osservazioni su di esse.* Trans. Lorenzo Bianconi. Turin, 1985. 196p.

Italian translation of item 132, with commentary.

135. Mann, Alfred. "Mattheson as Biographer of Handel." In *New Mattheson Studies*, pp. 345–52. Ed. George J. Buelow and Hans Joachim Marx. Cambridge: Cambridge University Press, 1983. ML 55 M327 N5 1983. ISBN 0–521–25115–X.

Handelian biography begins with Mattheson's *Ehrenpforte* article (item 136). Mattheson's importance as a source, especially for the Hamburg years, is underscored by Burney's recognition (item 123). Contrasts the increasingly cool Handel-Mattheson correspondence with the warm relationship maintained by Handel and Telemann.

136. Mattheson, Johann. "Händel." In *Grundlage einer Ehrenpforte, woran der tüchtigsten Kapellmeister, Komponisten, Musikgelehrten, Tonkünstler . . . Leben, Werke, Verdienste . . . erscheinen sollen*, pp. 93–101. Hamburg: by the author, 1740. Repr. Berlin: Liepmannsohn, 1910; Kassel: Bärenreiter, 1960. ML 105 M42.

Handel declined repeated invitations to submit an autobiography. Mattheson's is the first detailed account of

Eighteenth-Century Biographies 37

Handel's life and works. Emphasis on Mattheson's relationship with Handel, especially during the Hamburg years. Excerpts from three Handel letters. Available in item 139, pp. 27–37. Facs. repr. in *Händel-Jahrbuch* 17 (1971): 89–115 (Handel and Telemann articles).

137. Nicolson, Harold. *The Development of English Biography.* London: Leonard and Virginia Woolf at the Hogarth Press, 1927. Hogarth Lectures on Literature series. Repr. 1933. 158p. CT 21 N5.

Chronological outline of English biography as a literary form, with emphasis on major works. Outlines concept of "pure" biography, as distinct from funeral orations or fictionalized and subjective accounts. Useful in interpreting English biographies.

138. Reichardt, Johann Freidrich. "Georg Friedrich Händels Jugend." In *Georg Friedrich Händel: Beiträge zu seiner Biographie aus dem 18. Jahrhundert*, pp. 179–93. Taschenbücher zur Musikwissenschaft, 32. Wilhelmshaven: Heinrichshofen, 1979. ML 410 H13 G35. ISBN 3-7959- 0268-1.

Originally published as a monograph in Berlin in 1785. Biography up to and including Italian years (late 1706–1710). Information comes from Mainwaring and Mattheson, partly by way of Hiller. Also available in *Händel-Jahrbuch* 5 (1959): 183–98.

139. Siegmund-Schultze, Walther, ed. *Georg Friedrich Händel: Beiträge zu seiner Biographie aus dem 18. Jahrhundert.* Taschenbücher zur Musikwissenschaft, 32. Wilhelmshaven: Heinrichshofen, 1979. 311p. ML 410 H13 G35. ISBN 3-7959-0268-1.

Collection of eighteenth-century biographical accounts. Helpful introduction and annotations. Contains items 124, 125, 133, 136, 138. Also a 1770 German translation of the *Gentleman's Magazine* biography of 1760 (based on Mainwaring), J.A. Hiller's Handel entry in *Lebensbeschreibungen berühmter Musikgelehrten und Tonkünstler neuerer Zeit* (1784), E.L. Gerber's Handel article in the *Historisch-biographisches Lexikon der Tonskünstler* (1790 and 1812), C.F.D. Schubart's discussion of Handel in *Ideen zu einer Ästhetik der Tonkunst* (ca. 1790, pub. posth. 1806) and an excerpt from J.G. Herder's *Adrastea* (1802). Modern German translation of item 125 contains only the Handel section. First pub. 1977 by Verlag Philipp Reclam jun., Leipzig.

140. Smith, William C. "More Handeliana." *Music and Letters* 34 (1953): 11–24.

    Suggests reasons to doubt Coxe's authorship of item 125. But see Young's introduction to item 125, vi–vii. Discusses the two J.C. Smiths, Handel's will, the Water Music sources, and Handel portraits.

141. Stauffer, Donald. *The Art of Biography in 18th-Century England*. 2 vols. Princeton: Princeton University Press, 1941. 572p. Suppl. 293p. CT 34 G7 S67.

    Authoritative comprehensive work on the subject, written in a particularly attractive style. Brief mentions of item 123, item 132, and of Hawkins as a biographer. Second volume or bibliographic supplement contains alphabetical and chronological lists of English biographies and autobiographies 1700–1800.

2. Biographies, Comprehensive Studies, and Collections of Essays

The early nineteenth century produced a dearth of scholarly, original or substantial Handel biographies. In the middle years of the century, Friedrich Chrysander began his pioneering effort to write a comprehensive critical biography (item 145). Because of its overwhelming detail and wealth of information on the works themselves, it has overshadowed the biography of Victor Schoelcher (item 170), published a year earlier in England. Schoelcher's work should be recognized as the beginning of a trend toward the searching of contemporary documents

Comprehensive Studies 39

in order to reconcile the factual contradictions of the early accounts and fill in the gaps in Handel's life-story—a trend which continued in England during the early years of our century and is still a significant branch of research.

On the other hand, the continuing Handel cult in England, coupled with the new availability of biographical detail, spawned a number of charming biographies of an essentially popular nature, containing nothing original or scholarly, which have been omitted from this survey.

142. Abraham, Gerald, ed. *Handel: A Symposium.* London: Oxford University Press, 1954. 328p. ML 410 H13 A66.

Contains ten essays on various aspects of Handel's life and works (items 255, 381, 434, 514, 563, 594, 639, 670, 689, 693) as well as a catalogue of works by William C. Smith (item 380), a brief chronology, a bibliography and index. Musical examples.

143. Alexandre-Debray, Janine. *Haendel.* Paris: Ramsay, 1980. 452p. ML 410 H13 A75. ISBN 2–85956–156–0.

Biography in novelistic style. Bibliography, discography.

144. Burrows, Donald. "Handel: His Life and Work." In *Handel: A Celebration of His Life and Times*, pp. 7–17. Ed. Jacob Simon. London: National Portrait Gallery, 1985. ML 410 H13. ISBN 0–904017–68–0.

Polished biographical sketch, incorporating recent research and exceedingly well informed comments. Brevity appropriate to its place in an exhibition catalogue; no detailed discussions of works.

145. Chrysander, Friedrich. *G.F. Händel.* 3 vols. Leipzig: Breitkopf und Härtel, 1858–1867, repr. 1912. 495, 481, 224p. ML 410 H13 C3.

The classic critical biography, it remains incomplete, stopping at 1740. Volume 1 contains the first two books, *Jugendzeit und Lehrjahre in Deutschland 1685–1706* and *Die große Wanderung 1707–1720.* Volume 2 contains *Zwanzig Jahre bei der italienischen Oper in London 1720–1740.* Volume 3 contains the beginning of Book 4, *Uebergang zum Oratorium 1738–1759.*

Though some of its information has naturally been superseded by succeeding generations of scholarship, it remains a model of attention to detail, and many of its special insights still provide an irreplaceable guide. The writer, editor of the great Händel-Gesellschaft collected edition, was able to speak with authority on even the lesser known works. No index, but see item 146.

146. _____. *G.F. Händel-Register.* Prepared by Siegfried Flesch. Leipzig: VEB Deutscher Verlag für Musik; Hildesheim: Georg Olms, 1967. 55p. ML 410 H13 C32.

A general index and an index of Handel's works to item 145.

147. Dean, Winton. *The New Grove Handel.* New York: Norton, 1983. 185p. ML 410 H13 D24. ISBN 0-393-30086-2.

Publication in paperback form of the authoritative Handel article in *The New Grove Dictionary of Music and Musicians* (1980). Outlines biography clearly and concisely, using the most up-to-date information. Brief discussions of the music. Extremely detailed and authoritative works-list by Anthony Hicks (item 379). Bibliography contains additions to the 1980 version. Index, plates.

148. Dent, Edward J. *Handel.* London: Duckworth, 1934. 140p. ML 410 H13 D41 1934.

Concise biographical account, enlivened by the author's sophisticated insights into the music of the time.

149. Deutsch, Otto Erich. *Handel: A Documentary Biography.* London: A. and C. Black, 1955. 942p. ML 410 H13 D47.

Year-by year account of Handel's life, using Mainwaring (item 132) as a skeleton and presenting annotated transcriptions in English of all documents, letters, newspaper items, advertisements, contemporary comments, etc. known to the com-

Comprehensive Studies

piler. Indispensable research tool. Model for the more up-to-date item 151. Plates, indexes, extensive bibliography.

150. Flower, Sir Newman. *George Frideric Handel: His Personality and His Times*. London: Cassell. 1959. First published 1923; revised 1947, 1959. 399p. ML 410 H13 F5 1959.

As stated in the Preface, concentrates on Handel the Man, without technical discussions of the music. In spite of its novelistic style, it presents some documentary material for the first time. Appendix entitled "Handel's Difficulties with His Singers and Notes on His Score Corrections." Bibliography compiled by William C. Smith. Index, Plates.

151. *Händel-Handbuch IV: Dokumente zu Leben und Schaffen*. Kassel: Bärenreiter, 1985. 621p. ML 134 H3 H3. ISBN 3-7618-0717-1.

Prepared by various scholars who are named in the Preface. Based on Deutsch's pioneering documentary biography (item 149), this impressive volume presents all known contemporary documents with concise commentary in German.

152. *Handel and the Fitzwilliam*. Cambridge: Fitzwilliam Museum, 1974. 45p. ML 141 C3 H3.

Contains the catalogue of an exhibition of Handeliana and the programs of three concerts given in conjunction with it. Also items 207, 273, 761, and 847. Plates.

153. Hoffmann, Hans. *Georg Friedrich Händel: Vom Opernkomponisten zum Meister des Oratoriums*. Marburg an der Lahn: Francke-Buchhandlung, 1983. 106p. ML 410 H13 H64 1983. ISBN 3-88224-317-1.

Concludes that the 1737 visit to Aix-en-Provence was the most crucial turning-point in Handel's life. Ignores modern scholarship and is poorly documented. Bibliography.

154. Hogwood, Christopher. *Handel.* London: Thames and Hudson, 1984. 312p. ML 410 H13 H66 1984.

   Presents a life of the composer firmly rooted in documentary sources and enlivened by the special insights of the author. Sparkling anecdotes and well-chosen quotations appear frequently, set apart from the main text. Superbly illustrated. Chronological table by Anthony Hicks. Excellent bibliography, indexes.

155. Keates, Jonathan. *Handel: The Man and His Music.* London: Victor Gollancz Ltd., 1985. 346p. ML 410 H13 K4 1985. ISBN 0-575-03573-0.

   Presents a thoroughly readable chronological account with intelligent, non-technical discussions of the music. Documentation is unobtrusive, but the fruits of up-to-date research are considered. No musical examples. Eleven plates, indexes.

156. Labie, Jean-François. *George Frédéric Haendel.* Paris: Laffont, 1980. 862p. ML 410 H13 L17. ISBN 2-221-00566-X.

   Lengthy biography interspersed with short whimsical essays on related issues. Weakened by a lack of understanding of eighteenth-century English culture. Presents outdated information on the early years. Works-list contains a number of spurious pieces. Plates, chronology, indexes.

157. Landon, H.C. Robbins. *Handel and His World.* London: Weidenfeld and Nicolson, 1984. 256p. ML 410 H13 L18. ISBN 0-297-78498-6.

   Called by the author a "documentary survey," it is a sort of elaborate gloss of Mainwaring (item 132). Concentrates especially on a few examples of English choral and ceremonial music. Lavishly illustrated. Musical examples. Select bibliography, index.

158. Lang, Paul Henry. *George Frideric Handel.* New York: W.W. Norton, 1966. 731p. ML 410 H13 L2. ISBN 0-393-00815-0.

Comprehensive Studies 43

Elegant critical biography followed by discussions of musical style. Contains impressive and provocative material on historical and musical background. Emphasis is on insight rather than documentation. (German translation by Eva Ultsch. Basel, 1979).

159. _____. "Handel: 300 Years On." *Musical Times* 126 (1985): 77–84.

A compressed "life and works" in the author's inimitably elegant style. Illustration.

160. Leichtentritt, Hugo. *Händel.* Stuttgart: Deutsche Verlags-Anstalt, 1924. 871p. ML 410 H13 L4.

Detailed, comprehensive discussion of Handel's life and then his works. One of the best books of its kind. Especially revealing section on the history of the Handel "movement." Chronological tables of biography and works present not only a convenient summary of what was known about Handel in 1924, but also a useful index to the book. Index of names, no illustrations, no musical examples. Short bibliography.

161. Marx, Hans Joachim, ed. *Händel und Hamburg: Ausstellung anläßlich des 300. Geburtstages von Georg Friedrich Händel in der Staats- und Universitäts-bibliothek Hamburg—Carl von Ossietzky.* Hamburg: Karl Dieter Wagner, 1985. 179p. ML 410 H13 H234. ISBN 3–88979–009–7.

Beautifully designed catalogue of the Hamburg exhibition celebrating the Handel tercentenary. Description of each item concludes with a short bibliography. Twenty-six plates. Index of names, plates; bibliography. Introductory essays listed separately as items 184, 213, 223, 450, 489, 886, 922.

162. Müller-Blattau, Joseph. *Georg Friedrich Händel: Der Wille zur Vollendung.* Die Großen Meister der Musik. Potsdam: Akademische Verlagsgesellschaft Athenaion M.B.H., 1933. 160p. ML 410 H13 M93.

Deals first with biography, then with the works. Lavishly illustrated with portraits, musical examples, title pages etc. Bibliography, index.

163. _____. *Georg Friedrich Händel: Der Wille zur Vollendung.* Mainz: Schott, 1959. 204p. and 36p. of Plates.

Revision of item 162 in a less attractive format. Does not always achieve its goal of keeping up with new research.

164. Müller, Erich H. *The Letters and Writings of George Frideric Handel.* London: Cassell, 1935. 99p. ML 410 H13 A3.

Includes the annotated texts of most of Handel's extant letters, his will, the preface to *Suites de pièces pour le clavecin* (1720), and the dedication of *Radamisto* (1720) to George I. All but one of the letters in French and German are translated into English in an appendix. Index of names and work titles. The only work discussed in any detail is *Belshazzar* (1744). For additional letters, see Deutsch (item 149) pp. 93, 202, 557, 860, 602, 606, 677. See also items 203 and 224.

165. Mueller von Asow, Hedwig and Erich H. *Georg Friedrich Händel: Biographie, Briefe und Schriften.* Lindau am Bodensee: Frisch & Perneder, 1949. Repr. Hildesheim: Olms, 1977. 219p. ML 410 H13 G46. ISBN 3-487-06331-X.

Revised version of item 164, with notes and translations in German and including Mattheson's translation of Mainwaring (item 133).

* Robinson, Percy. *Handel and His Orbit.* London: Sherratt and Hughes, 1908. Repr. New York: Da Capo Press, 1979. 223p. ML 410 H13 R5 1979. ISBN 0-306-79522-1.

Cited below as item 361.

166. Pecman, Rudolf. *Georg Friedrich Händel.* Prague: Editio Supraphon, 1985. ML 410 H13 P4 1985. 388p.

In Czechoslovakian. Plates, musical examples, indexes, works-list, bibliography. Table of contents for HHA.

167. Rockstro, William S. *The Life of George Fredrick Handel.* London: MacMillan, 1883. 452p. ML 410 H13 R6.

Comprehensive Studies

As stated in the introduction by Sir George Grove, an English alternative to the "excessive length" and density of Chrysander (item 145) and the "rampant partiality" of Schoelcher (item 170). Direct, factual presentation of biographical facts as they were known at the time. Index, works-list.

168. Rolland, Romain. *Haendel.* Paris: Alcan, 1910. 2nd. rev. ed. by Félix Raugel, Paris: Albin Michel, 1951. Repr. 1974. 308p. ML 410 H13 R67 1974. ISBN 2-226-00125-5.

The classic biography by this erudite Frenchman focuses on Handel's life and the general "esthétique" of his music. Appended material features discussions of various choral works, a works-list, bibliography, and discography. Musical examples, illustrations, no index. Has been translated into several languages, including English (trans. A. Eaglefield Hull, 1916. Repr. New York: AMS Press, 1971).

169. Rudolph, Johanna, *Händelrenaissance.* 2 vols. Berlin: Aufbau-Verlag, 1960-69. 244, 464p. ML 410 H13 R83.

Profound consideration of Handel's life and works from the point of view of social and political history, with a focus on ideology of Handel interpretations. Well-informed, but strongly affected by the author's political orientation. Organization is hard to fathom. Very few musical examples, all relegated to an appendix in Volume 2. Plates. Index.

170. Schoelcher, Victor. *The Life of Handel.* Trans. James Lowe. London: Robert Cocks & Co., 1857. Repr. New York: Da Capo Press, 1979. 443p. ML 410 H13 S3 1979. ISBN 0-306-79572-8.

The first to attempt to set straight some of the inaccuracies in chronology and other details inherited from the accounts of Mainwaring, Burney, and Hawkins. To accomplish this, the author had the keen historical sense to conduct a search of the journals from Handel's time, fixing a number of significant dates and also acquiring a feeling for the musical life of eighteenth-century England that is perhaps lacking in the work of Chrysander, his great German contemporary. Also informed by examination of the Handel sources in the Royal collection and at Fitzwilliam. Index.

171. Serauky, Walter. *Georg Friedrich Händel: Sein Leben—sein Werk.* 3 vols. Kassel: Bärenreiter, 1956–1958. 948, 565, 595p. ML 410 H13 S47.

Starts on volume 3 with Handel in the late 1730's, since the author's plan, thwarted by his death in 1959, was to pick up where Chrysander left off (item 145) and then go back and fill in the beginning. Informed by a wealth of detail, not all of it relevant, it is marred by a lack of understanding of eighteenth-century England. Musical examples, indexes.

172. Siegmund-Schultze, Walther. *Georg Friedrich Händel.* 3rd ed. Leipzig: VEB Deutscher Verlag für Musik, 1962. 234p. ML 410 H13 S54 1962.

Originally published in 1954 and revised in 1959. Concise biography, followed by chapters on the operas, oratorios, instrumental music, and Handel's musical style generally. Detailed analyses of "Io ti bacio" from *Ariodante* and "Glory to God" from *Messiah*. Chronological table, cursory works-list and bibliography, index of names.

173. _____. *Georg Friedrich Händel: Thema mit 20 Variationen.* Halle (Saale), 1965. 158p.

Begins with an essay entitled "Theme," which generalizes on the greatness of Handel using Beethoven's famous quotation as a motto. Offers twenty short chapters on topics as general as Handel's cantatas and as specific as the Dejanira scene in *Hercules.*

174. _____. *Georg Friedrich Händel: Sein Leben, sein Werk.* Munich: Paul List, 1984. 375p. ML 410 H13 S55 1984. ISBN 3–471–78624–4.

Attempts to bring together recent research into an up-to-date view of Handel. Biography with illustrations is followed by a series of essays on various topics, most with musical ex-

Comprehensive Studies 47

amples. No detailed references or footnotes. Works-list, chronological table, short bibliography, index of names.

175. Simon, Jacob, ed. *Handel: A Celebration of His Life and Times*. London: National Portrait Gallery, 1985. 296p. ML 410 H13. ISBN 0-904017-68-0.

Published for the exhibition held from November 8, 1985 to February 23, 1986, at the National Portrait Gallery. Valuable introductory essays (items 144, 274, 784). Maps, sketches, and engravings of London during Handel's time, even a plan of his house. Portraits of Handel and his contemporaries, manuscripts, documents, first editions, etc. Excellent commentary and detailed descriptions for all the items, including suggestions for further reading. Appendices include an inventory of musical instruments belonging to the Duke of Chandos, documents pertaining to Handel's naturalization, Handel's library and his collection of paintings. Index of exhibit titles. Lavishly illustrated and exquisitely prepared.

176. Smith, William C. *Concerning Handel: His Life and Works*. London: Cassell, 1948. 299p. ML 410 H13 S59.

Eight essays by a distinguished British Handelian. Includes items 240, 241, 242, 243, 244, 319, 320, 321. Plates, index.

177. Streatfeild, Richard A. *Handel*. London: Methuen & Co., 1909. 2nd ed., 1910. Repr. New York: Da Capo Press, 1964. 366p. ML 410 H13 S7 1964.

Relates Handel's life story, making use of much original work on the early years. Discusses operas, oratorios and other choral works, and instrumental music. Encourages a historical perspective on the question of Handel's borrowings (Appendix C). Index. The reprint of the 1910 edition features a useful introduction by J. Merrill Knapp.

178. Weinstock, Herbert. *Handel*. New York: Knopf, 1946. 2nd ed. 1959. Repr. Westport, Connecticut: Greenwood Press, 1979. 328p. & indexes. ML 410 H13 W27. ISBN 0-313-21109-4.

Second edition of this novelistic biography differs very little from the first. Short bibliography.

179. Young, Percy. *Handel.* London: Dent, 1947. Rev. 1965, 1975. 244p. ML 410 H13 Y58. ISBN 0-460-03161-9.

Attractive, concise, biographical account, followed by essays on Handel's music. Appendices include short catalogue of works, bibliography, and newly-presented documents on Handel's finances. Musical examples. Index.

3. Studies of Particular Biographical Issues

Some of the most fruitful biographical studies have uncovered significant details about Handel's association with various institutions and courts. Ursula Kirkendale's discoveries in the Ruspoli archives in Rome (item 210) laid the groundwork for a new understanding of the early Italian period. In addition, scholars have investigated Handel's short tenure at Hanover, the somewhat elusive years at Cannons, and his association with the Chapel Royal. The following list also contains the most significant books and articles on Handel's relationship with various individuals and on other personal details such as health and appearance.

180. Becker, Heinz. "Georg Friedrich Händel: Opernkomponist und Kosmopolit." In *Karlsruher Händel-Vorträge*, pp. 21-34. Ed. Kurt R. Pietschmann and Gabriele Eikermann. Karlsruhe: Badisches Staatstheater Karlsruhe, 1985. ML 410 H13 K37.

Not examined.

* Beeks, Graydon F. "Handel and Music for the Earl of Carnarvon." In *Bach, Handel, Scarlatti: Tercentenary Essays*, pp. 1-20. Ed. Peter Williams. Cambridge: Cambridge University Press, 1985. ML 410 B13. ISBN 0-521-25217-2.

Cited below as item 616.

Particular Issues 49

181. Bell, A. Craig. *Handel before England.* Darley: Grian-Aig Press, 1975. 60p. ML 410 H13 B45.

   Charming but somewhat superficial account of the early years. Many musical examples. Indexes.

182. Braun, Werner. "Beiträge zu G.F. Händels Jugendzeit in Halle (1685–1703)." *Wissenschaftliche Zeitschrift der Martin-Luther-Universität Halle-Wittenberg* VIII, 4 (1959): 851–62.

   Broadens what item 111 presented about Halle in the early 1700's. Fascinating information about the intellectual climate. Demonstrates that, although musical opportunities at the Dom were limited, concerted music was performed there on special occasions.

183. _____. "Händel contra Mattheson. Bedingungen einer Konfrontation." *Concerto* 2/5 (1985): 24–29.

   Summarizes relations between the two composers, noting the musical connections as well as biographical. Plates.

184. _____. "Händel und der Dichter Barthold Heinrich Brockes." In *Händel und Hamburg: Ausstellung anläßlich des 300. Geburtstages von Georg Friedrich Händel*, pp. 85–97. Ed. Hans Joachim Marx. Hamburg: Karl Dieter Wagner, 1985. ML 410 H13. ISBN 3-88979-009-7.

   Outlines the relationship between Handel and the Hamburg poet Brockes, with emphasis on the *Brockespassion* and especially on the *Neun deutsche Arien*.

185. Burrows, Donald. "Thomas Gethin: A Handel Tenor." *Musical Times* 116 (1975): 1003–1006.

   Discusses the only tenor soloist regularly named in the autographs of Handel's Chapel Royal anthems.

186. _____. "Handel and the 1727 Coronation." *Musical Times* 118 (1977): 469–73.

Assembles documentary evidence relating to the 1727 Coronation of George II. Prints order of service. Also contains a reproduction of a lost Handel portrait, discussed by Betty Matthews in a letter to the editor in page 474.

*   _____. "Handel and the Foundling Hospital." *Music and Letters* 58 (1977): 269–84.

Cited below as item 623.

*   _____. "Handel and the English Chapel Royal during the Reigns of Queen Anne and King George I." Ph.D. dissertation. Open University, 1981.

Cited below as item 625.

187.   _____. "Handel and Hanover." In *Bach, Handel, Scarlatti: Tercentenary Essays*, pp. 35–60. Ed. Peter Williams. Cambridge: Cambridge University Press, 1985. ML 55 B14 1985. ISBN 0–521–25217–2.

Presents newly discovered letters and other documents which reveal much about Handel's tenure in Hanover and his early years in England. Paper studies suggest that *Apollo e Dafne* was completed in Hanover and that he composed five duets (nos. 3, 4, 8, 11, 12) there.

188.   Chrysander, Friedrich. "Der Bestand der königlichen Privatmusik und Kirchen-Kapelle in London, 1710–1755." *Vierteljahrsschrift für Musikwissenschaft* 8 (1892): 514–31.

Presents fragmentary documentary information on the English royal musical establishments for selected years between 1710 and 1755, derived from John Chamberlayne's *Magnae Britanniae Notitia*. Handel is listed as "Musik-Master" to the princesses from 1728.

189.   Coopersmith, J.M. "List of Portraits, Sculptures etc. of Georg Friedrich Händel." *Music and Letters* 13 (1932): 156–67.

Particular Issues 51

Lists paintings, miniatures, prints, sculptures, "metal pieces," and caricatures.

190. Cudworth, Charles. "Mythistorica Handeliana." In *Festskrift Jens Peter Larsen*, pp. 161–66. Ed. Nils Schiørring, Henrik Glahn and Carsten E. Hatting. Copenhagen: Wilhelm Hansen, 1972. ML 55 L23 F5. ISBN 87-7455-000-4.

Good-natured essay suggesting that many Handelian anecdotes are fictional.

191. Dart, Thurston. "Bononcini Sets Handel a Test." *Musical Times* 112 (1971): 324–25.

Announces the discovery in the Fitzwilliam Museum of a cantata which the author believes to be the "exercise" set by Bononcini for the boy Handel, according to a story related in Mainwaring's *Memoirs* (item 132). Musical examples.

192. Daub, Peggy. "Handel and Frederick." *Musical Times* 122 (1981): 733.

Responds to an article by Derek McCulloch (pp. 525–29) in which he misguidedly suggests that the Prince's attitude to Handel was uniformly hostile.

193. Della Seta, Fabrizio. "Due partiture di Benedetto Marcello e un possibile contributo Haendeliano." *Nuova rivista musicale italiana* 17 (1983): 341–82.

Concludes that Handel and Marcello met in Venice during the winter of 1707–1708, and again during 1709–1710. Points to similarities in specific works, especially the last aria of Marcello's serenata *La morte d'Adone* and "Vo' far guerra" from *Rinaldo*. The Handel connection helps the author to assign the serenata a date of 1710. Plates, example.

194. Fabbri, Mario. *Alessandro Scarlatti e il Principe Ferdinando de' Medici*. Florence: L.S. Olschki, 1961. 120p. ML 410 S22 F3.

Contains the texts of three letters from the correspondence of Prince Ferdinand, showing that Handel visited Düsseldorf in 1710 but did not go to Innsbruck, and giving details on his relationship with the Medicis.

195. _____. "Nuova luce sull'attività fiorentina di Giacomo Antonio Perti, Bartolomeo Cristofori e Giorgio F. Haendel." *Chigiana* 21 (1964): 143–90.

Important new material on Handel's whereabouts during 1709 and his relationships with the Medici family and with the composer Giacomo Antonio Perti.

196. Farncombe, Charles. "G.F. Handel Seen through Other Eyes. Testimonies and Judgments of the Composer's English Contemporaries." In *Georg Friedrich Händel: Ausstellung aus Anlaß der Händel-Festspiele des Badischen Staatstheaters Karlsruhe 1985*, pp. 41–58. Ed. Klaus Häfner and Kurt Pietschmann. Karlsruhe: Badische Landesbibliothek, 1985. ML 141 K36 H33. ISBN 3-88705- 013–4.

Sort of a biographical summary of Handel from his arrival in England to his death, with quotations from letters and poems by his contemporaries. Illustrations. German translation by Felix Heinzer on pp. 59–80.

197. Fleischhauer, Günter. "Berührungspunkte mit der Antike und Antikem Gedankengut im Lebensweg G.F. Händels." *Konferenzbericht Halle (Saale) 1983*, pp. 26–36.

Speculates on contacts with the literature and thought of Classical antiquity which Handel most likely had at various points in his life. Outlines, for example, the program of Classical studies in the Halle Gymnasium he probably attended. Useful references.

198. Greenacombe, John. "Handel's House: A History of No. 25 Brook Street, Mayfair." *London Topographical Record* 25 (1985): 111–30.

Detailed history of the house which Handel occupied from 1723 until his death, with notes on Handel's activities in the house, voting record in local elections, church membership,

Particular Issues 53

etc. Description of the layout of the house and subsequent additions to it. Photographs, illustration, ground plans.

199. Gress, Johannes. "Händel in Dresden (1719)." *Händel-Jahrbuch* 9 (1963): 135–51.

Examines the documentary evidence on Handel's 1719 trip to Dresden, adding information about musical events there at the time.

200. Häfner, Klaus. "Georg Friedrich Händel." In *Georg Friedrich Händel: Ausstellung aus Anlaß der Händel-Festspiele des Badischen Staatstheaters Karlsruhe 1985*, pp. 7–24. Ed. Klaus Häfner and Kurt Pietschmann. Karlsruhe: Badische Landesbibliothek, 1985. ML 141 K36 H33. ISBN 3-88705-013-4.

One of those "Handel the Man" essays, but well written and occasionally provocative. Several illustrations.

201. Hall, James S. "John Christopher Smith: Handel's Friend and Secretary." *Musical Times* 96 (1955): 132–34.

Announces the discovery of the burial date of the elder Smith and presents a transcript of his will. German translation in the *Händel-Jahrbuch* 3 (1957): 126–32.

202. _____. "John Christopher Smith: His Residence in London." *Händel-Jahrbuch* 3 (1957): 133–37.

Identifies and describes the three London residences of the elder Smith.

* _____. "Handel among the Carmelites." *Dublin Review* 233 (1959): 121–31.

Cited below as item 632.

203. Hicks, Anthony. "An Auction of Handeliana." *Musical Times* 114 (1973): 892–93.

Describes a remarkable group of letters, some by Handel and others by Charles Jennens, which was sold in July 1973.

Gives details of the information therein, including previously unknown facts about the librettos of *Messiah, L'Allegro, Saul, The Occasional Oratorio,* and possibly *Israel in Egypt.*

204. _____. "Handel's Early Musical Development." *Proceedings of the Royal Musical Association* 103 (1976–77): 80–90.

    Reviews recent scholarship on Handel's Italian period. Contends that only *Almira*, the trio sonata in g minor op. 2 no. 2, and the *Laudate pueri* setting in F, are surviving authentic works from before 1707. Examines these, and offers a broad survey of works composed in Rome during 1707.

205. Hodgkinson, Terence. "Handel at Vauxhall." *Victoria and Albert Museum Bulletin* 1/4 (1965): 1–13.

    Gives details on the Handel statue by Roubiliac, including information on its commission by Jonathan Tyers in 1738 and a description of its surroundings at Vauxhall Gardens. Lavishly illustrated.

206. Jackson, David M. "Bach, Handel, and the Chevalier Taylor." *Medical History* 12 (1968): 385–93.

    A cursory examination of the opthalmological conditions of Bach and Handel and their treatments. That Taylor operated on Bach is certain; whether he did the same with Handel is not clear. Included is an interesting account of the treatment of ocular disorders, especially cataracts, in the mid-eighteenth century.

207. Kerslake, John. "The Likeness of Handel." In *Handel and the Fitzwilliam*, pp. 24–27. Cambridge: Fitzwilliam Museum, 1974. ML 141 C3 H3.

    Surveys and describes significant portraits and statues. Plates of the portraits by Denner, Mercier, and Hudson (1756) and of the model for Roubiliac's Vauxhall statue (ca. 1738).

208. Keynes, Milo. "Handel's Illnesses." *The Lancet* no. 8208/9 (1980): 1354–55.

Particular Issues 55

Argues that Handel's attacks of 1737 and 1743 have been misdiagnosed as strokes and were in fact bad bouts of recurrent muscular rheumatism. These severe attacks coincided with depression, characteristic of Handel's cyclothymic temperament, but there is no evidence of symptoms associated with strokes. Notes on the attempted cures for Handel's blindness.

209. _____. "Handel and His Illnesses." *Musical Times* 123 (1982): 613–14.

    Very similar to item 208.

210. Kirkendale, Ursula. "The Ruspoli Documents on Handel." Journal of the *American Musicological Society* 20 (1967): 222–73, 518.

    Presents thirty-eight entries from documents in the Fondo Ruspoli in the Archivio Segreto Vaticano originating between May 16, 1707, and October 10, 1711. Reveals that Handel was highly active in Rome from mid-July into September or even November of 1708. Provides crucial information for the dating of a number of chamber cantatas.

211. Knapp, J. Merrill. "Mattheson and Handel: Their Musical Relations in Hamburg." In *New Mattheson Studies*, pp. 307–26. Ed. George J. Buelow and Hans Joachim Marx. Cambridge: Cambridge University Press, 1983. ML 55 M327 N5 1983. ISBN 0–521–25115–X.

    Evaluates Mattheson's claim to have taught Handel how to write for the stage. Discusses Mattheson's *Cleopatra* and Handel's *Almira*, emphasizing their differences in style. Musical examples.

212. Lowenthal, Ruth. "Handel and Newburgh Hamilton: New References in the Strafford Papers." *Musical Times* 112 (1971): 1063–66.

    Gives details on the position in Lord Strafford's household of Handel's librettist Newburgh Hamilton. Presents the references to Hamilton and Handel in the letters of the Strafford children to their father during the seasons of 1736–37 and 1738–39.

213. Maertens, Willi. "Händels Freundschaft mit Telemann." In *Händel und Hamburg: Ausstellung anläßlich des 300. Geburtstages von Georg Friedrich Händel*, pp. 109–16. Ed. Hans Joachim Marx. Hamburg: Karl Dieter Wagner, 1985. ML 410 H13 H234. ISBN 3-88979-009-7.

Describes the life-long relationship between Handel and Telemann, comparing and contrasting the different directions of their lives and careers. Lists opportunities they had to become familiar with each other's music, suggesting that each had an influence on the other.

214. Mann, Alfred. "Eine Kompositionslehre von Händel." *Händel-Jahrbuch* 10–11 (1964–65): 35–57.

Identifies a group of Handel autographs in the Fitzwilliam Museum as teaching materials, most likely prepared for Princess Anne, George II's oldest daughter. Offers generous musical examples with commentary, showing that the lessons focused mostly on counterpoint and figured bass.

215. _____. "Artist and Teacher." *Current Musicology* 9 (1969): 141–46.

Shows how, in his role as teacher, Handel remained at all times the active composer. Musical examples.

216. _____. "Zum deutschen Erbe Händels." In *50 Jahre Göttinger Händel-Festspiele*, pp. 48–56. Ed. Walter Meyerhoff. Göttingen: Bärenreiter, 1970. ML 410 H13 M59.

Discusses the surviving works thought to have been composed in Germany. Pleads for a mature scholarly perspective on the question of Handel's nationality. Provides an excellent summary of the German musical tradition inherited by Handel.

217. _____, ed. *Georg Friedrich Händel: Aufzeichnungen zur Komponistenlehre*. Hallische Händel-Ausgabe Supple-

Particular Issues

ment, Bd. 1. Kassel: Bärenreiter, 1978. 100p. M 3 H262 1978 BD.1.

Selects from the group of Fitzwilliam autographs described in item 214 the manuscripts expressly prepared for teaching purposes, putting them in logical sequence and presenting photographic reproductions. Provides penetrating commentary on the materials, which focus on figured bass and counterpoint, with especially interesting fugal examples. Extensive preface, musical examples. Text appears in both German and English.

218. _____. "Handel's Successor: Notes on John Christopher Smith the Younger." In *Music in Eighteenth-Century England: Essays in Memory of Charles Cudworth*, pp. 135–45. Ed. Christopher Hogwood and Richard Luckett. Cambridge: Cambridge University Press, 1983. ML 55 C85. ISBN 0–521–23525–1.

Examines the life of J.C. Smith with special reference to his relationship with Handel and his own talents as conductor and composer. Identifies Smith as Handel's successor in a number of senses—as oratorio conductor and even composer, and as Royal Music Master. Comments on the functions of conductors at oratorio performances, pointing out that the great tradition of the composer as conductor was coming to an end in the later eighteenth century.

219. _____. "Handel the Organist." *American Organist* 19 (1985): 68–70.

Using early sources, shows that Handel's brilliance as a performer reflected his training in the German contrapuntal organ tradition.

220. _____. "Bach and Handel As Teachers of Thorough Bass." In *Bach, Handel, Scarlatti: Tercentenary Essays*, pp. 245–57. Ed. Peter Williams. Cambridge: Cambridge University Press, 1985. ML 55 B14 1985. ISBN 0–521–25217–2.

Explains that Bach and Handel "placed the teaching of composition in the framework of vocal and instrumental performance." Presents examples of teaching materials by Bach and Handel, showing that the emphasis of the instruction was on polyphonic part-writing.

221. _____. "An Unknown Detail of Handel Biography." *Bach: The Quarterly Journal of the Riemenschneider Bach Institute* 16/2 (1985): 3–5.

Reports on an annotation in a Minneapolis copy of Hawkins' *General History* (item 129), once owned by the oboist Redmond Simpson. Simpson describes a "paraletic stroke" suffered by Handel in Dublin in 1742. In German in *Händel-Jahrbuch* 31 (1985): 61–62.

222. Marx, Hans Joachim. "Händel in Rom—seine Beziehung zu Benedetto Card. Pamphilj." *Händel-Jahrbuch* 29 (1983): 107–18.

Presents copyists' bills from the accounts of Cardinal Pamphilj's household. Sheds light on the composition of the cantatas *Delirio amoroso* (HWV 99) and *Il Consiglio* (HWV 170) and the oratorio *Il trionfo del tempo e del disinganno* (HWV 46a).

223. _____. "Händels Beziehung zu Johann Mattheson." In *Händel und Hamburg: Ausstellung anläßlich des 300. Geburtstages von Georg Friedrich Händel*, pp. 65–73. Ed. Hans Joachim Marx. Hamburg: Karl Dieter Wagner, 1985. ML 410 H13 H234. ISBN 3-88979-009-7.

Describes the relationship between Handel and Mattheson, giving biographical details and citing Mattheson's references to Handel's music in his critical works. Contends that the *Six Fugues or Voluntarys*, published in 1735 as opus 3, were composed in Hamburg around 1705, and not later in England.

224. _____. "Ein unveröffentlichter Brief Händels in Harvard." *Göttinger Händel-Beiträge* 2 (1986): 221–25.

Presents a previously unpublished Handel letter from 1750. Includes a plate of the second page. Briefly discusses the letter's contents and background.

225. Matthews, Betty. "Handel—More Unpublished Letters." *Music and Letters* 42 (1961): 127–31.

Presents excerpts from a series of letters written by Anthony Ashley-Cooper to James Harris during the years 1746–57. They refer to Handel's good health and spirits, and to performances of oratorios, in particular *Theodora*. Offers a plate showing a little Larghetto composed by Handel during a visit to St. Giles. Amplification of details provided by Winton Dean in a letter on pp. 395–96.

226. _____. "Handel and the Corfes." *Musical Times* 112 (1971): 231–32.

Identifies James Corfe as a singer who sang small parts and in the chorus of Handel's operas and oratorios from about 1735.

227. _____. "Handel and the Royal Society of Musicians." *Musical Times* 125 (1984): 79–82.

Chronicles the history of the Royal Society of Musicians, which was originally called the Society of Decay'd Musicians, and its relationship with Handel and Handelians.

228. McCarthy, Margaret W. "Handel and Pope." *College Music Symposium* 25 (1985): 52–58.

Evaluates an eighteenth-century remark comparing Handel to Pope, with special reference to *Israel in Egypt* and *The Rape of the Lock*.

229. McLean, Hugh. "Bernard Granville, Handel and the Rembrandts." *Musical Times* 126 (1985): 593–601.

Expansive accounts of Bernard Granville and his sister Mary Delaney, and their relations with Handel. Discusses the Handel-Granville exchange of two Rembrandts, giving an inventory of Handel's art collection as it was put up for auction early in 1760.

230. _____. "Granville, Handel and 'Some Golden Rules'." *Musical Times* 126 (1985): 662–65.

Continuation of item 229. Traces the fate of the Handeliana in the Granville collection. Speculates that a document entitled "Some Golden Rules for the attaining to play Through Bass," while not written by Handel, could have some connection with the composer.

231. Morelli, G., ed. *Handel in Italia.* Venice: Istituto Italiano Antonio Vivaldi della Fondazione Giorgio Cini, 1981.

    Not examined.

232. Moser, H.J. *Der junge Händel und seine Vorläufer in Halle.* Der rote Turm, 5. Halle (Saale): Gebauer Schwetschke, 1929. 16p. ML 410 H13 M7.

    Briefly discusses Halle composers as far back as Scheidt. Notes on Handel's family and his activities in Halle. Informed speculation about his responsibilites at the Dom. Colored by nationalistic bias.

233. Ober, William B. "Bach, Handel, and 'Chevalier' John Taylor, M.D. Ophthalmiater." *New York State Journal of Medicine* 69/12 (1969): 1797–1807.

    Stops short of making definite diagnoses of Bach and Handel's vision problems in this thorough piece of detective work. Several possibilities are presented, with the author indicating his own preferences. Unflattering portrait of Taylor and his methods.

234. Rackwitz, Werner. *Il caro sassone: Georg Friedrich Händel, Lebensbeschreibung in Bildern.* Leipzig: VEB Deutscher Verlag für Musik, 1986. 204p. ML 410 H13 R15 1986.

    Collection of plates and illustrations showing Handel's associates and contemporaries and historical illustrations of the cities and buildings where he lived and worked. A few documents, autographs and stage sets. Short bibliography, index.

235. Ringer, Alexander L. "Handel and the Jews." *Music and Letters* 42 (1961): 17–29.

Contends that Handel's attitude to the Jews exerted a profound influence on his music, and especially on the treatment of Old Testament stories in the oratorios. Enlightening comments on the religious *milieu* in which the composer grew up.

236. Roscoe, Christopher. "Two 18th-Century Non-events." *Musical Times* 112 (1971): 18–19.

 Brings to light evidence from a Dublin newspaper showing that a performance of *Samson* was planned for Handel's 1742 stay there.

237. Sasse, Konrad. "Neue Daten zu Johann Christoph Schmidt." *Händel-Jahrbuch* 3 (1957): 115–25.

 Summarizes documentary research into the early life of the elder Smith, Handel's close friend and musical associate.

238. Schickling, Dieter. *Georg Friedrich Händel in Briefen, Selbstzeugnissen und Zeitgenössischen Dokumenten.* Zürich: Manesse Verlag, 1985. 267p. ML 410 H13 A34. ISBN 3-7175-1688-4.

 Offers a selected series of letters and other contemporary documents arranged chronologically. Bibliographical note, chronological table, checklist of operas and oratorios. Plates.

239. Smith, William C. "George III, Handel and Mainwaring." *Musical Times* 65 (1924): 789–95.

 Presents the complete set of manuscript annotations, possibly by George III himself, in a surviving copy of Mainwaring's biography (item 132). These provides details on numerous minor biographical issues. Plates.

240. _____. "Finance and Patronage in Handel's Life." In *Concerning Handel: His Life and Works*, pp. 9–64. London: Cassell, 1948. ML 410 H13 S59.

 Substantial account of this important aspect of Handel's professional life. Includes available documents and figures relevant to the composer's business dealings and relationships with patrons.

241. _____. "Gustavus Waltz: Was He Handel's Cook?" In *Concerning Handel: His Life and Works*, pp. 165–94. London: Kassell, 1948. ML 410 H13 S59.

Establishes through an exhaustive investigation that Waltz, though famous as Handel's "cook," had a long and fairly distinguished career as a singer and actor, and possibly as an instrumentalist. Interesting notes on London theatrical productions.

242. _____. "Handel's Failure in 1745: New Letters." In *Concerning Handel: His Life and Works*, pp. 145–61. London: Cassell, 1948. ML 410 H13 S59.

Draws attention to two letters from Handel printed in the *Daily Advertiser* during January, 1745. Concludes from these and other evidence that, although the 1744–45 oratorio season was a financial disaster, 1745 was by no means a year of unmitigated failure.

243. _____. "Handel the Man." In *Concerning Handel: His Life and Works*, pp. 3–6. London: Cassell, 1948. ML 410 H13 S59.

Transcript of a short speech given at the 1939 Halle Handel celebrations. General comments on Handel's character.

244. _____. "Some Handel Portraits Reconsidered." In *Concerning Handel: His Life and Works*, pp. 111–42. London: Cassell, 1948. ML 410 H13 S59.

Discusses but does not resolve various issues surrounding a Handel portrait by the English painter Francis Kyte and a series of engravings by the Dutch artist Jacobus Houbraken.

245. Sorenson, Scott. "Valentine Snow, Handel's Trumpeter." *Journal of the International Trumpet Guild* 4 (1979): 5–11.

Assembles all known information on the soloist for whom Handel wrote many virtuoso parts. Well documented.

246. Steblin, Rita. "Did Handel Meet Bononcini in Rome?" *Music Review* 45 (1984): 179–93.

Speculates that Handel may have written the cantata *Stelle, perfide stelle* on the occasion of Bononcini's return from Rome to Vienna in the late spring of 1706. Proposes a possible chronology for Handel's travels during the mysterious year 1705–1706. Examines in detail two cantata manuscripts in the Österreichische Nationalbibliothek. Tables, plates, illustrations.

247. Streatfeild, Richard A. *Handel, Canons and the Duke of Chandos.* London: C. Whittingham and Co., 1916. ML 410 H13 S8.

Not examined.

248. Strohm, Reinhard. "Händel in Italia: Nuovi contributi." *Rivista italiana di musicologia* 9 (1974): 152–74.

Milestone article in the research on Handel's Italian period. Suggests that he was invited to Italy not by Gian Gastone de' Medici, but by Ferdinand. Announces discovery of the libretto of *Rodrigo*, entitled *Vincer se stesso è la maggior vittoria*. Speculates that Antonio Salvi, Ferdinand's court poet, may have been its librettist. Discusses Handel's visits to Venice; his relationship with Vincenzo Grimani, the librettist of *Agrippina*; and Handel's meeting with Steffani in Italy.

249. _____. "Handel's Italian Journey as a European Experience." In *Essays on Handel and Italian Opera*, pp. 1–14. Cambridge: Cambridge University Press, 1985. ML 410 H13. ISBN 0–521–26428–6.

General and somewhat speculative discussion of Handel's Italian years (1706–10). Comments on *Vincer se stesso (Rodrigo)*, *Agrippina*, *La Resurrezione*, *Dixit Dominus*, *Salve regina*, *Donna che in ciel*, *Aci, Galatea e Polifemo* and on the cantatas, especially as they reflect social trends and political events. First published in Italian in *Handel in Italia*, ed. G. Morelli (Venice: Istituto Italiano Antonio Vivaldi della Fondazione Giorgio Cini, 1981).

250. Szonntagh, Eugene L. "New Works of Schuetz, Bach, Scarlatti, and Handel Discovered." *Diapason* 76/5 (1985): 10–11.

    Joke celebrating the composers' birthdays. Musical examples.

251. Taylor, Carole. "Handel and Frederick, Prince of Wales." *Musical Times* 125 (1984): 89–92.

    Concludes that Prince Frederick's hostility to Handel has been exaggerated. Examination of the prince's household accounts reveals his support for Handel. Contains important information on royal patronage.

252. Timms, Colin. "Handel and Steffani: A New Handel Signature." *Musical Times* 114 (1973): 374–77.

    Announces the discovery of a dated Handel signature in a copy of chamber duets by Agostino Steffani. Discusses the implications for Handel biography. Surveys the Handel chamber duets, with special reference to the influence of Steffani. Plates, musical examples.

253. Vlad, Roman. "Nei nomi di J.S. Bach e G.F. Haendel." *Nuova rivista musicale italiana* 19 (1985): 75–93.

    Holds that the "Canon triplex" in Bach's hand in the 1746 portrait by Elias Gottlieb Haussmann embodies a complex series of numerological relationships uniting the names of Bach and Handel. Suggests that Bach borrowed part of the theme from Handel. Musical examples, illustrations, and an arrangement by the author of solutions to the canon.

254. Williams, Peter. "A Newly Discovered Handel Organ." *Musical Times* 117 (1976): 1031–33.

Describes the recently restored choir organ in the Liebfrauenkirche at Halle, where Handel studied with and assisted Friedrich Wilhelm Zachow. Plate.

255. Young, Percy. "Handel the Man." In *Handel: A Symposium*, pp. 1–11. Ed. Gerald Abraham. London: Oxford University Press. 1954. ML 410 H13 A66.

Easygoing and somewhat speculative consideration of the composer's character and personality.

256. ———. "Händels Verhältnis zur englischen Sprache." *Händel-Jahrbuch* 21–22 (1975–76): 41–52.

Investigates Handel's relationship to the English language in terms of speaking, writing, and text-setting.

257. Zanetti, Emilia. "Haendel in Italia." *Approdo musicale* 3/12 (1960): 3–73.

Presents valuable information on Rome at the time of Handel's early Italian travels. Discusses works he composed there, especially *La resurrezione*, various cantatas and the Latin church music. Speculates on his relations with Corelli and the Scarlattis, his meeting with Steffani and his religious learnings. Notes on the 1729 trip to Italy. Followed by an annotated discography of the pieces composed in Italy.

III

SOURCES

When Handel died, he left his "Musick Books" to his old friend John Christopher Smith, who passed them on to his son in 1763. Smith the younger presented the Handel autographs to George III, and they are now in the Royal Music Collection in the British Library. The conducting scores, manuscript copies with autograph additions, went to Smith's stepdaughter Lady Rivers and eventually to Chrysander, and they are now in the State and University Library of Hamburg.

The magnificent collection of manuscript copies made for Charles Jennens was left to his relative the Earl of Aylesford in 1773 and now survives in the Newman Flower Collection at the Manchester Public Library. In the Fitzwilliam Museum at Cambridge are autograph sketches and fragments, autograph manuscripts of some shorter works, and the Barrett Lennard collection of copies made during the 1760s. Other important manuscript sources exist in private collections, some of which are described in item 282.

Chrysander issued facsimiles of the *Messiah* and *Jephtha* autographs. The Tenbury Wells conducting score of *Messiah* appeared in a 1974 facsimile edition by H. Watkins Shaw.

The early printed editions of Handel's works are catalogued and described in item 268. Very few of these represent complete works, and not all were issued with Handel's consent.

In the case of the operas, contemporary word-books offer crucial information. During 1988, Garland Publishing Inc. will be issuing a series entitled *The Librettos of Handel's Operas*, edited by Ellen T. Harris, which will offer complete facsimiles of seventy librettos of Handel's operas, including first performances and twenty-eight revisions.

Also underway is a comprehensive catalogue of Handel's autographs, being prepared by Donald Burrows and Martha Ronish (see item 271).

For information about the sources of specific pieces, the reader is advised to consult the prefaces to HHA volumes, as well as the separately published critical reports. Sources are listed in the *Händel-Handbuch* I–III (item 377), and in the works-list (item 379) of the New Grove Dictionary article, published separately as *The New Grove Handel* (item 147).

1. Catalogues

258. Clausen, Hans Dieter. *Händels Direktionspartituren ("Handexemplare")*. Hamburger Beiträge zur Musikwissenschaft, Band 7. Hamburg: Verlag der Musikalienhandlung Karl Dieter Wagner, 1972. 281p. ML 93 C44.

   Contains a complete catalogue of surviving conducting scores. Summarizes revisions and performance indications. Illustrations of watermarks, plates, bibliography. Instructions for using catalogue given in English as well as German (pp. 76–88).

259. Duck, Leonard W. "The Aylesford Handel Manuscripts: A Preliminary Check-list." *Manchester Review* 10 (1965): 228–32.

   Introduces and presents a brief list of the important collection, then newly acquired by the Manchester Public Library.

260. Ewerhart, Rudolf. "Die Händel-Handschriften der Santini-Bibliothek in Münster." *Händel-Jahrbuch* 6 (1960): 111–50.

Catalogues 69

Descriptive catalogue of the Handel manuscripts in the Santini collection at Münster. Especially important for cantatas and the two Italian oratorios, as they were copied during Handel's years in Italy, and several contain autograph annotations.

261. Fellowes, Edmund H. *The Catalogue of Manuscripts in the Library of St. Michael's College Tenbury.* Paris: Editions de L'Oiseau lyre, 1934. 319p. ML 136 T4 S3.

Includes the *Messiah* conducting score and various anthems and keyboard works in early collections. Brief descriptions, index.

262. Fuller-Maitland, J.A. and Mann A.H. *Catalogue of the Music in the Fitzwilliam Museum Cambridge.* London: Cambridge University Press, 1893. 298p. ML 136 C35 F5.

Pages 157–227 contain "Manuscripts and Sketches by G.F. Handel," a chapter by A.H. Mann describing in considerable detail the numerous autograph materials and early copies in the collection. (Does not contain the Barrett Lennard collection, presented in 1902).

263. *Handschriften und ältere Drucke der Werke Georg Friedrich Händels in der Musikbibliothek der Stadt Leipzig.* Leipzig: Musikbibliothek der Stadt Leipzig, 1966. 46p. ML 136 L4 M84.

Lists early copies and prints of Handel's music in the Leipzig Musikbibliothek. Indexes, bibliography.

264. Kinsky, Georg. *Manuskripte, Briefe, Dokumente von Scarlatti bis Stravinsky: Katalog der Musikautographen-Sammlung Louis Koch.* Stuttgart: Hoffmannsche Buchdruckerei Felix Krais, 1953. 361p. ML 138 K63.

Includes an autograph fragment of the cantata "Qual ti riveggio o Dio," the autograph of the trio "Se tu non lasci amore" and a Handel letter to his brother-in-law from February 1731. Detailed descriptions, provenance, background, musical examples, complete reproductions of the letter. Index.

265. Krause, Peter. *Handschriften und ältere Drucke der Werke Georg Friedrich Händels in der Musikbibliothek der Stadt Leipzig.* Leipzig: Musikbibliothek der Stadt Leipzig, 1966. 46p. ML 136 L4 M84.

Lists items in the city of Leipzig's collection, including early prints and some early copies, especially of chamber cantatas. Also contains the early German editions by J.O.H. Schaum (1821–25) and the complete series *The Works of Handel* published by the Handel Society between 1843 and 1858. Indexes.

266. Neville, Don J. "Opera 1600–1750 in Contemporary Editions and Manuscripts, Part 2." *Studies in Music from the University of Western Ontario* 4 (1979): 1–325.

Detailed catalogue of the University's early prints. Handel works are found on pp. 165–91. Plates, index.

267. Ronish, Martha J. "The Autograph Manuscripts of George Frideric Handel: A Catalogue." Ph.D. dissertation. University of Maryland, 1984.

A comprehensive catalogue of Handel autographs, it proposes chronologies based on the evidence of paper studies. Indexes. Not examined.

268. Smith, William C. *Handel. A Descriptive Catalogue of the Early Editions.* 2nd. ed. Oxford: Basel Blackwell, 1970. 378p. ML 134 H356 1970.

Includes all prints up to Handel's death as well as first editions and prints of special significance up to the early nineteenth century. Descriptions are detailed and far-ranging, including cross references, lists of singers named, origins of texts, citations of advertisements, etc. Superbly indexed. Second edition contains a supplement.

269. Squire, William Barclay. *British Museum. Catalogue of the King's Music Library. Part 1: The Handel Manuscripts.* London: British Museum, 1927. 143p. ML 138 B74 K4 pr. 1.

General Studies 71

Lists and describes the autographs and copies now in the British Library. Notes additions, deletions and special performance indications, especially where the manuscripts differ from Chrysander's edition. This magnificent collection includes a great many of the surviving Handel autographs. Plates, index.

270. Walker, Arthur D. *George Frideric Handel. The Newman Flower Collection in the Henry Watson Music Library.* Manchester: Manchester Public Libraries, 1972. 134p. ML 136 M2 H308.

Brief entries index the Aylesford Manuscripts, the printed music and printed librettos. Index of Handel's works, general index.

2. General Studies on Sources

271. Burrows, Donald J. "Paper Studies and Handel's Autographs: A Preliminary Report." *Göttinger Händel-Beiträge* I (1984): 103–15.

Summarizes the history of Handel paper studies. Outlines the problems encountered and methods devised for the author's work with Martha Ronish on a comprehensive catalogue of Handel's autographs. Suggests possible implications of this research. Presents as examples the entries on *Esther* (1718?) and *Muzio Scevola* Act III.

272. Heawood, Edward. *Watermarks Mainly of the 17th and 18th Centuries.* Monumenta chartae papyriceae historiam illustrantia I. Hilversum: The Paper Publications Society, 1950. Repr. 1957, 1970. 154p., 533 pl. (= pages of examples). "Addenda and Corrigenda" published in 1970.

Reproductions of the author's tracings and drawings of 4078 watermarks arranged by type and indexed by type (eg. "crown," "Fleur-de-Lis" etc.), and by names, letters, and dates found in the watermarks. General introduction, list of sources, and references to the watermarks.

273. Hicks, Anthony. "Handel Manuscripts." In *Handel and the Fitzwilliam*, pp. 10–13. Cambridge: Fitzwilliam Museum, 1974. ML 141 C3 H3.

   Surveys the major collections of Handel sources.

274. _____. "Handel: The Manuscripts and the Music." In *Handel: A Celebration of His Life and Times*, pp. 18–24. Ed. Jacob Simon. London: National Portrait Gallery, 1985. ML 410 H13. ISBN 0–904017–68–0.

   Excellent general introduction to the Handel sources. Traces the history of Handel's manuscripts from the time of his bequest to J.C. Smith. Notes on compositional method, outlining the process by which scores were copied and parts prepared. Description of word-books, early printed editions, and secondary copies. Summary of the major collections.

275. Hudson, Frederick. "Concerning the Watermarks in the Manuscripts and Early Prints of G.F. Handel." *Music Review* 20 (1959): 7–27.

   Calls for a catalogue of the watermarks in Handel sources. Guides the reader to works on English paper studies. Outlines some of the general problems faced by researchers. Summarizes source studies for the author's edition of the Opus 3 concertos. Illustrations.

276. _____. "The Study of Watermarks As a Research Factor in Undated Manuscripts and Prints: Beta-Radiography with Carbon-14 Sources." In *International Musicological Society: Report of the Eleventh Congress, Copenhagen 1972*, vol. 1., pp. 447–53. Ed. Henrik Glahn, Søren Sørenson and Peter Ryom. Copenhagen: Edition Wilhelm Hansen, 1974, ML 36 I6 1972. ISBN 87–7455–026–8.

   Provides a detailed explanation of the most refined method of recording watermarks. Select bibliography, list of centres in Europe and America where the service is provided.

General Studies 73

277. King, Alec Hyatt. *Handel and His Autographs.* London: British Museum, 1967. 32p., 20 plates. ML 93 K37.

Sketches the history of the autographs in the British Museum (now British Library). Outlines Handel's practices with regard to manuscripts, giving examples of performance indications, methods of dating, etc. Plates give examples from twenty different manuscripts. Short bibliography.

* Larsen, Jens Peter. *Handel's Messiah: Origins, Composition, Sources.* New York: Norton, 1972. 2nd edition. 337p. ML 410 H13 L2 1972. ISBN 0-393-00657-3.

Cited below as item 523.

278. _____. "Charakter und Bedeutung von zeitgenössischen Händel-Quellen." *Händel-Jahrbuch* 27 (1981): 141-48.

Translation of general remarks on the study of Handel sources made at the Handel Symposium in New York in 1979.

279. _____. "Probleme der Händel-Überlieferung." *Musikforschung* 34 (1981): 137-61.

Incorporates an extended discussion of Handel source problems into a somewhat critical evaluation of Clausen's work (item 258). Discusses the problem of multiple versions and the critical evaluation of sources, with emphasis on the identity and function of copyists.

280. La Rue, Jan. "Watermarks and Musicology." *Acta musicologica* 33 (1961): 120-46.

Introduces the subject and summarizes features of watermarks in America, England, Germany, Austria, France, Italy, the Netherlands, Scandinavia, Spain, and Switzerland. Illustrations, bibliography.

281. _____. s.v. "Watermarks." *New Grove Dictionary of Music and Musicians.* Ed. Stanley Sadie. London: Macmillan, 1980. Vol. 20, pp. 228-31. ML 100 G8863. ISBN 0-333-23111-2.

Introduces and defines the subject, with illustrations and a bibliography.

282. Smith, William C. *A Handelian's Notebook.* London: Adam and Charles Black, 1965. 179p. ML 410 H13 S595.

Offers a series of chatty and informative essays on various aspects of English Handel research and practice, including a summary of opera and staged oratorio performances from 1925 to 1964. Notes on German festivals and opera performances from 1920 to 1960. Describes several important private collections of Handeliana. Indexes.

3. Special Studies of the Sources

283. Barber, Elinore. "Early Handel Prints and a Handel Manuscript in the Bach Institute's Vault Collection." *Bach: The Quarterly Journal of the Riemenschneider Bach Institute* 16/2 (1985): 6–17.

Describes in detail an eighteenth-century manuscript copy of the Utrecht Jubilate in a German version, as well as seven early Handel prints. Plates.

* Baselt, Bernd. "Die Bühnenwerke Georg Friedrich Händels: Quellenstudien und thematisches Verzeichnis." 2 vols. Habilitationsschrift (Musicology). Martin-Luther-Universität Halle-Wittenberg, 1974.

Cited below as item 401.

284. Beechey, Gwilym. "A Late Eighteenth-Century Print of Handel's *Samson.*" *Musical Opinion* 108 (1985): 294–96.

Discusses a print from about 1787. Gives examples of nineteenth-century distortions of passages from *Samson*. Musical examples, plates.

* Beeks, Graydon F. "Handel's Chandos Anthems: The 'Extra' Movements." *Musical Times* 119 (1978): 621–23.

Special Studies

Cited below as item 612.

* _____. "Handel's Chandos Anthems: More 'Extra' Movements." *Music and Letters* 62 (1981): 155–61.

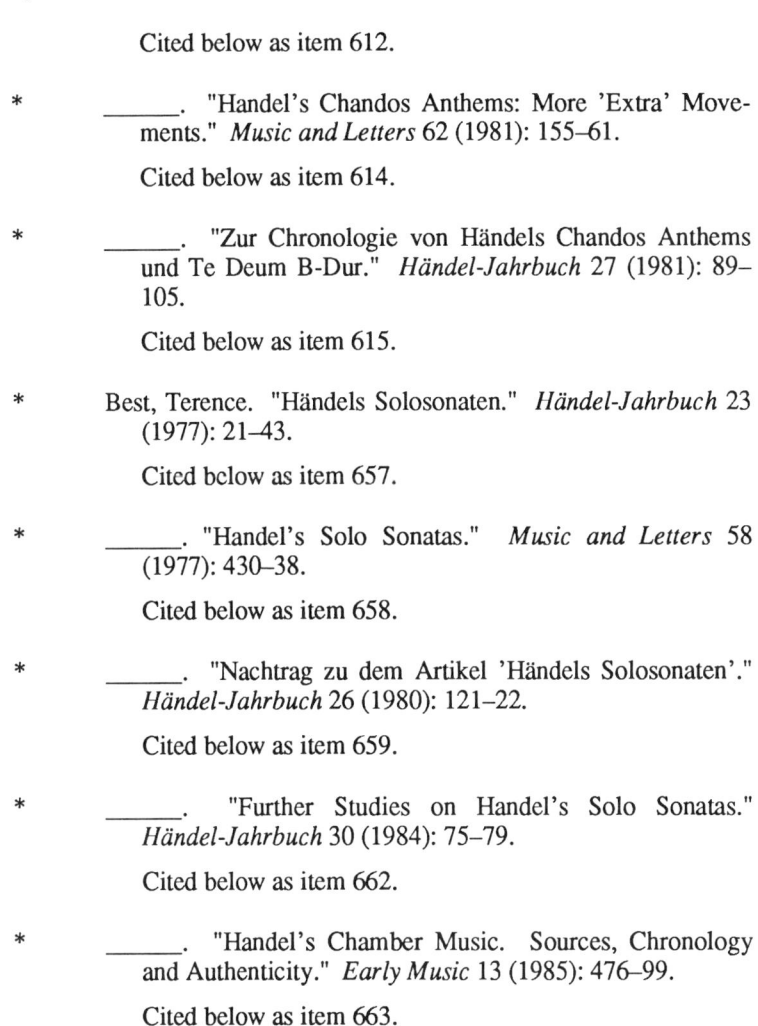

Cited below as item 614.

* _____. "Zur Chronologie von Händels Chandos Anthems und Te Deum B-Dur." *Händel-Jahrbuch* 27 (1981): 89–105.

Cited below as item 615.

* Best, Terence. "Händels Solosonaten." *Händel-Jahrbuch* 23 (1977): 21–43.

Cited below as item 657.

* _____. "Handel's Solo Sonatas." *Music and Letters* 58 (1977): 430–38.

Cited below as item 658.

* _____. "Nachtrag zu dem Artikel 'Händels Solosonaten'." *Händel-Jahrbuch* 26 (1980): 121–22.

Cited below as item 659.

* _____. "Further Studies on Handel's Solo Sonatas." *Händel-Jahrbuch* 30 (1984): 75–79.

Cited below as item 662.

* _____. "Handel's Chamber Music. Sources, Chronology and Authenticity." *Early Music* 13 (1985): 476–99.

Cited below as item 663.

* Bill, Oswald. "Die Liebesklage der Armida. Händels Kantate HWV 105 im Spiegel Bachscher Aufführungspraxis." In *Georg Friedrich Händel: Ausstellung aus Anlaß der Händel-Festspiele des Badischen Staatstheaters Karlsruhe 1985*, pp. 25–40. Ed. Klaus Häfner and Kurt Pietschmann.

Karlsruhe: Badische Landesbibliothek, 1985. ML 141 K36 H33. ISBN 3-88705-013-4.

Cited below as item 584.

* Boyd, Malcolm. "*La solitudine*: A Handel Discovery." *Musical Times* 109 (1968): 1111–14.

Cited below as item 585.

285. _____. "Music Manuscripts in the Mackworth Collection at Cardiff." *Music and Letters* 54 (1973): 133–41.

Describes the collection, which includes manuscript copies of cantatas and arias by Handel. One of these is a unique copy of a version of the cantata "L'aure grate, il fresco rio."

286. Brown, Patricia. "Introduction to Robert Dalley-Scarlett and His Collection." *Studies in Music* 5 (1971): 87–89.

Chatty introduction to the supplementary pamphlet "Early Published Handel Scores in the Dalley-Scarlett Collection," a descriptive catalogue listing eighty-two early prints now in the Fisher Library, University of Sydney (Australia).

* Burrows, Donald J. "Handel's Peace Anthem." *Musical Times* 114 (1973): 1230–32.

Cited below as item 622.

287. _____. "Sir John Dolben's Music Collection." *Musical Times* 120 (1979): 149–51.

Describes a collection, now at the Royal College of Music, which includes early copies of the Coronation Anthems and the A Major Te Deum.

288. _____. "Sources for Oxford Handel Performances in the First Half of the Eighteenth Century." *Music and Letters* 61 (1980): 177–85.

Examines performing materials associated with Oxford in the early eighteenth century, showing that the musicians there had access not only to Handel prints but also to copies of unpublished works by members of the Smith circle. Identifies an early copy of movements from the *Water Music*.

289. _____. "The Composition and First Performance of Handel's *Alexander's Feast*." *Music and Letters* 64 (1983): 206–11.

Describes in detail the five main sources connected with the early stages of *Alexander's Feast*.

* _____. "Walsh's Editions of Handel's Opera 1–5: The Texts and Their Sources." In *Music in Eighteenth-Century England: Essays in Memory of Charles Cudworth*, pp. 79–102. Ed. Christopher Hogwood and Richard Luckett. Cambridge: Cambridge University Press, 1983. ML 55 C85. ISBN 0–521–23525–1.

Cited below as item 666.

* _____. "Handel and Hanover." In *Bach, Handel, Scarlatti: Tercentenary Essays*, pp. 35–60. Ed. Peter Williams. Cambridge: Cambridge University Press, 1985. ML 55 B14 1985. ISBN 0–521–25217–2.

Cited above as item 187.

290. _____. "The Sources of *Alexander's Feast*." *Music and Letters* 66 (1985): 87–88.

In a letter to the editor, responds to the correspondence of Barry Cooper in the 1984 issue. Gives substantial additional details on sources.

291. _____. "The Autographs and Early Copies of *Messiah*: Some Further Thoughts." *Music and Letters* 66 (1985): 201–19.

Shows how the author's recent paper studies have affected the understanding of the *Messiah* sources. Evaluates the significance of newly-rediscovered copies and the London wordbook. Includes a summary of paper characteristics for the principal sources, as well as a table detailing *Messiah* performances from 1742 to 1754. Plates, musical examples.

*   Cooper, Barry. "The Organ Parts to Handel's *Alexander's Feast*." *Music and Letters* 59 (1978): 159-79.

Cited below as item 548.

*   _____. "Keyboard Sources in Hereford." *Research Chronicle of the Royal Musical Association* 16 (1980): 135-39.

Cited below as item 669.

292. Coopersmith, J.M. "Some Adventures in Handel Research." *Papers Read by Members of the American Musicological Society* 1937, pp. 11-23.

An early study of Handel orthography, enlivened by discussion of modern Handel forgeries. Musical examples, fuzzy reproductions.

293. _____. "The First Gesamtausgabe: Dr. Arnold's Edition of Handel's Works." *Notes* 4 (1947): 277-91; 439-49.

Clears up areas of confusion with regard to the first collected edition, including the dates of publication. Gives details about the early years of the project. Surveys subscription lists, gives table of contents.

*   Dean, Winton. *Handel's Dramatic Oratorios and Masques.* London: Oxford University Press, 1959. 694p. ML 410 H13 D35.

Cited below as item 503.

294. _____. "Handel's Early London Copyists." In *Bach, Handel, Scarlatti: Tercentenary Essays*, pp. 75-98. Ed. Peter Williams. Cambridge: Cambridge University Press, 1985. ML 55 B14 1985. ISBN 0-521-25217-2.

Concludes on the basis of systematic study of early copies that there were two "circles" of copyists for Handel manu-

Special Studies

scripts before the "Smith circle" discovered by Larsen (item 523). Suggests that Handel's friend J.C. Smith was enlisted as a copyist around 1718, and that he learned the trade from the violist D. Linke. Plates, tables, illustrations.

295. _____. "The Musical Sources for Handel's *Teseo* and *Amadigi*." In *Slavonic and Western Music: Essays for Gerald Abraham*, pp. 63–80. Ed. Malcolm Brown and Roland Wiley. Oxford: Oxford University Press, 1985. ML 55 A18 1984. ISBN 0-8357-1594-9.

Describes the manuscript sources for the two operas, including tables summarizing details.

* Dean, Winton and J. Merrill Knapp. *Handel's Operas 1704–1726*. Oxford: Clarendon Press, 1987. 751p. ML 410 H13 D37 1986. ISBN 0-19-315219-3.

Cited below as item 433.

296. Ewerhart, Rudolf. "New Sources for Handel's *La resurrezione*." *Music and Letters* 41 (1960): 127–35.

Announces the discovery in the Santini collection (Münster) of the conducting score from the first performance of *La resurrezione*. Discusses its significant implications, especially with regard to the overture and the sequence of the first few numbers.

297. Feustking, Friedrich C. "Die durch Blut und Mord erlangete Liebe, oder Nero." *Händel-Jahrbuch* 23 (1977): 60–135.

Photographic reproduction of the libretto printed for the February 1705 production of *Nero*.

298. Fuld, James J. "The First Complete Printing of Handel's *Messiah*." *Music and Letters* 55 (1974): 454–57.

Examines a unique copy of *Messiah* in the Royal Academy of Music. Speculates that *Messiah* may originally have been issued in three parts, in an edition unknown to William C. Smith (see item 268).

* Gudger, William D. "Handel's Organ Concertos in Walsh's Arrangements for Solo Keyboard." *Organ Yearbook* 10 (1979): 63–82.

Cited below as item 684.

299. Hall, James S. "The Importance of the Aylesford Handel Manuscripts." *Brio* 4/1 (1967): 7–11.

Demonstrates with a few well-chosen examples from *L'Allegro* and *Acis and Galatea* the crucial importance of the Aylesford copies.

* Hill, Cecil. "Die Abschrift von Händels 'Wassermusik' in der Sammlung Newman Flower." *Händel-Jahrbuch* 17 (1971): 75–88.

Cited below as item 686.

300. Hinsch, Hinrich. "Faksimile-Wiedergabe des Librettos *Der beglückte Florindo*." *Händel-Jahrbuch* 30 (1984): 21–73.

Photographic reproduction of the libretto printed for the 1708 Hamburg production. Introduction by Bernd Baselt.

301. ———. "Faksimile-Wiedergabe des Librettos *Die verwandelte Daphne*." *Händel-Jahrbuch* 31 (1985): 17–59.

Photographic reproduction of the libretto printed for the 1708 Hamburg production.

302. Hirsch, Paul. "Dr. Arnold's Handel Edition (1787–1797)." *Music Review* 8 (1947): 106–16.

Covers the same ground as item 293, coming to many of the same conclusions about the dates and early history of Arnold's edition. Gives table of contents, prospectus, advertisement, plates, etc.

303. Hopkinson, Cecil. "Handel and France: Editions Published There During His Lifetime." *Edinburgh Bibliographical Society Transactions* 3 (1948–55): 223–48.

Special Studies

> Gives complete bibliographic details on prints of Handel's music issued in France during the 1730s, '40s and '50s. Included were keyboard pieces, instrumental chamber music, concertos, and overtures.

304. Hudson, Fredrick. "The Earliest Paper Made by James Whatman the Elder (1702–1759) and Its Significance in Relation to G.F. Handel and John Walsh." *Music Review* 38 (1977): 15–32.

    Establishes that Whatman's paper was being used as early as December, 1740, when it appears in Walsh's *Select Harmony*, part IV. Investigates Whatman in light of Watermarks in Walsh/Handel prints ca. 1739–41. Lists relevant prints in the National Library of Scotland. Plates.

305. _____. "The New Bedford Manuscript Part-Books of Handel's Setting of *L'Allegro*." *Notes* 33 (1977): 531–52.

    Describes three newly-discovered part-books from around 1780. Notes on the history of the Shaw Musical Society. Illustrations of watermarks, plates.

306. Johnstone, H. Diack. "An Unknown Book of Organ Voluntaries." *Musical Times* 108 (1967): 1003–1007.

    Describes a manuscript collection from the mid-eighteenth century, which includes an E major fugue attributed to John Stanley and Handel. Musical examples.

307. Kinnear, Betty and Robert Illing. *Georg Frederick Handel, Solo Cantatas: A Photographic Reproduction of the 18th-Century Manuscript Collection in the Fisher Library of the University of Sydney.* Adelaide: issued privately, 1975. 274p. ML 96.4 H2 C3 1975.

    Photographic reproduction with a few introductory comments of a mid-eighteenth century manuscript containing fifty-two Italian cantatas.

308. _____. *An Illustrated Catalogue of the Early Editions of Handel in Australia.* Adelaide: issued privately, 1977. 255p.

Contains a substantial number of early editions, including about half the operas, two thirds of the oratorios, most of the sacred music, and half the instrumental music. Each entry appears with a reproduction of the title page and features a detailed description including references to item 268.

309. Knapp, J. Merrill. "The Autograph Manuscripts of Handel's *Ottone.*" In *Festskrift Jens Peter Larsen*, pp. 167–80. Ed. Nils Schiørring, Henrik Glahn, Carsten E. Hatting. Copenhagen: Wilhelm Hansen, 1972. ML 55 L23 F5. ISBN 87-7455-000-4.

Compares the autograph sources of *Ottone* with Chrysander's Händel Gesellschaft edition. Table.

310. _____. "The Autograph of Handel's *Riccardo primo.*" In *Studies in Renaissance and Baroque Music in Honor of Arthur Mendel*, pp. 331–58. Ed. Robert L. Marshall. Kassel: Bärenreiter, 1974. ML 55 M415 S7. ISBN 3-7618-0412-1.

Discusses the background, literary sources, and libretto of the opera. Compares the autograph with the Hamburg score used by Chrysander in the old Händel Gesellschaft edition. Musical examples.

311. _____. "The Hall Handel Collection." *Princeton University Library Chronicle* 36 (1974): 3–18.

Offers background on James S. Hall and describes his Handel collection of prints, early copies, and other items now in the Princeton University Library. Of particular interest is an early copy of *Belshazzar*. Beautiful reproductions.

* _____. "Die drei Fassungen von Händels *Il trionfo del tempo.*" In *Konferenzbericht Halle (Saale) 1981*, pp. 86–94.

Cited below as item 519.

312. _____. "Editionstechnische Probleme bei Händels Opern, im Besonderen bei *Teseo, Poro, Ezio,* und *Deidamia.*" In *Konferenzbericht Halle (Saale) 1982*, pp. 22–32.

In an attempt to explain how source studies affect modern performance, takes the reader through the process of editing a Handel opera. Shows, using four examples, how the problems may vary.

* Kubik, Reinhold. *Händels Rinaldo: Geschichte, Werk, Wirkung.* Neuhausen: Hänssler-Verlag, 1982. 264p. ML 410 H13 K8. ISBN 3-7751-0594-8.

Cited below as item 451.

313. Kümmerling, Harald. "Heinrich Bokemeyers Kopie von Händels erster Fassung des *Laudate pueri dominum.*" *Händel-Jahrbuch* 1 (1955): 102-104.

Describes a copy of Handel's *Laudate pueri* in F made by the Wolfenbüttel cantor Heinrich Bokemeyer around 1720. Cites in detail the variants between the copy and Handel's autograph, used by Chrysander for his edition. In some cases, Bokemeyer's version probably corrects errors, and its text setting is superior.

* Lasocki, David. "A New Look at Handel's Recorder Sonatas II: The Autograph Manuscripts." *Recorder and Music* 6 (1978): 71-79.

Cited below as item 695.

* _____. "A New Look at Handel's Recorder Sonatas III: The Roger and Walsh Prints: A New View." *Recorder and Music* 6 (1979): 130-32.

Cited below as item 696.

314. Lenneberg, Hans and Laurence Libin. "Unknown Handel Sources in Chicago." *Journal of the American Musicological Society* 22 (1969): 85-100.

Describes copies originating in the Smith circle in the mid-eighteenth century. The Chandos anthems, the Birthday Ode and parts of *Acis and Galatea, La resurrezione,* etc. are involved. Tables, plates, illustrations.

315. Mann, Alfred. "Zur Frage der Datierung durch Wasserzeichen. Mit einem Brief von Frederick Hudson." *Händel-Jahrbuch* 26 (1980): 123-28.

Remarks on the special problems of chronology inherent in a collection of fragments, referring to the author's HHA volume "Aufzeichnungen zur Kompositionslehre." Presents a German translation of a letter by Fredrick Hudson offering information on the collection and on the use of watermarks generally.

*   Marx, Hans Joachim. "Ein Beitrag Händels zur Accademia Ottoboniana in Rom." *Hamburger Jahrbuch für Musikwissenschaft* 1 (1974): 69-86.

    Cited below as item 596.

*   _____. "Zur Kompositionsgeschichte von Händels Pastoralkantate *Apollo e Dafne*." *Göttinger Handel-Beiträge* I (1984): 70-85.

    Cited below as item 598.

*   Mayo, John. "Handel's Italian Cantatas." Ph.D. dissertation. University of Toronto, 1977.

    Cited below as item 599.

*   Nielsen, N.K. "Handel's Organ Concertos Revisited." *Dansk aarbog for musikforskning* 3 (1963): 3-26.

    Cited below as item 706.

*   Pestelli, Giorgio. "Haendel e Alessandro Scarlatti: Problemi di attribuzione nel MS A 7663 Cass. della biblioteca del Conservatorio 'Nicolo Paganini' di Genova." *Rivista italiana di musicologia* 7 (1972): 103-14.

    Cited below as item 708.

316. Picker, Martin. "Handeliana in the Rutgers University Library." *Journal of the Rutgers University Library* 29 (1965): 1-12.

Special Studies

Gives details on more than forty items in the Rutgers collection, including thirty eighteenth-century editions of operas, organ concertos, oratorios, odes, and anthems. Mentions early manuscript copies of anthems, duets, and the Birthday Ode, as well as an 1804 German adaptation of the Funeral Anthem.

* Redlich, Hans F. "The Oboes in Handel's Opus 6." *Musical Times* 109 (1968): 530–31.

Cited below as item 715.

317. Serwer, Howard. "Die Anfänge des Händelschen Oratoriums (*Esther* 1718)." In *Konferenzbericht Halle (Saale) 1981*, pp. 34–45.

Discusses in great detail the sources for the original version of *Esther*. Suggests plausibly that it was composed in 1718.

318. Smith, William C. "Recently-Discovered Handel Manuscripts." *Musical Times* 78 (1937): 312–15.

Describes the autograph of the final chorus of *Floridante*, a page of an unidentified aria, and an early copy of four additional arias used in the 1717 revival of *Rinaldo*. Plates.

319. _____. "*Acis and Galatea* in the Eighteenth Century." In *Concerning Handel: His Life and Works*, pp. 197–265. London: Cassell, 1948. ML 410 H13 S59.

Describes editions and outlines performances of *Acis and Galatea* through the eighteenth century.

320. _____. "The Earliest Editions of *Messiah*." In *Concerning Handel: His Life and Works*, pp. 67–108. London: Cassell, 1948. ML 410 H13 S59.

Lists and describes nine early editions of *Messiah*.

321. _____. "The Earliest Editions of the *Water Music*." In *Concerning Handel: His Life and Works*, pp. 269–87. London: Cassell, 1948. ML 410 H13 S59.

Describes early editions up to the 1760s, giving a thematic index of the first editions for orchestra and harpsichord. Briefly discusses the Barrett Lennard copy in the Fitzwilliam Museum, Cambridge. Plates.

*   ———. "*Samson*: The Earliest Editions and Handel's Use of the Dead March." *Händel-Jahrbuch* 3 (1957): 105–14.

Cited below as item 537.

322. Squire, William Barclay. "Handel in Contemporary Song-Books." *Musical Antiquary* 4 (1912–13): 102–11.

Attempts to identify the songs printed under Handel's name before 1800. Brief descriptions, identifications of adaptations and doubtful or spurious items as far as possible.

323. Stahura, Mark W. "The Publishing Copy Text of Handel's *Samson*." *Journal of Musicology* 4 (1985): 207–16.

Discusses in detail a secondary copy of *Samson* with Handel's annotations. Tables.

*   Steblin, Rita. "Did Handel Meet Bononcini in Rome?" *Music Review* 45 (1984): 179–93.

Cited above as item 246.

324. Streatfeild, Richard A. "The Granville Collection of Handel Manuscripts." *Musical Antiquary* 2 (1910–11): 208–24.

Gives background on Handel's friend Bernard Granville (1709–75) and describes the manuscripts (now in the British Library). In some cases, notes that these early copies represent versions different from Chrysander's edition. The rarest item is the autograph of the trio "Se tu non lasci amore," in Basel (see item 264). See also W.H. Cummings in *Musical Antiquary* 3 (1911): 59–60.

*   Stutzenberger, David R. "'Belshazzar,' an Oratorio by George Frideric Handel: An Edition, Critical Report and Performance Tape." DMA dissertation. University of Maryland, 1980.

Special Studies 87

Cited below as item 541.

325. Talbot, Michael. "Some Overlooked Manuscripts in Manchester." *Musical Times* 115 (1974): 942–44.

Lists and briefly describes non-Handelian manuscripts in the Newman Flower collection. Since much of the music originated in Italy during the time of Handel's early visit there, it seems likely that the manuscripts originally belonged to him.

326. Timms, Colin. "Handelian and Other Librettos in Birmingham Central Library." *Music and Letters* 65 (1984): 141–67.

Describes an important collection of librettos in Birmingham, two of which are unique copies of librettos for Handel productions. Especially interesting information on the pasticcio *Ormisda*. Appends an annotated list of all sixty-one librettos.

* Tobin, John. *Handel at Work.* London: Cassell, 1964. 84p. ML 410 H13 T6.

Cited below as item 370.

* _____. *Handel's Messiah: A Critical Account of the Manuscript Sources and Printed Editions.* London: Cassell, 1969. 279p. ML 410 H13 T63.

Cited below as item 543.

327. Watanabe, Keiichiro. "Die Kopisten der Handschriften von den Werken G.F. Händels in der Santini-Bibliothek, Münster." *Ongaku Gaku* 16 (1970): 225–62.

Identifies by handwriting characteristics eleven copyists of Handel manuscripts in the Santini collection, in addition to Angelini and Alessandro Scarlatti. Illustrations.

328. _____. "The Lost Manuscript Copy of Handel's 'Gloria Patri' (The former Nanki Music Library MS 0.52.3)."

Toho Gakuen College of Music, Faculty Bulletin 3 (1977): 42–66.

Discusses the history of the lost copy of the "Gloria patri" which is meant to conclude *Nisi Dominus*. Notes on the copyists of this and other works from the Italian period.

329. _____. "The Paper Used by Handel and His Copyists during the Time of 1706–1710." *Ongaku gaku* 27 (1981): 129–71.

Taking as his starting point five autograph manuscripts with date and place noted, the author has made a thorough scientific study of the papers used by Handel and his copyists during the Italian period. The conclusions, which are of particular interest with regard to *Apollo e Dafne*, are presented in a series of detailed Appendixes, including watermark tracings, manuscripts arranged according to paper, manuscripts in alphabetical order of the works, and copyists of each manuscript.

330. Zobeley, Fritz. "Werke Händels in der Graf von Schönbornschen Musikbibliothek." *Händel-Jahrbuch* 1931, pp. 98–116.

Carefully describes an early manuscript copy of *Rodelinda*, a copy of the Cluer edition of *Scipio*, and a collection of arias from *Rodrigo* and *Agrippina*. Discusses at length two concertos doubtfully attributed to Handel. Musical examples, illustration of watermark.

4. Compositional Method and Borrowings

The study of Handel's borrowings has an intriguing history of its own. Nineteenth-century English Handelians were shocked when they began to discover their hero's "thievery." During the early years of the twentieth century, a few enlightened scholars, notably Percy Robinson, published defenses of Handel, showing that borrowing was a common and accepted practice in his time. Nowadays it is generally recognized that borrowing was integral to Handel's compositional method, and that the study of it may answer old questions and open up new areas of exploration.

* Ardry, Roger W. "The Influence of the Extended Latin Sacred Works of Giacomo Carissimi on the Biblical Oratorios of George Frederic Handel." Ph.D. dissertation. The Catholic University of America, 1964. 142p.

Cited below as item 491.

331. Baselt, Bernd. "Zum Parodieverfahren in Händels frühen Opern." *Händel-Jahrbuch* 21–22 (1975–76): 19–39.

Shows that the seven operas composed between 1707 and 1715 are an especially rich field for the study of Handel's self-borrowings. Appendix lists the parodies in *Rodrigo*, *Agrippina*, *Rinaldo*, *Il pastor fido*, *Teseo*, *Lucio Cornelio Silla*, and *Amadigi*. Reflects on the types, causes and implications of Handel's parody techniques.

332. _____. "Miscellanea Handeliana." In *Der Komponist und sein Adressat: Musikästhetische Beiträge zur Autor-Adressat-Relation*, pp. 60–88. Ed. Siegfried Bimberg. Wissenschaftliche Beiträge der Martin-Luther-Universität Halle-Wittenberg 1976. Halle: Martin-Luther-Universität, 1976.

Examines "wandering melodies" in Handel's sketches generally. Discusses aspects of Handel's relationship with Gottlieb Muffat. Introduces a document written by Chrysander concerning plans for an 1857 staged performance of *Acis and Galatea*. (Not examined; see the RILM abstract).

333. _____. "Schöpferische Beziehungen zwischen G. Ph. Telemann und G. F. Händel—G. Ph. Telemanns *Harmonischer Gottesdienst* als Quelle für Händel." In *Die Bedeutung Georg Philipp Telemanns für die Entwicklung der europäischen Musikkultur im 18. Jahrhundert: Bericht über die Internationale Wissenschaftliche Konferenz anläßlich der Georg-Philipp-Telemann-Ehrung der DDR Magdeburg 12. bis 18. März 1981*, Teil 2, pp. 4–14. Ed. Günter Fleischhauer, Wolf Hobohm, Walter

Siegmund-Schultze. Magdeburg: 1985.

Discusses in detail numerous Handel borrowings from Telemann's cantata cycle *Harmonischer Gottes-Dienst*, published in Hamburg in 1725–26. Shows that Handel borrowed from at least fifty of the cantatas for works composed between 1727 and 1748. Excellent musical examples.

334. Bennett, Joseph. "Handel and Muffat." *Musical Times* 36 (1895): 149–52; 667.

Discusses, using many musical examples, Handel's borrowings from Gottlieb Muffat's *Componimenti musicali*. Muses on the practice of borrowing. Briefly points out a borrowing from Mattheson in a Handel Allemande and a somewhat doubtful example in *Messiah* from Buxtehude.

* Burrows, Donald J. "Handel's Peace Anthem." *Musical Times* 114 (1973): 1230–32.

Cited below as item 622.

* Dean, Winton. *Handel's Dramatic Oratorios and Masques*. London: Oxford University Press, 1959. 694p. ML 410 H13 D35.

Cited below as item 503.

335. _____. "Handel and Keiser: Further Borrowings." *Current Musicology* 9 (1969): 73–80.

Identifies hitherto unrecognized borrowings from Keiser's *Octavia* in *Ariodante* and *Orlando*. Traces Handel's use over five decades of a remarkable intervallic figure from *Octavia*. Musical examples.

* Dean, Winton and J. Merrill Knapp. *Handel's Operas 1704–1726*. Oxford: Clarendon Press, 1987. 751p. ML 410 H13 D37 1986. ISBN 0–19–315219–3.

Cited below as item 433.

Compositional Method 91

336. Derr, Ellwood. "Handel's Procedures for Composing with Materials from Telemann's 'Harmonischer Gottes-Dienst' in 'Solomon'." *Göttinger Händel-Beiträge* I (1984): 116–46.

Investigates in the most profound way Handel's use of Telemann's materials in *Solomon*, appending a list of additional notes that draw upon the *Harmonischer Gottes-Dienst*. Hypothesizes that "Handel was able to encode and store large quantities of music in long-term memory . . . and that the guise of the recalled data in new pieces results from conscious crafting procedures." Extensive musical examples.

* Drummond, Pippa. *The German Concerto: Five Eighteenth-Century Studies*. Oxford: Oxford University Press, 1980. 402p. ML 1263. ISBN 0-19816122-0.

Cited below as item 671.

* Gellrich, Gerhard. "Muffat in Händels Werkstatt." *Die Musikforschung* 13 (1960): 50–51.

Cited below as item 679.

337. Gudger, William D. "Handel's Last Compositions and His Borrowings from Habermann (Part 1)." *Current Musicology* 22 (1976): 61–72.

Reveals previously unidentified borrowings in the B flat organ concerto (HWV 308) from a set of six masses published as opus 1 by Franz Johann Habermann (1706–83). Study of Handel's use of Habermann's themes and his re-working of the first movement emphasizes the progressive tendencies in the concerto, including *galant* phrase structures and elements of the Classical concerto form.

338. _____. "Handel's Last Compositions and His Borrowings from Habermann (Part 2)." *Current Musicology* 23 (1977): 28–45.

Shows that Handel borrowed more often than was previously known from the six masses of F.J. Habermann

(1706–83) for the choruses in *Jephtha*. Examines related autograph sketches to illuminate the borrowing procedure. Examples, appendix listing sketches and fragments related to *Jephtha*.

339. _____. "A Borrowing from Kerll in *Messiah*." *Musical Times* 118 (1977): 1038–39.

Points out a borrowing from a canzona by Johann Caspar Kerll in "Let All the Angels of God" in *Messiah*. Outlines the borrowing process as it is revealed in sketches. Reviews Handel's borrowings from Kerll. Musical examples.

* _____. "Skizzen und Entwürfe für den Amen-Chor in Händels *Messias*." *Händel-Jahrbuch* 26 (1980): 83–114.

Cited below as item 509.

* _____. "Sketches and Drafts for *Messiah*." *American Choral Review* 27/2–3 (1985): 31–44.

Cited below as item 510.

340. Kimbell, David. "Aspekte von Händels Umarbeitungen und Revisionen eigener Werke." *Händel-Jahrbuch* 23 (1977): 45–67.

Deals with Handel's arrangements and revisions of his own works, dividing his study into 1) transcriptions 2) revisions and 3) new versions that reflect changing tastes. As an example of the latter, *Il trionfo del tempo* and *The Triumph of Time and Truth* are examined to reveal aspects of the composer's late oratorio style under the influence of the English Enlightenment. Musical examples from *Il trionfo* and from various keyboard works.

341. Larsen, Jens Peter. "Reflections on Handel's 'Borrowing' Practices." In the modern reprint of Percy Robinson's *Handel and His Orbit*, pp. v–xii. New York: Da Capo Press, 1979. ML 410 H13 R5 1979. ISBN 0–306–79522–1.

Compositional Method

General comments on the early twentieth-century conflict about the morality of Handel's borrowing. Speculates on the reasons for this practice.

342. Leavis, Ralph. "Three Impossible Handel Borrowings." *Musical Times* 123 (1982): 470–71.

Presents, with musical examples, passages by Gabrieli (?), Corelli, and Rameau which seem to have furnished significant thematic material for Handel (in *Israel in Egypt*, *Messiah*, and *Joseph*), but which exist only in sources that have no connection with Handel. Adds two items to Winton Dean's list of borrowings in the oratorios (item 503).

343. Lutz, Martin. "Parodie und Entlehnung bei Händel." In *Georg Friedrich Händel: Ausstellung aus Anlaß der Händel-Festspiele des Badischen Staatstheaters Karlsruhe 1985*, pp. 81–94. Ed. Klaus Häfner and Kurt Pietschmann. Karlsruhe: Badische Landesbibliothek, 1985. ML 141 K36 H33. ISBN 3-88705-013-4.

Explores the notion of parody in the Baroque period and particularly in Handel's works. Distinguishes between parody and borrowing. Plates.

344. Mann, Alfred. "Handelian Rehearsal and Performance Practice." *College Music Symposium* 9 (1969): 97–100.

Shows that the free applications of the *concertato* principle in Handel's choral works represent not only compositional decisions but also solutions to practical problems. Musical examples.

* Marx, Hans Joachim. "Ein Beitrag Händels zur Accademia Ottoboniana in Rom." *Hamburger Jahrbuch für Musikwissenschaft* 1 (1974): 69–86.

Cited below as item 596.

* ———. "Zur Kompositionsgeschichte von Händels Pastoralkantate *Apollo e Dafne*." *Göttinger Händel-Beiträge* I (1984): 70–85.

Cited below as item 598.

345. Massenkeil, Günther. "Zum Verhältnis Carissimi-Händel." *Händel-Jahrbuch* 28 (1982): 43–51.

Discusses in detail Handel's use in *Samson* of the final chorus of Carissimi's *Jephta*. Shows that "He Chose a Mournful Muse" from *Alexander's Feast* is indebted to a solo passage from *Jephta*. Comments on the interest in Carissimi's music in England during and before Handel's time, pointing out that the relationship between the two composers may be more complex than hitherto realized. Musical examples.

* Mayo, John. "Handel's Italian Cantatas." Ph.D. dissertation. University of Toronto, 1977.

Cited below as item 599.

346. Prout, Ebenezer. "Urio's Te Deum and Handel's Use Thereof." *Monthly Musical Record* 1 (1871): 139–41.

Cites numerous examples of Handel's borrowings from the Te Deum, especially in the Dettingen Te Deum and *Saul*. Expresses the view that most of Handel's themes are borrowed. Musical examples.

347. _____. "Handel's Obligations to Stradella." *Monthly Musical Record* 1 (1871): 154–56.

Mentions several Handel borrowings from Stradella's serenata, published by Chrysander. Reveals much about the late nineteenth-century attitude to musical borrowing. Musical examples.

348. _____. "Graun's Passion Oratorio and Handel's Knowledge of It." *Monthly Musical Record* 24 (1894): 97–99; 121–23.

Chronicles in a chatty way the author's discovery and study of borrowing in *Il trionfo del Tempo* (1737) and *The Triumph of Time* from an early Brunswick Passion by Carl Heinrich Graun. Exemplifies typical nineteenth-century shock at the "robbery." Musical examples.

349. Reich, Herbert. "Händels *Trauer-Hymne* und die *Musikalischen Exequien* von Schütz." *Musik und Kirche* 36 (1966): 74–78.

Suggests that Handel referred to Schütz' *Musikalischen Exequien* in his *Funeral Anthem*. Cites a borrowing. Musical examples.

350. _____. "Händel's Chorbearbeitung einer Orgelfuge von Joh. Phil. Krieger." *Musik und Kirche* 36 (1966): 172–77.

Discusses the close relationship between an organ fugue by J.P. Krieger and "She put on righteousness" from the *Funeral Anthem*.

351. Roberts, John H. "Handel's Borrowings from Telemann: An Inventory." *Göttinger Händel-Beiträge* I (1984): 147–71.

Attempts to provide a comprehensive list of Handel's borrowings from Telemann's *Harmonischer Gottes-Dienst*, *Musique de table*, and *Sonates sans basse*. Argues effectively against the belief that Handel borrowed only rarely from other composers before 1736 and also against the notion that he borrowed only because of haste, illness or lack of inspiration.

352. _____. "Introduction." In *Reinhard Keiser's "Adonis" and "Janus"*, pp. xv–xx. Handel Sources: Materials for the Study of Handel's Borrowing, 1. New York: Garland Publishing Inc., 1986. M 1500 K26 A2. ISBN 0–8240–6475–5.

Provides background on Keiser's two operas, as well as a list of Handel's borrowings from them.

353. _____. "Introduction." In *Reinhard Keiser's "La forza della virtù"*, pp. xi–xvii. Handel Sources: Materials for the Study of Handel's Borrowing, 2. New York: Garland Publishing Inc., 1986. M 1500 K26 F6. ISBN 0–8240–6476–3.

Offers background on Keiser's opera and its sources, as well as a list of Handel's borrowings from it.

354. _____. "Introduction." In *Reinhard Keiser's "Claudius" and "Nebucadnezar"*, pp. xv–xxvi. Handel Sources: Materials for the Study of Handel's Borrowing, 3. New York: Garland Publishing Inc., 1986. M 1500 K26 C6. ISBN 0-8240-6477-1.

Presents brief background and notes on the sources of the two Keiser works, as well as an extensive list of Handel's borrowings from them.

355. _____. "Introduction." In *"Ambleto" by Francesco Gasparini and Others, and Giovanni Porta's "Numitore"*, pp. vii–xvi. Handel Sources: Materials for the Study of Handel's Borrowing, 4. New York: Garland Publishing Inc., 1986. M 1500 A5 I7. ISBN 0-8240-6478-X.

Provides background on the pasticcio *Ambleto* and Porta's opera *Numitore*, citing Handel's numerous borrowings from them.

356. _____. "Introduction." In *Carl Heinrich Graun's Passion "Kommt her und schaut" and Antonio Lotti's "Mass"*, pp. ix–xvi. Handel Sources: Materials for the Study of Handel's Borrowing, 5. New York: Garland Publishing Inc., 1986. M 2020 G75 L3. ISBN 0-8240-6479-8.

Offers background on Graun's early Passion setting and Lotti's Mass, listing Handel's borrowings from both.

357. _____. "Introduction." In *Alessandro Scarlatti's "Il Pompeo"*, pp. ix–xiv. Handel Sources: Materials for the Study of Handel's Borrowing, 6. New York: Garland Publishing Inc., 1986. M 1500 S28 P5. ISBN 0-8240-6480-1.

Offers background on *Pompeo* and introduces some of the complex problems associated with Handel's borrowings from Scarlatti. Lists borrowings from *Pompeo*.

Compositional Method

358. _____. "Introduction." In *Alessandro Scarlatti's "Dafni"*, pp. vii–xiv. Handel Sources: Materials for the Study of Handel's Borrowing, 7. New York: Garland Publishing Inc., 1986. M 1500 S28 D3. ISBN 0-8240-6481-X.

    Discusses *Dafni*'s background and sources, and lists Handel's borrowings from it.

359. _____. "Introduction." In *Giovanni Bononcini's "Il Xerse"*, pp. ix–xvi. Handel Sources: Materials for the Study of Handel's Borrowing, 8. New York: Garland Publishing Inc., 1986. M 1500 B7244 X5. ISBN 0-8240-6482-8.

    Gives background on *Il Xerse* and lists borrowings not only from it but from Bononcini's 1706 opera *La regina creduta re*.

360. _____. "Introduction." In *Agostino Steffani's "La lotta d'Hercole con Acheloo"*, pp. ix–xviii. Handel Sources: Materials for the Study of Handel's Borrowing, 9. New York: Garland Publishing Inc., 1986. M 1500 S82 L5. ISBN 0-8240-6483-6.

    Gives background for and lists borrowings from not only Steffani's opera but also from miscellaneous sources, including works by Giovanni Legrenzi, Domenico Sarro, Andrea Stefano Fiorè, Giuseppe Vignati, and Giuseppe Orlandini.

361. Robinson, Percy. *Handel and His Orbit*. London: Sherratt and Hughes, 1908. Repr. New York: Da Capo Press, 1979. 223p. ML 410 H13 R5 1979. ISBN 0-306-795223-1.

    Not a biography, it discusses certain points of biography, especially as regards the Italian years (ca. 1706–10). Defends Handel the borrower against the morally earnest attack of Sedley Taylor (item 369), calling for an understanding of the eighteenth-century view. Argues somewhat whimsically that the Erba *Magnificat* and Urio *Te Deum* were actually by Handel. New forward by Jens Peter Larsen (item 341).

362. _____. "Was Handel a Plagiarist?" *Musical Times* 80 (1939): 573–77.

Reviews the debate on borrowing since the 1908 publication of his book (item 361). Shows that Handel never tried to conceal his borrowings, suggesting that they added a level of meaning in *Alexander's Feast*.

363. Seiffert, Max. "Franz Johann Habermann (1706–1783)." *Kirchenmusikalisches Jahrbuch* 18 (1903): 81–94.

Cites borrowings from Habermann's masses in Handel's *Jephtha*. Extensive musical examples.

364. _____. "Georg Philipp Telemanns *Musique de table* als Quelle für Händel." *Bulletin de la Société 'Union Musicologique'* 4 (1924): 1–28.

Gives a lengthy introduction to Telemann's *Musique de table*, followed by a discussion of Handel borrowings (some debatable) in *Alexander's Feast, Atalanta, Samson, Belshazzar, Hercules, Judas Maccabaeus*, and selected concertos. Musical examples.

365. Shedlock, John S. "Handel's Borrowings." *Musical Times* 42 (1901): 450–52; 526–28; 596–600; 756.

Reviews the nineteenth-century discovery by the English of Handel's "plagiarism." Analyzes borrowings from a whole range of composers, astutely recognizing some as stylistic similarity or adherence to convention. A fascinating document.

366. _____. "Handel and Habermann." *Musical Times* 45 (1904): 805–806.

Reviews the evidence on Handel's borrowings from Habermann's masses.

367. Siegmund-Schultze, Walther. "Zu Händels Schaffensmethode." *Händel-Jahrbuch* 7–8 (1961–62): 69–136.

Rather than focusing on the evidence of the sources, the author discusses the essential qualities of Handel's style, showing how they affected his use of musical materials. Discusses two areas: 1) parody and 2) the revision of individual works and movements. Contends that Handel's musical inspiration is most often related to a verbal text, and that the sources of many borrowings in instrumental pieces were first texted or associated with texted works. Generous musical examples.

368. Silbiger, Alexander. "Scarlatti Borrowings in Handel's Grand Concertos." *Musical Times* 125 (1984): 93–95.

Identifies and discusses eight borrowings in the Opus 6 concertos from Domenico Scarlatti's *Essericizi per cembalo*, published in London in 1738. These must have been obvious to Handel's contemporaries, and may indeed have given Charles Avison the idea of turning Scarlatti sonatas into grand concertos. Although Handel may have been influenced by Scarlatti's "perfect binary symmetry" and phrase structures, a comparison of their styles confirms that they differ essentially. Musical examples.

* Strohm, Reinhard. "Francesco Gasparini's Later Operas and Handel." In *Essays on Handel and Italian Opera*, pp. 80–92. Cambridge: Cambridge University Press, 1985. ML 410 H13 S75 1985. ISBN 0–521–26428–6.

Cited below as item 479.

369. Taylor, Sedley. *The Indebtedness of Handel to Works by Other Composers.* Cambridge: Cambridge University Press, 1906. Repr. New York: Johnson Reprint Corporation, 1971. 196p. ML 410 H13 T2 1971.

Presents evidence of borrowings in the works of Handel from nine continental composers. In a misunderstanding of Baroque practices which is typical of the period, points an accusing finger at Handel for pilfering the music of his contemporaries. Well-indexed, copious musical examples. New foreword by Paul Henry Lang.

370. Tobin, John. *Handel at Work.* London: Cassell, 1964. 84p. ML 410 H13 T6.

Offers reproductions with commentary of many of the alterations in the autograph manuscript of *Messiah*. Plates, examples, index.

371. Williams, Peter. "The Acquisitive Minds of Handel and Bach: Some Reflections on the Nature of 'Influences'." In *Charles Brenton Fisk, Organ Builder: Essays in His Honor*, vol. 1, pp. 267–81. Ed. Barbara Owen, Fenner Douglass, and Owen Jander. Easthampton, Massachusetts: Westfield Center for Early Keyboard Studies, 1985. ML 55 F538 C475 1986. ISBN 0–9616755–1–9.

Ponders the complexity of the "influence" question. Shows that various harpsichord pieces feature conventional modes of expression while others bear subtle relationships to works by other composers. Suggests implications for Handel's borrowing process. Deals particularly with the suites HWV 449, 452, 438, and 426.

372. Wollenberg, Susan. "Handel and Gottlieb Muffat: A Newly-Discovered Borrowing." *Musical Times* 113 (1972): 448–49.

Handel had access to some of Muffat's unpublished works. The second movement of the Organ Concerto in A opus 7 no. 2 contains a borrowing from a Muffat ricercar in F.

373. Zimmerman, Franklin B. "Handel's Purcellian Borrowings in His Later Operas and Oratorios." In *Festschrift Otto Erich Deutsch zum 80. Geburtstag*, pp. 20–30. Ed. Walter Gerstenberg, Jan LaRue, and Wolfgang Rehm. Kassel: Bärenreiter, 1963. ML 55 D5 F4.

Evaluates the extent of Purcell's influence on Handel during the latter years, citing examples of borrowings in major vocal works from 1741 to 1749. Musical examples.

374. _____. "Musical Borrowings in the English Baroque." *Musical Quarterly* 52 (1966): 483–95.

Investigates, with musical examples, borrowing practices in the works of English composers during the century bounded by Purcell's birth and Handel's death. Focuses on Purcell, Blow, and Handel, referring to Handel's borrowings from Blow in *Susanna* and possibly from Purcell in the Hallelujah chorus of *Messiah*.

375. _____. "Händels Parodie-Ouvertüre zu *Susanna*: Eine neue Ansicht über die Entstehungsfrage." *Händel-Jahrbuch* 24 (1978): 19–30.

    Shows how Handel used the overture to John Blow's Ode to St. Cecilia of 1684 ("Begin the Song") in his own overture to *Susanna*. Revealing comments on borrowing procedures. Musical examples.

376. _____. "Purcellian Passages in the Compositions of G.F. Handel." In *Music in Eighteenth-Century England: Essays in Memory of Charles Cudworth*, pp. 49–58. Ed. Christopher Hogwood and Richard Luckett. Cambridge: Cambridge University Press, 1983. ML 55 C85. ISBN 0-521-23525-1.

    Contends that Handel's Purcellian borrowings belong to a special class of compositional procedure, in which most often the spirit or effect of the model is retained, while the notes are changed. Suggests that Handel became increasingly open to Purcell's influence in later years. Musical examples to document borrowings.

IV

LIST OF HANDEL'S WORKS

1. Works-Lists, Catalogues, and Collected Editions

The number and diversity of Handel's works, together with source problems and questions of authenticity and chronology, present difficulties for compilers of works-lists and catalogues. Early lists by the nineteenth-century Handelians Julian Marshall and Victor Schoelcher, preserved in the British Library and in the Mann Library, King's College, Cambridge, are described in item 282, pp. 94–97. Modern lists and catalogues are given below.

377. Baselt, Bernd. *Händel-Handbuch.* 5 vols. Kassel: Bärenreiter, 1978–. ML 134 H3 H3.

> Complete thematic catalogue. Intended as a supplement to the *Hallische Händel-Ausgabe.* Each entry gives textual sources, description of performing forces, locations in collected editions, composition and performance dates, musical incipits for every movement, list of sources, extensive commentary with notes on borrowings, and selected bibiliography. An indispensable research tool. Because of ongoing research, the user should be prepared to seek up-to-the-minute supplements to information on sources, especially watermarks, and borrowing. Indexes.

Volume 1. *Lebens- und Schaffensdaten. Thematisch-systematisches Verzeichnis: Bühnenwerke.* 1978. 540p. ISBN 3-7618-0610-8.

Chronological summary of biography by Siegfried Flesch. Thematic catalogue of all stage works, except for the fragments and pasticcios which appear in Volume 3. Reviewed by Winton Dean in *Music and Letters* 64 (1983): 232-34.

Volume 2. *Thematisch-systematisches Verzeichnis: Oratorische Werke, vokale Kammermusik, Kirchenmusik.* 800p. ISBN 3-7618-0715-5.

Thematic catalogue of oratorios, odes, serenatas, vocal chamber music, and church music. Reviewed by Mary Ann Parker-Hale in *Journal of the American Musicological Society* 39 (1986): 655-63.

Volume 3. *Thematisch-systematisches Verzeichnis: Instrumentalmusik, Pasticci und Fragmente.* 1986. 442p. ISBN 3-7618-0716-3.

Thematic catalogue of the instrumental music. Appendix to the stage works, including operatic fragments and pasticcios.

Volume 4. *Dokumente zu Leben und Schaffen.* 1985. 621p. ISBN 3-7618-0717-1.

Cited above as item 151.

Volume 5. *Bibliographie.* (to appear)

378. Bell, A. Craig. *Handel: Chronological Thematic Catalogue.* Darley: Grian-Aig Press, 1972. 454p. ML 134 H16 B4.

The first published thematic catalogue. Lists performing editions. Contains no incipits for unpublished works. Gives few details, especially on the Italian cantatas. Indexes.

379. Hicks, Anthony. "Works." In Winton Dean, *The New Grove Handel*, pp. 118-66. New York: Norton, 1983. ML 410 H13 D24. ISBN 0-393-30086-2.

Authoritative list of works which first appeared with the Handel article in the *New Grove Dictionary of Music and Musicians*. Gives textual sources, manuscript sources, dates of composition and/or performances under the composer, useful remarks and locations in collected editions. For information on early prints, refers the reader to item 268.

380. Smith, William C. "Catalogue of Works." In Gerald Abraham, ed., *Handel: A Symposium*, pp. 275-310. London: Oxford University Press, 1954. ML 410 H13 A66.

The best catalogue before item 379. Contains no musical incipits, but offers informed commentary. Admits to being incomplete. Does not list Italian cantatas by name. An expanded version of the list prepared by Smith for the fifth edition of *Grove's Dictionary* (1954), it appears in German in the 1956 *Händel-Jahrbuch*.

Handel was the first composer for whom a complete works edition was planned. Prepared by Samuel Arnold during the years 1787 to 1797, it was by no means complete. Half a century later, sixteen volumes of *The Works of Handel* were printed for the Handel Society in London (1844-58).

More modern times have produced two collected editions of Handel's works. The first, published during the years 1858 to 1902 under the editorship of the German scholar Friedrich Chrysander, was a monumental achievement of persistence, dedication and care. It was originally published by the Händel-Gesellschaft, hence its designation HG. In 1966, the Gregg Press issued a reprint in a reduced format, and this is the version in which the series exists in many music libraries today.

Like most nineteenth-century editions, Chrysander's does not meet modern standards of authenticity, accuracy or completeness. He was unaware of or did not include numerous pieces, was prevented by financial constraints from publishing others, was unfamiliar with many important sources located in Great Britain, and distorted a number of works, notably operas.

The new edition, entitled *Hallische Händel-Ausgabe* (Halle Handel Edition), began to appear in 1955. During those early years, the goals and standards of the project were unclear. Recent volumes reflect more reliable scholarly achievements and are accompanied by separately published critical reports.

Given below is a checklist which owes much to items 377 and 379. Upon consulting these more detailed catalogues, the reader will find that they are not always in complete agreement on matters of authenticity and chronology.

For the operas and oratorios, the dates relate to first performances. Otherwise, dates refer to the exact or approximate times of composition or publication, as noted.

Most of Handel's opera librettos are adaptations of earlier works. In this list, these adaptations have been indicated in the briefest form. The identity of the adaptor is not always certain.

As a rule, doubtful and spurious works do not appear. Brackets around HHA numbers indicate that the volumes in question are still in preparation at the time of writing.

Vocal Music: Operas

2. Vocal Music

HG = Handel Gesellschaft edition
HHA = Hallische Händel-Ausgabe
HWV = Händel Werk-Verzeichnis (item 377)

HWV   HG   HHA

OPERAS

1	Almira	1705	55	[II,1]
	[Der in Kronen erlangte			
	Glücks-Wechsel, oder Almira,			
	Königin von Castilien]			
	(Feustking)			
2	Nero	1705		
	[Die durch Blut und Mord			
	erlangte Liebe]			
	(Feustking)			
	music lost			
5	Rodrigo	1707	56	[II,2]
	[Vincer se stesso è la maggior			
	vittoria]			
	(adaptation of Silvani)			
3	Der beglückte Florindo	1708		
	(Hinsch)			
	most music lost, but see item 403			
4	Die verwandelte Daphne	1708		
	(Hinsch)			
	most music lost, but see item 403			
6	Agrippina	1710	57	[II,3]
	(Grimani)			
7	Rinaldo	1711	58	[II,4]
	(Rossi, after Tasso)	rev. 1731		
8	Il pastor fido	1712	59	[II,5]
	(Rossi, after Guarini)	rev. 1734		[II,31]
9	Teseo	1713	60	[II,6]
	(Haym, after Quinault)			

LIST OF HANDEL'S WORKS

10	Lucio Cornelio Silla (Rossi)	1713	61	[II,7]
11	Amadigi di Gaula (Haym, after de la Motte)	1715	62	II,8
12	Radamisto (Haym, adapt. of Lalli)	1720	63	[II,9]
13	Muzio Scevola (Rolli, adapt. of Stampiglia) only Act III by Handel	1721	64	[II,10]
14	Il Floridante (Rolli, adapt. of Silvani)	1721	65	[II,11]
15	Ottone, Rè di Germania (Haym, adapt. of Pallavicino)	1723	66	[II,12]
16	Flavio, Rè de' Longobardi (Haym)	1723	67	[II,13]
17	Giulio Cesare in Egitto (Haym, adapt. of Bussani)	1724	68	II,14
18	Tamerlano (Haym, adapt. of Piovene)	1724	69	[II,15]
19	Rodelinda, Regina de' Longobardi (Haym, adapt. of Salvi)	1725	70	[11,16]
20	Publio Cornelio Scipione (Rolli, adapt. of Salvi)	1726	71	[II,17]
21	Alessandro (Rolli, adapt. of Mauro)	1726	72	[II,18]
22	Admeto, Rè di Tessaglia (adapt. of Aureli)	1727	73	[II,19]
23	Riccardo Primo Rè d'Inghilterra (Rolli, adapt. of Briano)	1727	74	[II,20]
24	Siroe, Rè di Persia (Haym, adapt. of Metastasio)	1728	75	[II,21]
25	Tolomeo, Rè d'Egitto (Haym, adapt. of Capece)	1728	76	[II,22]
26	Lotario (adapt. of Salvi)	1729	77	[II,23]
27	Partenope (adapt. of Stampiglia)	1730	78	[II,24]
28	Poro, Rè dell'Indie (adapt. of Metastasio)	1731	79	[II,25]
29	Ezio (adapt. of Metastasio)	1732	80	II,26

Vocal Music: Operas

30	Sosarme, Rè di Media (adapt. of Salvi)	1732	81	[II,27]
31	Orlando (adapt. of Capece)	1733	82	II,28
32	Arianna in Creta (adapt. of Pariati)	1734	83	[II,29]
33	Ariodante (adapt. of Salvi)	1735	85	II,32
34	Alcina (adapt. of 1728 lib. after Ariosto)	1735	86	[II,33]
35	Atalanta (adapt. of Valeriano)	1736	87	[II,34]
36	Arminio (adapt. of Salvi)	1737	89	[II,35]
37	Giustino (adapt. of Beregan)	1737	88	[II,36]
38	Berenice, Regina d'Egitto (adapt. of Salvi)	1737	90	[II,37]
39	Faramondo (adapt. of Zeno)	1738	91	[II,38]
40	Serse (adapt. of Minato/Stampiglia)	1738	92	[II,39]
41	Imeneo (adapt. of Stampiglia)	1740	93	[II,40]
42	Deidamia (Rolli)	1741	94	[II,41]

UNCOMPLETED OPERAS

A2	Genserico (after Beregan)	1727–28
A5	Titus L'Empereur (after Racine)	ca. 1731–32

OPERAS—ARRANGEMENTS AND PASTICCIOS

A1	Elipidia, over li rivali generosi (adapt. of Zeno) <small>music by Vinci, Orlandini, Lotti, Capelli</small>	1725
A3	Ormisda (adapt. of Zeno) <small>music by Orlandini, Vinci, Hasse, Leo</small>	1730
A4	Venceslao (adapt. of Zeno) <small>music by Vinci, Hasse, Lotti, Capelli, Orlandini</small>	1731
A6	Lucio Papiro dittatore (Zeno/Frugoni) <small>music by Giacomelli, Porpora</small>	1732
A7	Catone (Metastasio) <small>music by Leo, Hasse, Porpora, Vinci, Vivaldi</small>	1732
A8	Semiramide riconosciuto (Metastasio) <small>music by Vinci, Hasse, Leo</small>	1733
A9	Caio Fabbricio (Zeno) <small>music by Hasse, Vinci, Leo</small>	1733
A10	Arbace (Metastasio) <small>music by Vinci, Hasse, Porta</small>	1734
A11	Oreste (adapt. of Barlocci) <small>pasticcio of own works</small>	1734
A12	Didone abbandonata (Metastasio) <small>music by Vinci, Hasse, Giacomelli, Vivaldi</small>	1737
A13	Alessandro Severo (adapt. of Zeno) <small>pasticcio of own works</small>	1738

Vocal Music: Oratorios 111

A14	Giove in Argo (adapt. of Lucchini) pasticcio of own works	1739		

ORATORIOS

46a	Il trionfo del tempo e del disinganno (Pamphili)	1707	24	[I,4]
47	Oratorio per la resurrezione di nostro signor Gesù Cristo (Capece)	1708	39	[I,3]
48	Der für die Sünde der Welt gemartete und sterbende Jesus (Brockes)	1719	15	I,7
50b	Esther (Pope, Arbuthnot, Humphreys)	1732	41	[I,10]
51	Deborah (Humphreys)	1733	29	[I,11]
52	Athalia (Humphreys)	1733	5	[I,12]
46b	Il trionfo del tempo e della verità (Pamphili and anon. additions)	1737	20,24	[I,4]
53	Saul (Jennens)	1739	13	I,13
54	Israel in Egypt	1739	16	[I,14]
56	Messiah (Jennens)	1742	45	I,17
57	Samson (Hamilton)	1743	10	[I,18]
59	Joseph and His Brethren	1744	42	[I,20]
61	Belshazzar (Jennens)	1745	19	[I,21]
62	Occasional Oratorio (Hamilton)	1746	43	[I,23]
63	Judas Maccabaeus (Morell)	1747	20	[I,24]
64	Joshua (Morell?)	1748	17	[I,26]

65	Alexander Balus (Morell)	1748	33	[I,25]
66	Susanna	1749	1	I,28
67	Solomon	1749	26	[I,27]
68	Theodora (Morell)	1750	8	[I,29]
70	Jeptha (Morell)	1752	44	[I,32]
71	The Triumph of Time and Truth (Morell)	1757	20	[I,33]

ODES AND SERENATAS

72	Aci, Galatea e Polifemo	1708	53	[I,5]
74	Ode for the Birthday of Queen Anne (A. Philips?)	1713	46A	I,6
73	Il Parnasso in festa	1734	54	[II,30]
75	Alexander's Feast (Dryden, additions by Hamilton)	1736	12	I,1
76	Ode for St. Cecilia's Day (Dryden)	1739	23	[I,15]

ENGLISH PASTORALS, MASQUES, MUSIC DRAMAS, AND THEATER MUSIC

43	The Alchemist (music for Jonson's play)	1710	—	
49a	Acis and Galatea	1718	3	[I,9]
50a	Esther [Haman and Mordecai] (Pope and Arbuthnot)	1718?	40	[I,10]
55	L'Allegro, il Penseroso ed il Moderato (Jennens and Milton)	1740	6	I,16
58	Semele (Congreve)	1744	7	[I,19]

Vocal Music: Cantatas 113

60	Hercules (Broughton)	1745	4	[I,22]
44	Comus (music for Milton's play)	1745	—	
45	Alceste (Smollett)	1749-1750	46B	[I,30]

CHAMBER CANTATAS

At present, very few of the cantatas have been assigned dates of composition with any degree of certainty. Most were composed during Handel's Italian sojourn (ca. 1707–10), but a few are associated with his years in England (HWV 85, 87, 89, 97, 109, 119, 124, 121). On the other hand, some of the duets are associated with Hanover (HWV 178, 183, 185, 194, 197, 199).

77	Ah! che pur troppo è vero	50	[V,1]
78	Ah! crudel, nel pianto mio	52A	[V,3]
79	Alla caccia (Diana cacciatrice)	—	[V,3]
80	Allor ch'io dissi	50	[V,1]
81	Alpestre monte	52A	[V,3]
82	Amarilli vezzosa (Il duello amoroso)	—	[V,3]
83	Arresta il passo (Aminta e Fillide)	52A/B	[V,3]
84	Aure soavi, e lieti	50	[V,1]
85	Behold where weeping Venus stands (Venus and Adonis)	—	
86	Bella ma ritrosetta	—	[V,1]
87	Carco sempre di gloria	52A	[V,3]
88	Care selve, aure grate	50	[V,1]
89	Cecilia, volgi un sguardo	52A	[V,3]
90	Chi rapì la pace al core	50	[V,1]
91a–b	Clori, degli occhi miei	50	[V,1]
92	Clori, mia bella Clori	52A	[V,3]
93	Clori, ove sei?	50	[V,1]
94	Clori, sì, ch'io t'adoro	—	[V,1]

95	Clori, vezzosa Clori	—	[V,1]
96	Cor fedele	52B	[V,4]
	(Clori, Tirsi e Fileno)		
97	Crudel tiranno Amor	52A	[V,3]
98	Cuopre tal volta il cielo	52A	[V,3]
99	Da quel giorno fatale	52A	[V,3]
	(Il delirio amoroso)		
100	Da sete ardente afflitto	50	[V,1]
101a–b	Dal fatale momento	—	[V,1]
102a–b	Dalla guerra amorosa	50	[V,1]
103	Deh! lasciate e vita e volo	50	[V,1]
104	Del bel idolo mio	50	[V,1]
105	Dietro l'orme fugaci	52A	[V,3]
	(Armida abbandonata)		
106	Dimmi, o mio cor	50	[V,1]
107	Ditemi, o piante	50	[V,1]
108	Dolce mio ben, s'io taccio	50	[V,1]
109a–b	Dolce pur d'amor l'affanno	50	[V,1]
110	Dunque sarà pur vero	52A	[V,3]
	(Agrippina condotta a morire)		
111a–b	E partirai, mia vita?	50	[V,1]
112	Figli del mesto cor	50	[V,1]
113	Figlio d'alte speranze	52A	[V,3]
114	Filli adorata e cara	50	[V,1]
115	Fra pensieri quel pensiero	50	[V,1]
116	Fra tante pene	50	[V,1]
117	Hendel, non può mia musa	—	[V,1]
118	Ho fuggito amore anch'io	51	[V,1]
119	Echiggiate, festeggiate, Numi eterni, in questo dì	52A	[V,3]
120a–b	Irene, idolo mio	50	[V,1]
121a–b	L'aure grate, il fresco rio	50	[V,1]
	(La Solitudine)		
122	La terra è liberta	52B	[V,4]
	(Apollo e Dafne)		
123	Languia di bocca lusinghiera	52B	[V,4]
124	Look down, harmonious Saint	52A	[V,3]
	(The Praise of Harmony)		
125a–b	Lungi da me, pensier tiranno	50	[V,1]
126a–c	Lungi da voi, che siete poli	50	[V,1]
127a–c	Lungi dal mio bel nume	50	[V,1]

Vocal Music: Cantatas

128	Lungi n'andò Fileno	50	[V,1]
129	Manca pur quanto sai	50	[V,1]
130	Mentre il tutto è in furore	50	[V,1]
131	Menzognere speranze	50	[V,1]
132a–d	Mi palpita il cor	50	[V,1]
133	Ne'tuoi lumi, o bella Clori	50	[V,1]
134	Nel dolce dell'oblio (Pensieri notturni di Filli)	52B	[V,4]
135a–b	Nel dolce tempo	50	[V,1]
136a–b	Nell'africane selve	50	[V,1]
137	Nella stagion che di viole e rose	50	[V,1]
138	Nice, che fa? che pensa?	51	[V,2]
139a–b	Ninfe e pastori	51	[V,2]
140	No se emenderá jamás	52B	[V,4]
141	Non sospirar, non piangere	51	[V,2]
142	Notte placida e cheta	—	[V,4]
143	Oh come chiare e belle (Olinto pastore, Tebro fiume, Gloria)	52B	[V,4]
144	O lucenti, o sereni occhi	51	[V,2]
145	Oh numi eterni (La Lucrezia)	51	[V,2]
146	Occhi miei, che faceste?	51	[V,2]
147	Partì, l'idolo mio	51	[V,2]
148	Poichè giuraro amore	51	[V,2]
149	Qual sento io non conosciuto	—	[V,2]
150	Qual ti riveggio, oh Dio (Ero e Leandro)	—	[V,4]
151	Qualor crudele, sì, ma vaga Dori	51	[V,2]
152	Qualor l'egre pupille	51	[V,2]
153	Quando sperasti, o core	51	[V,2]
154	Quel fior che all'alba ride	—	[V,2]
155	Sans y penser	—	[V,2]
156	Sarai contenta in dì	51	[V,2]
157	Sarei troppo felice	51	[V,2]
158a–c	Se pari è la tua fè	51	[V,2]
159	Se per fatal destino	51	[V,2]
160a–c	Sei pur bella, pur vezzosa (La bianca rosa)	51	[V,2]
161a–c	Sento là che ristretto	51	[V,2]
162	Siete rose rugiadose	51	[V,2]

163	Solitudini care, amata libertà	51	[V,2]
164a–b	Son gelsomino	51	[V,2]
	(Il gelsomino)		
165	Spande ancor a mio dispetto	52A	[V,3]
166	Splenda l'alba in oriente	51	[V,2]
167a–b	Stanco di più soffrire	51	[V,2]
168	Stelle, perfide stelle	51	[V,2]
	(Partenza di G.B.)		
169	Torna il core al suo diletto	51	[V,2]
170	Tra le fiamme	52B	[V,4]
	(Il consiglio)		
171	Tu fedel? tu costante?	52B	[V,4]
172	Udite il mio consiglio	51	[V,1]
173	Un'alma innamorata	52B	[V,4]
174	Un sospir a chi si muore	51	[V,2]
175	Vedendo amor	51	[V,2]
176	Venne voglia ad amore	51	[V,2]
	(Amore uccellatore)		
177	Zeffiretto, arresta il volo	51	[V,2]
178	A mirarvi io son intento	32	[V,5,6]
179	Ahi, nelle sorti umane	32	[V,5,6]
180	Amor, gioje mi porge	32	[V,5,6]
181	Beato in ver chi può	32	[V,5,6]
182a–b	Caro autor di mia doglia	32	[V,5,6]
183	Caro autor di mia doglia	32	[V,5,6]
184	Che vai pensando, folle pensier	32	[V,5,6]
185	Conservate raddoppiate	32	[V,5,6]
186	Fronda leggiera e mobile	32	[V,5,6]
187	Giù nei Tartarei regni	32	[V,5,6]
188	Langue, geme, sospira	32	[V,5,6]
189	No, di voi non vuò fidarmi	32	[V,5,6]
190	No, di voi non vuò fidarmi	32	[V,5,6]
191	Quando in calma ride	32	[V,5,6]
192	Quel fior che all'alba ride	32	[V,5,6]
193	Se tu non lasci amore	32	[V,5,6]
194	Sono liete, fortunate	32	[V,5,6]
195	Spero indarno	32	[V,5,6]
196	Tacete, ohimè, tacete	32	[V,5,6]
197	Tanti strali al sen mi scocchi	32	[V,5,6]
198	Troppo cruda, troppo fiera	32	[V,5,6]
199	Va, speme infida	32	[V,5,6]

Vocal Music: Songs

| 200 | Quel fior che all'alba ride | 32 | [V,5,6] |
| 201a–b | Se tu non lasci amore | 32 | [V,5,6] |

SONGS AND ARIAS

None of the miscellaneous songs and arias was published by Chrysander. They are to be included in volumes 5 and 6 of Series V in the HHA.

Problems of authenticity arise in the study of the English songs. Readers are advised to consult items 268 and 379.

202–10	Neun deutsche Arien
211	Aure dolci, deh, spirate
212	Con doppia gloria mia
213	Con lacrime si belle
214	Dell'onda instabile
215	Col valor del vostro brando
216	Impari del mio core
217	L'odio, sì, ma poi ritrovò
218	Love's but the frailty of the mind
219	Non so se avrai mai bene
220	Per dar pace al mio tormento
221	Quant' invidio tua fortuna
222	Quanto più amara fu sorte crudele
223	S'un dì m'appaga, la mia crudele
224	Sì, crudel, tornerà
225	Sperà chi sa perchè la sorte
226	The morning is charming (Hunting Song)
227	Vo' cercando tra fiori
228	24 English Songs

LATIN AND ITALIAN SACRED MUSIC

230	Ah, che troppo ineguali	1708	52B	[V,4]
231	Coelestis dum spirat aura	1707	—	[III,2]
232	Dixit Dominus	1707	38	III,1

233	Donna, che in ciel	1707	—	[III,2]
234	Giunta l'ora fatal (Il pianto di Maria) authenticity in question	1709	—	
235	Haec est regina	1707	—	
236	Laudate pueri before	1707	38	[III,2]
237	Laudate pueri	1707	38	[III,2]
238	Nisi Dominus without Gloria Patri in HG	1707	38	[III,2]
239	O qualis de coelo	1707	—	[III,2]
240	Saeviat tellus	1707	—	[III,2]
241	Salve regina	1707	38	[III,2]
242	Silete venti	ca. 1724	38	[III,2]
243	Te decus virginum	1707	—	[III,2]
244	Kyrie eleison	ca. 1740	—	[III,2]
245	Gloria in excelsis	ca. 1740	—	[III,2]
269	Amen, alleluia in d	ca. 1746–47	38	[III, suppl.]
270	Amen in F	ca. 1730–40	38	[III, suppl.]
271	Amen, alleluia in g	ca. 1730–40	38	[III, suppl.]
272	Alleluia, amen in d	ca. 1738–41	38	[III, suppl.]
273	Alleluia, amen in G	ca. 1738–41	38	[III, suppl.]
274	Alleluia, amen in a	ca. 1733–41	38	[III, suppl.]
275	Amen, alleluia in C	ca. 1730–40	—	[III, suppl.]
276	Amen, halleluja in F	ca. 1743–46	—	[III, suppl.]
277	Halleluja, amen in F	ca. 1746–47	—	[III, suppl.]

GERMAN CHURCH MUSIC

229	7 Church Cantatas lost	ca. 1700–03	—

ENGLISH CHURCH MUSIC

	Chandos anthems	1717–18		
246	O be joyful in the Lord		34	[III,4]
247	In the Lord put I my trust		34	[III,4]
248	Have mercy upon me		34	[III,4]
249a–b	O sing unto the Lord		36,34	[III,9; III,5]

Vocal Music: Church Music

250a–b	I will magnify thee		34	[III,5; III,9]
251a–d	As pants the hart		34,36	[III,9; III,5]
252	My song shall be alway		35	[III,5]
253	O come let us sing		35	[III,5]
254	O praise the Lord with one consent		35	[III,6]
255	The Lord is my light		35	[III,6]
256a–b	Let God arise		35	[III,6; III,9]
257	O praise the Lord, ye angels of his		36	

authenticity in question

	Coronation anthems	1727	14	[III,10]
258	Zadok the priest			
259	Let thy hand be strengthened			
260	The king shall rejoice			
261	My heart is inditing			
262	This is the day (Wedding anthem)	1734	36	[III,11]
263	Sing unto God (Wedding anthem)	1736	36	[III,11]
264	The ways of Zion (Funeral anthem)	1737	11	[III,12]
265	The king shall rejoice (Dettingen anthem)	1743	36	[III,13]
266	How beautiful are the feet (Peace anthem)	1749	—	[III,14]
268	Blessed are they that considereth the poor (Foundling Hospital anthem)	1749	36	[III,14]
278	Utrecht Te Deum	1713	31	[III,3]
279	Utrecht Jubilate	1713	31	[III,3]
280	Te Deum in D (Caroline)	1714?	37	[III,8]
281	Te Deum in B flat (Chandos)	ca. 1718	37	[III,7]
282	Te Deum in A	1722–26	37	[III,8]
283	Dettingen Te Deum	1743	25	[III,13]

284	Sinners obey the gospel word (The Invitation)	ca. 1746–47	—		
285	O Love divine (Desiring to Love)	ca. 1746–47	—		
286	Rejoice, the Lord is king (On the Resurrection)	ca. 1746–47	—		

3. Instrumental Music

ORCHESTRAL CONCERTOS

288	"Sonata a 5" in B flat	ca.	1707	21	IV,12
331	Concerto in F		1722	47	IV,13 Anh
312–17	Concerti grossi, op. 3	pub.	1734	21	IV,11
318	Concerto grosso in C		1736	21	IV,12
319–30	Twelve Grand Concertos in 7 parts, op. 6	pub.	1740	30	IV,14
302	"Oboe Concerto No. 1" in B flat	pub.	1740	21	IV,12
301	"Oboe Concerto No. 2" in B flat	pub.	1740	21	IV,12
287	"Oboe Concerto No. 3" in g	?pub.	1863	21	IV,12
335a	Concerto in D	ca.	1746–48	47	IV,12
335b	Concerto in F	ca.	1746–48	47	IV,12
332	Concerto a due cori in B flat	ca.	1747	47	IV,12
333	Concerto a due cori in F	ca.	1747	47	IV,12
334	Concerto a due cori in F	ca.	1747	47	IV,12

SOLO CONCERTOS

289–94	Six Concertos, op. 4 organ; no. 6 harp/organ	pub. 1738	28	IV,2
303	Concerto in d 2 organs	1738–39	48	IV,12
295–300	A Second Set of Six Concertos organ	pub. 1740	48	[IV,7]
343	Concerto in G harpsichord; version of Chaconne in G	ca. 1739	—	
304	Concerto in d organ	ca. 1746	48	IV,12
305a	Concerto in F organ	ca. 1748	48	IV,16
306–11	A Third Set of Six Concertos, op. 7 organ	pub. 1761	28	[IV,8]

SONATAS FOR SOLO INSTRUMENT WITH CONTINUO

362	recorder in a		27	IV,3
377	recorder in B flat		—	IV,18
365	recorder in C		27	IV,3
367	recorder in d in B for flute in HG		27	IV,18
369	recorder in F		27	IV,3
360	recorder in g		27	IV,3
—	flute in D	ca. 1707	—	IV,18
359a	flute in e		27	IV,3
357	oboe in B flat			
366	oboe in c		27	IV,4
363	oboe in F in G for flute in HG		27	IV,18
361	violin in A		27	IV,4
371	violin in D	ca. 1750	27	IV,4

359	violin in d		27	IV,4
	in e for flute in HG			
358	violin in G		—	IV,18
364	violin in g		27	IV,18
—	viola da gamba		—	

TRIO SONATAS

386	flute/violin and violin in b	pub. ca. 1730 as op. 2 no. 1	27	IV,10
387	2 violins in g	op. 2 no. 2	27	IV,10
388	2 violins in B flat	op. 2 no. 3	27	IV,10
	as no. 4 in HG			
389	flute/recorder/violin and violin in F	op. 2 no. 4	27	IV,10
	as no. 5 in HG			
390	2 violins in g	op. 2 no. 5	27	IV,10
	as no. 6 in HG			
391	2 violins in g	op. 2 no. 6	27	IV,10
	as no. 7 in HG			
396	2 violins or flutes in A	op. 5 no. 1	27	IV,10
397	2 violins or flutes in D	op. 5 no. 2	27	IV,10
398	2 violins or flutes in e	op. 5 no. 3	27	IV,10
399	2 violins or flutes in G	op. 5 no. 4	27	IV,10
400	2 violins or flutes in g	op. 5 no. 5	27	IV,10
401	2 violins or flutes in F	op. 5 no. 6	27	IV,10
402	2 violins or flutes in B flat	op. 5 no. 7	27	IV,10
386a	flute/recorder and violin in C		27	IV,10
	original version op. 2 no. 1			
	2 violins in F		27	IV,10
	original version op. 5 no. 6			
	2 recorders in F		—	
	edited by C. Hogwood London, 1981			

OVERTURES, SINFONIAS, AND SUITES

336	Overture in B flat	1707?	48	IV,15
337–38	Overture in D	1722–23	—	IV,15
339	Sinfonia in B flat		—	IV,15
341	"Handel's Water Piece" authenticity in question	1733	—	IV,13
342	Overture in F	ca. 1734	48	
347	Sinfonia in B flat	ca. 1745–47	—	IV,19
348	Water Music Suite in F	1717	47	IV,13
349	Water Music Suite in D			
350	Water Music Suite in G			
351	Music for the Royal Fireworks	1749	47	IV,13

Various additional marches and dance movements, many arranged from operatic excerpts, some for wind ensemble.

KEYBOARD MUSIC

	Suites de pièces pour le clavecin (London, 1720)	2	IV,1
426	Suite in A Prelude, Allemande, Courante, Gigue		
427	Suite in F Adagio, Allegro, Adagio, Allegro		
428	Suite in d Prelude, Allegro, Allemande, Courante, Air con 5 variazioni, Presto		
429	Suite in e Prelude, Allemande, Courante, Sarabande, Gigue		
430	Suite in E Prelude, Allemande, Courante, Air on 5 variazioni		
431	Suite in f sharp Prelude, Largo, Allegro, Gigue		

432	Suite in g Ouverture, Andante, Allegro, Sarabande, Gigue, Passacaille		
433	Suite in f Prelude, Allegro, Allemande, Courante, Gigue		
	Suite de pièces pour le clavecin (London, 1733)	2	IV,5
434	Suite in B flat Prelude, Sonata, Aria con variazioni, Minuet		
435	Chacone in G		
436	Suite in d Allemande, Allegro, Air, Gigue, Menuetto con 3 variazioni		
437	Suite in d Prélude, Allemande, Courante, Sarabande con 2 variazioni, Gigue		
438	Suite in e Allemande, Courante, Gigue		
439	Suite in g Allemande, Courante, Sarabande Gigue		
440	Suite in B flat Allemande, Courante, Sarabande Gigue		
441	Suite in G Allemande, Allegro, Courante, Aria, Menuetto, Gavotta con 8 variazioni, Gigue		
442	Prélude et Chaconne in G		
605–10	Six Fugues or Voluntarys, op. 3 (London, 1935)	2	IV,6

Numerous additional suites and individual pieces.

MUSIC FOR MUSICAL CLOCK

| 587–97 | Tunes for Clay's Musical Clock | ca. 1735–40 |
| 598–604 | Sonata by Mr. Handel for a Musical Clock | ca. 1735–40 |

V

STUDIES OF HANDEL'S MUSIC

1. General Studies of the Music

381. Abraham, Gerald. "Some Points of Style." In *Handel: A Symposium*, pp. 262–74. Ed. Gerald Abraham. London: Oxford University Press, 1954. ML 410 H13 A66.

    Deals with the paradox of Handel's individuality against his assimilation of the music of others and the styles of his time. Focuses on borrowing and revision, studies the phenomenon of the "recurrent generating motive." Musical examples.

382. Baselt, Bernd. "Einflüße der französischen Musik auf das Schaffen G.F. Händels." In *Der Einfluß der französischen Musik auf die Komponisten der ersten Hälfte des 18. Jahrhunderts: Konferenzbericht der IX. Wissenschaftlichen Arbeitstagung Blankenburg/Harz 26.–28. Juni 1981*, pp. 64–76. Ed. Eitelfriedrich Thom. Blankenburg/Harz: Rat des Bezirkes Magdeburg, 1982.

    Traces French influences on Handel's music through his career, focusing on overtures, dances (especially in *Ariodante* and *Alcina*) and orchestral suites (Water Music). Musical examples and a photo of the author reading the paper.

383. Becker, Heinz. "Klangstrukturen bei Händel." In *Karlsruher Händel Vorträge*, pp. 35–50. Ed. Kurt R. Pietschmann and Gabriele Eikermann. Karlsruhe: Badisches Staatstheater Karlsruhe, 1985. ML 410 H13 K37.

Argues that Handel was one of the first composers to use the orchestra, in the modern sense, for dramatic purposes. Explores various textural choices, particularly the *aria all'unisono*, in excerpts from *La resurrezione*, *Agrippina*, *Rinaldo*, *Radamisto*, and *Deidamia*. Musical examples.

384. Blandford, W.F.H. "Handel's Horn and Trombone Parts." *Musical Times* 80 (1939): 697–99; 746–47; 794.

Discusses Handel's use of horn and trombone parts in the English oratorios, operas after 1720, Water and Fireworks music *et al*. Notes on performance problems.

385. Castriota, Alessandra. "Le zampogne dell'Italia meridionale nella musica di Händel." *Nuova rivista musicale italiana* 19 (1985): 94–111.

Explores the influences of Italian rustic bagpipe music on Handel's music, especially in *Messiah*, with notes on *Apollo e Dafne* ("La terra è liberata"), *Il Parnasso in festa* and *The Triumph of Time and Truth*. Musical examples, illustrations.

386. Dent, Edward J. "Englische Einflüße bei Händel." *Händel-Jahrbuch* 1929, pp. 1–12.

Shows that, when Handel first arrived in England, he was too distant from the Purcellian tradition to continue it. The profound effects of English influence on his music did not really set in until his later years. Contends that he never really learned to compose recitative in the English style. Comes to the problematic conclusion that the most important lesson he learned from English music, the dramatic use of chorus, came not from the church but from the theater.

387. Fuller, David. "The 'Dotted Style' in Bach, Handel and Scarlatti." In *Bach, Handel, and Scarlatti: Tercentenary Essays*, pp. 99–117. Ed. Peter Williams. Cambridge: Cam-

General Studies   129

bridge University Press, 1985. ML 55 B14 1985. ISBN 0-521-25217-2.

Shows that persistent dotting became a widespread mannerism which appeared in the sonata, the ballroom dance, the Italian opera aria and the overture. Suggests that it had different meanings at different times, exploring some of these in the historical background and in selected works of the three "1685" composers. Musical examples.

388. Harris, Ellen T. "Handel's Pastoral Genre: Its Literary and Musical Antecedents." Ph.D. dissertation. University of Chicago, 1976. 445p.

Early version of item 440.

389. _____. "The Italian in Handel." *Journal of the American Musicological Society* 33 (1980): 468–500.

Calls into question the concept of a strong Italian influence on Handel's vocal music. Points out that there is no evidence of influence by Scarlatti on Handel. Based on detailed analysis of various cantatas, comes to the controversial conclusion that many stylistic distinctions between the two composers point to national differences. Tables, musical examples.

390. Jung, Hermann. *Die Pastorale: Studien zur Geschichte eines musikalischen Topos.* Neue Heidelberger Studien zur Musikwissenschaft, 9. Berne: Francke, 1980. 296p. ML 160 J8. ISBN 3-7720-1457-7.

Presents a history of the pastoral topos in music up to Bach and Handel. Handel uses all the pastoral styles of his time.

391. Leichtentritt, Hugo. "Handel's Harmonic Art." *Musical Quarterly* 21 (1935): 208–23.

Comments on the rich and varied harmonies in recitatives, as opposed to arias. Notes on large-scale tonal plans. Mentions passages with interesting harmonies. Musical examples.

392. Lewis, Anthony. "Handel and the Aria." *Proceedings of the Royal Musical Association* 85 (1958–59): 95–107.

Offers a general discussion of the arias, focusing on melodic inspiration, nature and function of the ritornello and use of orchestra. Asks why Handel's orchestration of accompaniments became less colorful in later years.

393. Lindemann, Frayda B. "Pastoral Instruments in French Baroque Music: Musette and Vielle." Ph.D. dissertation. Columbia University, 1978. 287p.

Shows how these two folk instruments were used in art music during the second half of the seventeenth century. Argues that the pastoral mannerisms associated with them were exploited by Bach and Handel in music for other instruments. Not examined.

394. Scholz, Rudolf. "Ein Thementypus der empfindsamen Zeit: Ein Beitrag zur Tonsymbolik." *Archiv für Musikwissenschaft* 24 (1967): 178–98.

Traces a certain melodic and harmonic gesture through numerous eighteenth and nineteenth-century examples, including eight by Handel, and speculates on its affective symbolism. Musical examples.

395. Siegmund-Schultze, Walther. "Das Siciliano bei Händel." *Händel-Jahrbuch* 3 (1957): 44–73.

Attempts to define specific characteristics of the siciliano. Investigates Handel's adoption of the style with reference to works throughout his career. Many musical examples.

396. _____. "Das Revolutionäre im Schaffen Georg Friedrich Händels." *Händel-Jahrbuch* 24 (1978): 7–18.

Views Handel's music in light of social upheavals of his time.

397. _____ and Walter Serauky. *Konzertführer Georg Friedrich Händel 1685–1759*. Mainz: Schott, 1984. 157p. ML 410 H13 G467 1984. ISBN 3–7957–2467–8.

A concert companion for popular use. Musical examples and non-technical discussions of forty-eight works and collections. Biographical sketch, index.

398. Telle, Karina. *Tanzrhythmen in der Vokalmusik Georg Friedrich Händels.* Beiträge zur Musikforschung, Bd. 3. Munich/Salzburg: Musikverlag Emil Katzbichler, 1977. 125p. ML 410 H13 T35. ISBN 3-87397-252-2.

Systematically identifies vocal numbers, both solo and choral, that take on the styles of the sarabande, minuet, gigue, gavotte, bourée and hornpipe. Discusses the characteristics of each dance type and supports designations with many musical examples. Bibliography, no index.

399. Williams, John G. "The Influence of English Music and Society on G.F. Handel." Ph.D. dissertation. University of Leeds, 1969. 318, 82p.

Concludes that Handel was influenced not only by his musical contemporaries in England, but also by English folk music and Tudor and Restoration composers, especially Purcell. Not examined.

400. Zgorzelecki, Andrzej. "Händel 'alla Polacca'." *Händel-Jahrbuch* 28 (1982): 53–57.

Lists in a chatty way Handel works that may have some connection to Polish musical idioms. Mentions loose connections between Handel practice and Poland.

2. Operas

401. Baselt, Bernd. "Die Bühnenwerke Georg Friedrich Händels: Quellenstudien und thematisches Verzeichnis." 2 vols. Habilitationsschrift (Musicology). Martin-Luther-Universität Halle-Wittenberg, 1974.

Deals with all operas and incidental music. Includes commentary on origins, performance history, sources, versions, and thematic borrowings. Not examined.

402. _____. "Händel auf dem Wege nach Italien." In *Konferenzbericht Halle (Saale) 1979*, pp. 10–21.

Presents evidence to support the view of Reinhard Keiser as an influential friend of Handel. Chrysander thought that Keiser's setting of *Almira* and the Nero story were composed in a spirit of rivalry with Handel, but it seems now that Keiser had already written *Almira* when Handel's was performed in Hamburg. Furthermore, it was probably Keiser who invited Handel to Hamburg in the first place.

403. _____. "Wiederentdeckung von Fragmenten aus Händels verschollenen Hamburg Opern." *Händel Jahrbuch* 29 (1983): 7–24.

Announces the discovery of three dance movements, in a collection of early keyboard pieces in the Aylesford collection, which are related to Handel's lost Hamburg operas. Two movements marked "Coro" are certainly associated with choruses in *Florindo* and *Daphne*, while a third matches a choral text from *Daphne*. Only excerpts are given. The pieces contain material later used in two Italian cantatas, "Amarilli vezzosa" (HWV 82) and "Qual sento io non conosciuto" (HWV 149), strengthening the arguments for their authenticity, especially in the case of the latter. Suggests that the B flat major Ouverture (HWV 336) thought by Hicks (item 379) to be the first version of the *Trionfo del tempo* overture, may also have been the overture to *Florindo*. Together with fragments discovered in the 1960's by Winton Dean and David Kimbell (item 442), this brings to seven the number of movements from *Florindo* and *Daphne* that can be reconstructed.

404. _____. "Zur Gestaltung des Alceste-Stoffes in Händels Oper 'Admeto'." In *Konferenzbericht Halle (Saale) 1983*, pp. 74–92.

Discusses in detail the dramatic and musical characteristics in *Admeto* (1727), especially as the libretto relates to its model by O. Mauro (Hannover, 1679) and ultimately to Euripedes' *Alceste*. Answers the question, "How did Handel reconcile ef-

Operas

fective characterization with the demands and capabilities of his singers?"

405. Bianconi, Lorenzo. "Orlando, dall'Arcadia agl'Inferni." In *Georg Friedrich Händel: Orlando*, pp. 119–209. Venice: Edizione dell'Ufficio Stampa del Gran Teatro La Fenice, 1985.

Not examined.

406. Bimberg, Guido. "Dramaturgische Strukturelement in den *Ezio*—Opern von Händel und Gluck." In *Konferenzbericht Halle (Saale) 1977*, pp. 41–46.

Compares the adaptations of Metastasio's *Ezio* libretto for settings by Handel (1732) and Gluck (1750). Emphasis on dramatic rather than strictly musical considerations.

407. _____. "Zur Dramaturgie der Händel-Opern." phil. Diss. Martin-Luther-Universität Halle-Wittenberg, 1979.

Not examined, but the author's RILM abstract indicates that it revolves around a novel concept of the dramatic process (*dramaturgische Verlaufsstruktur*), demonstrated by analyses of selected examples by Handel.

* _____. "Handlung und Affekt in Händels Opern." In *Konferenzbericht Halle (Saale) 1980*, pp. 24–31.

Cited below as item 732.

408. _____. "Notate zu einer Dramaturgie der Händel-Opern." *Händel-Jahrbuch* 28 (1982): 35–42.

Discusses dramatic concepts in Handel's operas, with special reference to excerpts from *Giulio Cesare* and *Alcina*.

409. _____. "Die Figurenkonzeption in Händels Oper 'Poro, re dell'Indie'." In *Konferenzbericht Halle (Saale) 1982*, pp. 82–93.

Investigates the musical and dramatic relationships among the characters in *Poro*, one of Handel's rare settings of a

Metastasian libretto. Handel had his own concepts of music, drama and characterization. Examines these in light of *seria* conventions. Tables.

410. _____. "Julius Caesar als Händelsche Operngestalt." In *Konferenzbericht Halle (Saale) 1983*, pp. 60–70.

   Points out that the Caesar of Handel—Haym—Bussani is not the stereotypical tyrant or enlightened monarch, but rather a multi-dimensional character. Caesar was particularly attractive to opera librettists and composers because his story combined love and war. Views the character in its eighteenth century socio-historical context.

411. _____. "Die Ezio-Historie im Wandel der opera seria bei Händel und Verdi." In *Konferenzbericht Halle (Saale) 1984*, pp. 102–21.

   Comparison of Handel's *Ezio* (1732) with Verdi's treatment of the same story in *Attila* (1846) demonstrates the significant changes that took place in dramatic thought and ideology. Suggests that, for Handel, the historical events were merely a background for intense human conflicts, while for Verdi the events take precedence as an allegory for the Italian independence struggle.

412. _____. *Dramaturgie des Händel-Opern*. Schriften des Händel-Hauses in Halle, 3. Halle (Saale): Händel-Haus, 1985. 111p. ML 410 H13 B55. ISSN 0232-3214/3.

   Not examined.

413. Brainard, Paul. "Aria and Ritornello: New Aspects of the Comparison Handel/Bach." In *Bach, Handel, Scarlatti: Tercentenary Essays*, pp. 21–33. Ed. Peter Williams. Cambridge: Cambridge University Press, 1985. ML 55 B14 1985. ISBN 0-521-25217-2.

   Study of Handel's compositional process as reflected in autograph sources points up the fact that many of his aria ritornellos constitute a kind of synopsis of prominent musical/textual events from the opening and closing portions of the

A section. Unlike Bach, Handel tended to make subtle modifications in restatements of ritornellos. Suggests that Bach's and Handel's "parody" or borrowing techniques differed fundamentally.

414. Braun, Werner. "Händel und die frühdeutsche Oper." In *Karlsruher Händel Vorträge*, pp. 51–85. Ed. Kurt R. Pietschmann and Gabriele Eikermann. Karlsruhe: Badisches Staatstheater Karlsruhe, 1985. ML 410 H13 K37.

    Offers a valuable discussion of Handel's Hamburg operas.

415. Brown, Leslie, E. "Metaphor and Music: The Landscape Garden in Eighteenth-Century Opera Sets." *Opera Quarterly* 2 (1984): 37–55.

    Investigates the relationships between the garden sets and the operas themselves with special reference to works by André Campra, Louis de La Coste, and Mozart, as well as Handel's *Serse* and *Giulio Cesare*. Musical examples.

416. Burrows, Donald. "Handel's London Theatre Orchestra." *Early Music* 13 (1985): 349–57.

    Gives background on opera and theatre in London during the early years of the eighteenth century. Summarizes available documents on the size and constitution of orchestras used for the performance of Handel's works. Presents as additional evidence the orchestra players' lists from the Lord Mayor's Day Royal Entertainments at the Guildhall in 1714 and especially 1727. Plan of Haymarket theatre, other plates, tables.

417. Celletti, Rodolfo. "Il virtuosismo vocale nel melodramma di Haendel." *Rivista italiana di musicologia* 4 (1969): 77–101.

    Investigates the style of virtuoso passages in Handel's operas. Musical examples.

418. Chisholm, Duncan. "The English Origins of Handel's Pastor fido." *Musical Times* 115 (1974): 650–51.

Discusses English adaptations of pastoral dramas in the late seventeenth and early eighteenth centuries. Includes important precedents for *Il pastor fido* and *Acis and Galatea*.

419. Cummings, Graham H. "The London Performances of Handel's Opera *Poro*." In *Konferenzbericht Halle (Saale) 1982*, pp. 62–81.

    Discusses London casts, but also delivers more than the title promises. Offers considerable analysis of the libretto and a penetrating analysis of Handel's adaptation of *Poro* for the 1736–37 season. Well-documented. Tables.

420. _____. "Reminiscence and Recall in Three Early Settings of Metastasio's *Alessandro nell'Indie*." *Proceedings of The Royal Musical Association* 109 (1982–83): 80–104.

    Shows how textual repetition for dramatic effect in Metastasio's libretto inspired different techniques of musical recall in the operas of Vinci, Handel (*Poro*), and Hasse. Tables, musical examples.

421. _____. "Handel's Poro: An Edition and Critical Study." Ph.D. dissertation. Birmingham, 1984.

    Not examined.

422. Dean Winton. "Handel's *Giulio Cesare*." *Musical Times* 104 (1963): 402–404.

    Assesses the libretto of *Giulio Cesare* (1724), giving a plot summary. Presents a sharply critical account of the HHA edition. Illustration.

423. _____. "Handel's *Riccardo primo*." *Musical Times* 105 (1964): 498–500.

    Describes historical context of the original production of *Riccardo primo* (1727), listing original cast. Gives detailed plot summary. Comments on the orchestra. Illustration.

424. _____. "Handel's Scipione." *Musical Times* 108 (1967): 902–904.

Operas 137

General discussion of *Scipione* (1726), including notes on the first production and a detailed plot summary. The source for Rolli's libretto is unknown.

425. _____. "Handel's *Amadigi*." *Musical Times* 109 (1968): 324–27.

Assesses the adaptation by Handel's London librettist (Giacomo Rossi?) of La Motte's *Amadis de Grèce* for *Amadigi* (1715). Gives plot summary and lists original cast and modern revivals. General comments on the music.

426. _____. *Handel and the Opera Seria*. Berkeley: University of California Press, 1969. 220p. MT 100 H3 D4.

Offers excellent insight into the conventions of opera seria. Based on Ernest Bloch lectures delivered at Berkeley in 1965–66. Not heavily documented. Viewed by the author as a preliminary survey. Examines operas by issue, for example libretto, orchestration, modern revivals, etc. No bibliography. Index of works, general index.

427. _____. "Handel's Wedding Opera." *Musical Times* 111 (1970): 705–707.

Using historical accounts, describes the original production of *Atalanta* (1736). Reprints the "Argument" from the libretto and lists the cast members. General comments on the music.

428. _____. "Handel's *Ottone*." *Musical Times* 112 (1971): 955–58.

One of a series of articles appearing in anticipation of revivals of Handel operas. Lists the original cast of *Ottone* and reprints the "Argument" from the original libretto. Discusses the plot with reference to the manner in which Haym adapted his model, *Teofane* by S.B. Pallavicino. General comments on the music. Illustration.

* _____. ed. *G. F. Handel: Three Ornamented Arias*. Oxford: Oxford University Press, 1973. M 1505 H13. ISBN 0–19–34512–2.

Cited below as item 739.

429. _____. "A French Traveller's View of Handel's Operas." *Music and Letters* 55 (1974): 172–78.

Presents an excerpt from *Voiage d'Angleterre d'Hollande et de Flandre fait en l'année 1728 Par Mr. Fougeroux Pierre Jacques*, a set of letters from a French traveller which survived in manuscript and was published in 1960. The excerpt, dealing with Fougeroux's impressions of a number of concerts, three operas by Handel (*Siroe, Tolomeo, Admeto*), and *The Beggar's Opera*, appears in the original French. Informed introduction and commentary.

430. _____. "Handel's *Sosarme*, a Puzzle Opera." In *Essays on Opera and English Music in Honour of Sir Jack Westrup*, pp. 115–47. Oxford: Blackwell, 1975. ML 55 E8. ISBN 0–631–15890–1.

Offers a detailed plot summary of *Sosarme* (1732), with stage directions from the original libretto. Contrary to accepted statements, the source for the libretto was not Matteo Noris's *Alfonso Primo*, and remains unknown. Theorizes that the adaptor was Paolo Rolli. Presents details on a number of source problems, including the contents of Handel's autograph, the 1734 version, and the fact that, when preparing performance scores, Smith sometimes began to copy before Handel had finished composing. Concludes with a critical discussion. Musical examples.

431. _____. "Händels kompositorische Entwicklung in den Opern der Jahre 1724/25." *Händel-Jahrbuch* 28 (1982): 23–24.

Discusses some of the fundamental compositional changes made during the creation of *Giulio Cesare, Tamerlano* and *Rodelinda*. Gives an example of a detailed musical change, as well as broad revisions such as the elimination or insertion of arias and scenes. All have significant effects on the dramas. Summarizes Haym's function as adaptor of older Italian librettos.

* _____. "The Musical Sources for Handel's *Teseo* and *Amadigi.*" In *Slavonic and Western Music: Essays for Gerald Abraham*, pp. 63–80. Ed. Malcolm Brown and Roland Wiley. Oxford: Oxford University Press, 1985. ML 55 A18 1984. ISBN 0–8357–1594–9.

   Cited above as item 295.

432. _____. "Zur Oper *Alessandro* von Georg Friedrich Händel." *Concerto* 2/3 (1985): 46–51.

   Briefly examines the background, libretto, and music of *Alessandro*, finding that the ariosos and accompanied recitatives are of particular interest. Plates.

433. _____ and J. Merrill Knapp. *Handel's Operas 1704–1726.* Oxford: Clarendon Press, 1987. 751p. ML 410 H13 D37 1986. ISBN 0–19–315219–3.

   Eagerly-awaited first of two volumes on Handel's operas, it will remain the definitive work for some time. Informed by detailed study of the sources, it offers essays on all the operas, each one dealing with libretto, music, text and history, as well as general chapters on performance practice, background in Germany, Italy, and England, and Handel's operatic career. Invaluable appendices on borrowings, Handel's singers, performances during Handel's life, and modern stage productions to the end of 1984. Thoroughly indexed, excellent short bibliography. Musical examples, plates.

434. Dent, Edward J. "The Operas." In *Handel: A Symposium*, pp. 12–65. Ed. Gerald Abraham. London: Oxford University Press, 1954. ML 410 H13 A66.

   Presents historical context of Handel's operas. Brief commentary on each opera. Dated but incisive discussions of issues related to modern revivals.

435. Ferrero, Mercedes Viale. "Antonio e Pietro Ottoboni e alcuni melodrammi da loro ideati o promossi a Roma." In *Venezia e il melodramma nel Settecento* vol. 1, pp. 271–

94. Ed. Maria Teresa Muraro. Venezia: San Giorgio Maggiore, 1978.

Discusses a recently discovered manuscript of a *Giulio Cesare* by Antonio Ottoboni, reproducing the scenic design drawings by Filippo Juvarra. Detailed appendixes include a list of operas on the same story.

* Feustking, Friedrich C. "Die durch Blut und Mord erlangete Liebe, oder Nero." *Händel-Jahrbuch* 23 (1977): 60–135.

Cited above as item 297.

436. Grout, Donald Jay. *A Short History of Opera.* 2nd edition. New York: Columbia University Press, 1965. ML 1700 G83.

General discussion of Handel's operas on pp. 157–68 is enlivened by the author's profound understanding of the subject, and especially of the aesthetics of Baroque musical drama. Brief survey of Handel's operatic career is of limited usefulness today because of new information, especially on the Hamburg works, the Italian period and the sources of librettos. Musical examples. Extensive bibliography. Index.

437. Gwacharija, Washa. "Orientalische Thematik im Schaffen Georg Friedrich Händels und anderer Komponisten des 18. Jahrhunderts." *Händel-Jahrbuch* 20 (1974): 81–102.

Briefly discusses eastern themes in eighteenth-century opera plots. Especially useful for its comparative lists; for example, it shows Handel's operas on oriental themes, along with works by other composers on the same stories.

438. _____. "Die historischen Grundlagen von G.F. Händels Oper 'Radamisto'." In *Konferenzbericht Halle (Saale) 1979,* pp. 59–65.

Clarifies historical background for the story of Radamisto as it is found in Tacitus and interpreted by seventeenth and eighteenth-century librettists.

439. _____. "Antike und östliche Quellen zum Feldzug des Alexander von Makedarien gegen den indischen Herrscher

Poros." In *Konferenzbericht Halle (Saale) 1982*, pp. 33–39.

Historical background to the Alexander-Poro story. Lists fourteen operas of the late seventeenth and eighteenth centuries based on stories of Alexander the Great.

440. Harris, Ellen T. *Handel and the Pastoral Tradition*. Oxford: Oxford University Press, 1980. 292p. ML 410 H13 H28. ISBN 0-19-315236-3.

Contains valuable information about the pastoral traditions of Germany, Italy, and England. Argues that Handel's adaptation of all three traditions was an important factor in his success not only as an opera composer but also as a composer of oratorios. Works by Handel discussed in detail include *Florindo, Daphne* (librettos), numerous Italian cantatas, *Il pastor fido, Arianna, Parnasso in festa, Ariodante, Alcina,* and *Atalanta*. Extensive bibliography, index.

* Hinsch, Hinrich. "Faksimile-Wiedergabe des Librettos *Der beglückte Florindo*." *Händel-Jahrbuch* 30 (1984): 21-73.

Cited above as item 300.

* _____. "Faksimile-Wiedergabe des Librettos *Die verwandelte Daphne*." *Händel-Jahrbuch* 31 (1985): 17-59.

Cited above as item 301.

441. Kimbell, David R.B. "The Libretto of Handel's *Teseo*." *Music and Letters* 44 (1963): 371-79.

Examines the relationship between Nicola Haym's libretto and its seventeenth-century French model by Philippe Quinault.

442. _____. "A Critical Study of Handel's Early Operas." phil. Diss. Oxford, 1968.

Not examined, but see item 403.

443. _____. "The Amadis Operas of Destouches and Handel." *Music and Letters* 49 (1968): 329–46.

Compares librettos of Handel's *Amadigi* and *Amadis de Grèce*, by Antoine Houdar de la Motte and set by Destouches in 1699, showing how the French drama changed when reworked in the Italian manner. To some extent, responsibility for the drama shifted from poet to composer.

444. Knapp, J. Merrill. "Handel, the Royal Academy of Music, and Its First Opera Season in London (1720)." *Musical Quarterly* 45 (1959): 145–67.

Readable account of the origins of the Academy. Discusses Italian opera in London, business considerations, Handel's search for singers. Contrary to most accounts, Handel was the chief musical figure at the beginning; Ariosti played only a minor role, and Bononcini missed the first season. Discusses the productions of the first season, including Porta's *Numitore*, a popular show by French comedians and Domenico Scarlatti's *Narciso*, with an extended commentary on Handel's *Radamisto*. Prints "Ombra cara" with ornamentation from a copy of ca. 1760–70.

445. _____. "Handel's *Giulio Cesare in Egitto*." In *Studies in Music History: Essays for Oliver Strunk*, pp. 389–404. Ed. Harold Powers. Princeton: Princeton University Press, 1968. ML 3797.1 P69 S9.

Offers plot summary and background of the libretto. Examines word-books for *Giulio Cesare* productions in 1724, 1725, and 1730. Suggests that the autograph score is really a working document, even a "series of sketches," giving the original plan of Act 1 in an appendix. Evaluates the Chrysander edition. Gives cast lists, and shows what was performed, in what order and in what keys for each of the three productions.

446. _____. "The Libretto of Handel's *Silla*." *Music and Letters* 50 (1969): 68–75.

Introduces a recently-discovered libretto for *Silla*, which contains important information on the origins of the opera. Compares the libretto to the text of Handel's setting.

447. _____. "Handel's *Tamerlano*: The Creation of an Opera." *Musical Quarterly* 56 (1970): 405–30.

Offers a detailed comparison of Nicola Haym's libretto with its model, a libretto by Count Agostino Piovene. Compares Gasparini's music for the Piovene text to Handel's setting of Haym's adaptation. Shows that Handel's autograph contains information about the working relationship between composer and librettist. Musical examples.

* _____. "The Autograph Manuscripts of Handel's *Ottone*." In *Festskrift Jens Peter Larsen*, pp. 167–80. Ed. Nils Schiørring, Henrik Glahn, Carsten E. Hatting. Copenhagen: Wilhelm Hansen, 1972. ML 55 L23 F5. ISBN 87-7455-0004.

Cited above as item 309.

* _____. "The Autograph of Handel's *Riccardo primo*." In *Studies in Renaissance and Baroque Music in Honor of Arthur Mendel*, pp. 331–58. Ed. Robert L. Marshall. Kassel: Bärenreiter, 1974. ML 55 M415 S7. ISBN 3-7618-0412-1.

Cited above as item 310.

448. _____. "Handel's First Italian Opera: *Vincer se stesso è la maggior vittoria* or *Rodrigo*." *Music and Letters* 62 (1981): 12–29.

Summarizes considerable recent research on *Vincer se stesso* or *Rodrigo*, Handel's Florentine opera of 1707. Examines librettos of *Rodrigo* and its 1699 model, *Il duello d'amore e di vendetta* by Francesco Silvani (music by Marc' Antonio Ziani). Handel was already a "practised Italianate musician" when he composed it. See also Winton Dean's letter to the editor, *Music and Letters* 63 (1982): 385–86.

449. _____. "Handel's Second Song on the London Stage, or *Agrippina a Londra*." *Musical Times* 123 (1982): 250–51.

Published to highlight the London revival of *Agrippina* by Kent Opera in April, 1982. Even before the successful *Rinaldo* production of 1711, at least two arias from *Agrippina* had been performed on the London stage. As discovered by William C. Smith (*Music and Letters* 16 (1935): p. 286), the first was sung in a 1710 pasticcio revival entitled *Pirro e Demetrio*. Knapp points out that a second aria from *Agrippina* was used in a January 1711 pasticcio of *Etearco*, based on Bononcini's 1707 work. Traces Handel's use of this aria from the early Naples *Aci, Galatea e Polifemo* to its final incarnation in *Jephtha*.

* _____. "Editionstechnische Probleme bei Händels Opern, im Besonderen bei *Teseo, Poro, Ezio* und *Deidamia*." In *Konferenzbericht Halle (Saale), 1982*, pp. 22–32.

Cited above as item 312.

450. Koller, Heide Christiane. "Händels Opern auf der Hamburger Bühne (1715–1736)." In *Händel und Hamburg: Ausstellung anläßlich des 300. Geburtstages von Georg Friedrich Händel*, pp. 117–21. Ed. Hans Joachim Marx. Hamburg: Karl Dieter Wagner, 1985. ML 410 H13 H234. ISBN 3-88979-009-7.

Lists productions of Handel's operas at the Goosemarket theater in Hamburg during the years 1715–36. In addition to the basic data about each work and its German version, there are helpful remarks describing the nature of the adaptation. Some of the musical adaptations were made by Mattheson, Keiser, and Telemann.

451. Kubik, Reinhold. *Händels Rinaldo: Geschichte, Werk, Wirkung*. Neuhausen-Stuttgart: Hänssler-Verlag, 1982. 264p. ML 410 H13 K8 1982. ISBN 3-7751-0594-8.

An exhaustive study of *Rinaldo*, with significant material on the autograph corrections, the versions of 1711 and 1731 and especially on the borrowings. Discussion of *Rinaldo* as

Operas

Baroque opera takes into account two Hamburg versions (1715 and 1723) and a setting by Leonardo Leo (1718). General appearance and literary style are somewhat awkward, but the reader is assisted by copious tables and musical examples. Bibliography, index of names.

452. Kunze, Stefan. "Händels dramatische Gegenstände." In *Karlsruher Händel Vorträge*, pp. 87–98. Ed. Kurt R. Pietschmann and Gabriele Eikermann. Karlsruhe: Badisches Staatstheater Karlsruhe, 1985. ML 410 H13 K37.

Not examined.

453. _____. "Musik und Szene in Händels Opern." In *Karlsruher Händel Vorträge*, pp. 99–109. Ed. Kurt R. Pietschmann and Gabriele Eikermann. Karlsruhe: Badisches Staatstheater Karlsruhe, 1985. ML 410 H13 K37.

Not examined.

454. Leopold, Silke. "'Who could like Handel with such art control the various passions of the warring soul?' Händel und die dramatische Musik." *Concerto* 2/2 (1985): 33–40.

Surveys Handel's operatic oeuvre. Plates.

455. Loewenberg, Alfred. *Annals of Opera 1597–1940*. 3rd ed. London: John Calder, 1978. 1756 columns. ML 102 O6 L6 1978. ISBN 0–7145–3657–1.

First published in 1943, it offers a chronological list of operas according to their dates of first performance. Handel's operas can be seen in their historical contexts. Includes dates and places of subsequent productions, including twentieth-century revivals. Indexed in great detail. Introduction by Edward J. Dent.

456. Lynch, Robert D. "Opera in Hamburg, 1718–1738: A Study of the Libretto and Musical Style." Ph.D. dissertation. New York University, 1979.

Not examined, but the RILM abstract describes an invaluable source for the study of Handel's Hamburg period.

Detailed study of more than 500 librettos and their sources, analysis of all extant music manuscripts of operas performed in Hamburg, with special emphasis on Handel's works. Appendixes include twenty-two arias representative of the repertory.

457. _____. "The Influence of Operatic Reform in Hamburg, 1700–38." *Current Musicology* 28 (1978): 76–85.

Discusses Hamburg opera librettos, concentrating on their connections with the Italian reform movement. Compares Feustking's libretto for Handel's *Almira* with the 1699 version by Pancieri.

458. Milhous, Judith. "Opera Finances in London, 1674–1738." *Journal of the American Musicological Society* 37 (1984): 567–92.

Presents budgets for each of the following: the Dorset Garden semi-operas (1674–1706); the first Italian opera companies (1708–13); Heidegger's companies (1713–17); the Royal Academy of Music, especially in the early stages; Handel's operas (1729–38). Points out that Italian opera was always a losing proposition financially. Revealing discussion, speculating on the reasons for the lack of realism among eighteenth-century impresarios.

459. _____ and Robert D. Hume. "Box Office Reports for Five Operas Mounted by Handel in London 1732–1734." *Harvard Library Bulletin* 26 (1978): 245–66.

Offers annotated transcriptions of reports of ticket sales and cash receipts for six nights of five operas during 1732–34. Taken from the Coke papers (see item 460), the figures show that Italian opera was bound to be a losing proposition. Plates, tables.

460. _____. *Vice Chamberlain Coke's Theatrical Papers 1706–1715.* Carbondale: Southern Illinois University Press, 1982. 274p. PN 2596 L6 V5. ISBN 0–8093–1024–4.

Edited papers of Vice Chamberlain Thomas Coke (1674–1727) give correspondence, contracts, financial records, and other documents for the London theatre seasons from 1705–06 through 1714–15. Most of the documents relating directly to Handel have already appeared in item 458, but the contexts are revealing. Introduction contains brief sections on opera on the London stage, the theatrical situation in London (1695–1715), Thomas Coke and the Vice Chamberlain's office, etc. Index.

461. _____. "New Light on Handel and the Royal Academy of Music in 1720." *Theatre Journal* 35 (1983): 149–67.

Describes eight manuscripts on deposit at the University of Nottingham Library. Gives information on the first season of the Royal Academy (spring of 1720). Prints minutes of planning meetings, projected expenses, box office estimates, lists of orchestra members with their salaries, projections for the 1720–21 season. Generally, the projections were optimistic. Handel's salary is still a mystery. Appendix contains the Subscribers' Prospectus for the Royal Academy.

462. _____. "Handel's Opera Finances in 1732–3." *Musical Times* 125 (1984): 86–89.

Describes and presents the complete text of a recently discovered manuscript concerning the finances of Handel and Heidegger's season at the Haymarket Theatre—a set of notes made to determine total cash received as of October 23, 1733. Summarizes sources of income and estimates total income for the year, showing that the company might barely have broken even.

463. Monson, Craig. "*Giulio Cesare in Egitto*: From Sartorio (1677) to Handel (1724)." *Music and Letters* 66 (1985): 313–43.

Demonstrates that Francesco Bussani's original libretto contains striking and doubtless intentional parallels with events of British military and political history. Compares librettos and portions of the scores, showing that Haym's libretto was based on Bussani's and that Handel may well have been influenced by Sartorio's music. Generous musical examples.

464. Osthoff, Wolfgang, "Haendels 'Largo' als Musik des goldenen Zeitalters." *Archiv für Musikwissenschaft* 30 (1973): 175–89.

Examines in detail the text of "Ombra mai fu," referring to poetic models. Compares Handel's setting with those of Cavalli and Bononcini. Musical examples.

465. Pecman, Rudolf. "Apostolo Zeno und sein Libretto *Il Venceslao* zu dem gleich namigen Pasticcio von Georg Friedrich Händel." In *Konferenzbericht Halle (Saale) 1979*, pp. 66–93.

Handel's 1731 pasticcio was based on a Zeno libretto. Gives background on Zeno, describes the libretto and lists settings by Carlo Francesco Pollarolo (1653?–1722), Francesco Mancini (1672–1737), and Antonio Gaetano Pampani (d. 1769).

466. _____. "Die Gestalt Cäsars in der Auffassung Händels und Beethovens." In *Konferenzbericht Halle (Saale) 1983*, pp. 71–73.

Suggests that both Handel and Beethoven eschewed the heroic aspects of Caesar. In *Giulio Cesare*, the emphasis is rather on an analysis of his most important character traits. In Beethoven's unrealized plans for a Caesar opera, he was looking for the positive side of Brutus, and saw Caesar as a model for Napoleon as dictator.

467. Poladian, Sirvart. "Handel as an Opera Composer." Ph.D. dissertation. Cornell University, 1946.

Not examined.

468. Powers, Harold S. "Il Serse trasformato." Part I in *Musical Quarterly* 47 (1961): 481–92. Part II in *Musical Quarterly* 48 (1962): 73–92.

Pioneering work on the nature of Handel's opera librettos. Part I focuses on the structure of the libretto for *Serse*, comparing Minato's original (Venice, 1654) with Stampiglia's revision (Rome, 1694). Stampiglia shifts the high points from recitative to aria. Part II examines the musical relationship between Bononcini's and Handel's settings of the Stampiglia version. Aspects of Handel's *Serse* (1738) have mistakenly been allied to the modern opera buffa, but they really represent a close association with seventeenth-century practice.

469. Rackwitz, Werner. "Die Herakles-Gestalt bei Händel." In *Festschrift zur Händel-Ehrung der Deutschen Demokratischen Republik 1959*, pp. 51-61. Leipzig: Deutscher Verlag für Musik, 1959. ML 410 H13 F35.

    Briefly reviews the legendary background, then surveys the Hercules characters in *Admeto*, *Alceste*, *The Choice of Hercules* and *Hercules*.

470. Sasse, Konrad. "Opera Register from 1712 to 1734 (Colman-Register)." *Händel-Jahrbuch* 5 (1959): 199-223.

    Presents an annotated list made by a London operagoer of operas performed during the years 1712-1734. Includes information on casts, prices, successes and failures, the movements of the royal family, and other interesting miscellany.

471. Scherer, Barrymore L. "Cross and Crescent." *Opera News* 48/10 (1984): 14-16.

    Discusses Torquato Tasso's *Gerusalemme Liberata* as a source for *Rinaldo*. Plates.

472. Siegmund-Schultze, Walther. "Antike Themen in Händels Opern und Oratorien." In *Konferenzbericht Halle (Saale) 1983*, pp. 7-25.

    Discusses Classical themes in Handel's vocal works. Makes interesting connections between humanisn, literary Classicism and concepts of Old Testament heroes like Saul, David, Samson, and Solomon. Contends that Handel avoided opera librettos with strong references to belief in oracles or Fate.

473. Smith, William C. "The 1754 Revival of Handel's *Admeto.*" *Music and Letters* 51 (1970): 141–49.

Describes the 1754 revival, showing that Handel was indeed involved, contrary to the general belief that he was not. Examines early librettos, as well as annotations in early prints. Discusses Handel's handwriting in the 1750s. Plates.

* Stompor, Stephan. "Die deutschen Aufführungen von Opern Händels in der ersten Hälfte des 18. Jahrhunderts." 3 vols. Ph.D. dissertation. Universität Halle, 1975. 275, 260, 89p.

Cited below as item 923.

474. _____. "Die deutsche Aufführungen von Opern Händels in der ersten Hälfte des 18. Jahrhunderts." *Händel-Jahrbuch* 24 (1978): 31–89.

Discusses Handel's early Hamburg operas in detail. Gives historical details on productions of Handel operas in Hamburg and Braunschweig during the 1720s and '30s.

* Strohm, Reinhard. "Händel in Italia: nuovi contributi." *Rivista italiana di musicologia* 9 (1974): 152–74.

Cited above as item 248.

* _____. "Italienische Opernarien des frühen Settecento." *Analecta musicologica* 16 (1976): 1–268, 1–342.

Cited above as item 25.

475. _____. "Handel, Metastasio, Racine: The Case of *Ezio.*" *Musical Times* 118 (1977): 901–903.

Discusses the tastes of London opera goers, who rejected *Ezio* after only five performances. Handel's choice of a Metastasian libretto was influenced by its origins in Racine's Britannicus (1669). At the time of *Ezio* (1732), he was inter-

Operas 151

ested in Racine's works, which inspired the oratorios *Athalia* and *Esther*.

476. _____. *Die italienische Oper im 18. Jahrhundert*. Taschenbücher zur Musikwissenschaft 25. Wilhelmshaven: Heinrichschofen, 1979. 398p. ML 1703 S87. ISBN 3-7959-0110-3.

Collection of essays on eighteenth-century Italian opera. Emphasis on librettos. Each essay begins with a useful bibliography. Index, extensive general bibliography. No musical examples.

477. _____. "Händels Londoner Operntexte." In *Bericht über den Internationalen Musikwissenschaftlichen Kongress Berlin 1974*, pp. 305-307. Ed. H. Kühn and P. Nitsche. Kassel: Bärenreiter, 1980. ISBN 3-7618-0592-6.

Examines the models for Handel's opera librettos. Shows that he played an important role, often choosing librettos that he knew from performances of settings by other composers. He preferred old-fashioned texts, especially from Rome and Florence.

478. _____. "Comic Traditions in Handel's *Orlando*." In *Essays on Handel and Italian Opera*, pp. 249-69. Cambridge: Cambridge University Press, 1985. ML 410 H13 S75 1985. ISBN 0-521-26428-6.

Suggests that the Neapolitan buffa singer Celeste Resse had a hand in the creation of the plots for many of the intermezzos in which she performed. Whoever adapted Capeci's *L'Orlando, overo La gelosa pazzia* for Handel, possibly Nicola Haym, introduced comic traits into the role of Dorinda, to be sung by La Celestina, now called Celeste Gismondi. Shows that this and other comic aspects of *Orlando* may well have been designed by Handel himself. Appendix lists La Celestina's comic roles.

479. _____. "Francesco Gasparini's Later Operas and Handel." In *Essays on Handel and Italian Opera*, pp. 80-92. Cam-

bridge: Cambridge University Press, 1985. ML 410 H13 S75 1985. ISBN 0-521-26428-6.

Originally published in Italian in *Francesco Gasparini (1661-1727): Atti del primo Convegno Internazionale.* Florence: Leo S. Olschki, 1982. Shows that *Faramondo*, previously thought to be completely original, is partly derived from Gasparini's opera of the same name (Rome, 1720). Suggests that Handel's ties to Roman musical traditions were stronger than we realize.

480. _____. "Handel and His Italian Opera Texts." In *Essays on Handel and Italian Opera*, pp. 34–79. Cambridge: Cambridge University Press, 1985. ML 410 H13 S75 1985. ISBN 0-521-26428-6.

Summarizes knowledge about all the Italian opera librettos, with preliminary remarks about *Almira*. Useful recent references. Handel never set new texts; the author suggests that, since his choices were often associated with his own past, it might be possible to draw conclusions about Handel the man from study of the librettos. Originally appeared in German in the *Händel-Jahrbuch* 1975-76.

481. _____. "Handel's *Ezio*." In *Essays on Handel and Italian Opera*, pp. 225–31. Cambridge: Cambridge University Press, 1985. ML 410 H13 S75 1985. ISBN 0-521-26428-6.

Discusses Handel's third and last setting of a Metastasian libretto. Valuable summary of the features that made his operas retrogressive for the 1730s. The recitatives of Italian operas had to be shortened for the London public, but Handel was often able to convey in an aria setting what was lost by cutting the recitative. Based on material from item 475.

482. _____. "Handel's Pasticci." In *Essays on Handel and Italian Opera*, pp. 164–211. Cambridge: Cambridge University Press, 1985. ML 410 H13 S75 1985. ISBN 0-521- 26428-6.

Good general introduction defines *pasticcio* and describes its special functions in London. Examines all nine of Handel's

Operas 153

pasticci. Detailed chronological list of the sinfonias and arias includes for each number the name of the singer, the opera from which it came, the original text of the aria and the singer of the original aria. Musical examples. First appeared in German in *Analecta Musicologica* 14 (1974): 208–67.

483. _____. "Metastasio's *Alessandro nell'Indie* and Its Earliest Settings." In *Essays on Handel and Italian Opera*, pp. 232–48. Cambridge: Cambridge University Press, 1985. ML 410 H13 S75 1985. ISBN 0–521–26428–6.

Compares Handel's setting (*Poro*, 1731) with those by Hasse and Vinci. Although Handel interfered with Metastasio's verses to a lesser extent than his Italian contemporaries, his concept of drama differed fundamentally from Metastasio's. Appendix 1 gives performances of *Alessandro nell'Indie* (*Poro*, *Cleofide*) from 1730 to 1745. Appendix 2 lists singers who appeared more than once in these operas. Musical examples.

484. _____. "Towards an Understanding of the *opera seria*." In *Essays on Handel and Italian Opera*, pp. 93–105. Cambridge: Cambridge University Press, 1985. ML 410 H13 S75 1985. ISBN 0–521–26428–6.

Encourages modern producers to view the operas as their eighteenth-century predecessors might have, not as marmoreal "works" with one sacred text. Puts forward four convincing reasons for Handel's uniqueness as a composer of *opera seria*. Originally published in German in item 832, pp. 51–70.

485. Trowell, Brian. "Handel as a Man of the Theatre." *Proceedings of the Royal Musical Association* 88 (1961–62): 17–30.

General remarks on Handel's operas aimed at re-evaluating them and performing them today. Musical example.

486. Wolff, Hellmuth Christian. *"Agrippina": Eine italienische Jugendoper Händels.* Wolfenbüttel: Kallmeyer, 1943. 36p.

Stresses the hitherto unrecognized comic elements of Handel's 1709 opera. Discusses the libretto, gives musical commentary. Plates, musical examples.

487. _____. "Typologie der Musik der italienischen Oper 1600–1750." *Opera w dawnej Polsce na dworze Wladyslawa* 4 (1973): 69–86.

A survey of musical forms in Italian opera from 1600 to 1750. In Polish. (Summary from RILM).

488. _____. "L'opera comica nel sec. XVII a Venezia e l'*Agrippina* di Händel (1709)." *Nuova rivista musicale Italiana* 7 (1973): 39–50.

Shows how *Agrippina* continues the Venetian tradition of Pietro Andrea Ziano, Carlo Pallavicini and others, in which *seria* titles sometimes disguised satiric comic operas or comedies. Musical examples.

489. _____. "Händel und die Gänsemarkt-Oper." In *Händel und Hamburg: Ausstellung anläßlich des 300. Geburtstages von Georg Friedrich Händel*, pp. 45–52. Ed. Hans Joachim Marx. Hamburg: Karl Dieter Wagner, 1985. ML 410 H13 H234. ISBN 3-88979-009-7.

Summarizes Handel's relationship with Hamburg, especially in the area of opera, from 1703 until the closing of the opera house in 1738. Suggests that, by re-setting two of Handel's librettos in the early 1740s, Karl Heinrich Graun in effect continued the Handel tradition in Berlin.

* Young, Percy M. "Die Problematik der Oper in England während der ersten Hälfte des 18. Jahrhundert." In *Konferenzbericht Halle (Saale) 1982*, pp. 7–21.

Cited above as item 103.

* Zottos, Ion P. "The Completest Concert, or Augustan Critics of Opera: A Documentary and Critical Study in English Aesthetics." Ph.D. dissertation. University of Pennsylvania, 1977. 338p.

Cited above as item 64.

3. Oratorios

490. Allen, Burt M. "The Dramatic Function of the Chorus in Handel's Oratorios." DMA dissertation. University of Kansas, 1977. 112p.

Identifies and examines thirteen dramatic functions of the choruses in Handel's oratorios. Not examined.

491. Ardry, Roger W. "The Influence of the Extended Latin Sacred Works of Giacomo Carissimi on the Biblical Oratorios of George Frederic Handel." Ph.D. dissertation. The Catholic University of America, 1964. 142p.

In attempting to evaluate Carissimi's influence on Handel, points out only one borrowing—the famous "Plorate filii Israel" from *Jephta* in Handel's "Hear Jacob's God" in *Samson*—but examines similarities in dramatic choral passages. Musical examples.

492. Arlt, Jerry Ann. "The Choruses in Three of Handel's Late Oratorios." DMA dissertation. Arizona State University, 1985. 144p.

Discusses thirty-four choruses in *Solomon*, *Theodora*, and *Jephtha*. Not examined.

493. Baselt, Bernd. "Händel und Bach: zur Frage der Passionen." In *Johann Sebastian Bach und Georg Friedrich Händel: 24. Händelfestspiele der Deutschen Demokratischen Republik*, pp. 58–66. Halle: Martin-Luther-Universität, 1975.

Proposes Johannn Mattheson as the composer of the disputed St. John Passion, once thought to be by Handel. Discusses Bach's knowledge of the work.

494. Becker, Heinz. "Die Brockes-Passion von Georg Friedrich Händel." *Musica* 22 (1968): 135–37.

Briefly gives background on Hamburg Passion settings and compares Handel's setting of Brockes' text to those by Keiser, Telemann, and Mattheson, which he implies were known to Handel.

* Beechey, Gwilym. "A Late Eighteenth-Century Print of Handel's *Samson.*" *Musical Opinion* 108 (1985): 294–96.

Cited above as item 284.

* Beeks, Graydon F. "Handel and Music for the Earl of Carnarvon." In *Bach, Handel, Scarlatti: Tercentenary Essays*, pp. 1–20. Ed. Peter Williams. Cambridge: Cambridge University Press, 1985. ML 55 B14 1985. ISBN 0-52125217-2.

Cited below as item 616.

495. _____. "Some Thoughts on Performing *Messiah.*" *American Choral Review* 27/2–3 (1985): 20–30.

Proposes a perfomance of *Messiah* based on the original version of the autograph score, rather than on one of the documented performances. This score was written before Handel crossed "the line from composer to impresario."

496. Benson, J. Allanson. *Handel's Messiah: The Oratorio and Its History.* London: Wm. Reeves, 1923. 69p. MT 115 H133 B3.

Early handbook, including briefest summaries of traditional knowledge about sources, early performances and aspects of performance practice. Musical examples.

497. Boetticher, Wolfgang. "Zum Problem eines Spätstils in Händels Oratorienschaffen." In *Konferenzbericht Halle (Saale) 1981*, pp. 95–103.

Attempts to isolate features of Handel's style in his late oratorios, especially *Jephtha* and *The Triumph of Time and Truth.* Harmonic practices and other elements link this style to the new Empfindsamer and Rococo styles.

498. Bredenfoerder, Elisabeth. *Die Texte der Händel-Oratorien.* Leipzig: Bernhard Tauchnitz, 1934. Kölnes Anglistische Arbeiten, 19. Repr. 1966. 71p. ML 410 H13 B85 1966.

 Examines the literary, aesthetic, and sociological contexts of the oratorio librettos. Bibliography.

499. Britsch, Edwin R. "Musical and Poetical Rhetoric in Handel's Setting of Brockes' Passion Oratorio: A Rhetorical Analysis of the Poem with a Study of Handel's Use of the Figurenlehre." Ph.D. dissertation. Florida State University, 1984. 222p.

 Concludes that Handel was familiar with poetic and musical rhetoric and applied this knowledge in his setting of Brockes' poem.

500. Burrows, Donald J. "Handel's Performances of *Messiah*: The Evidence of the Conducting Score." *Music and Letters* 56 (1975): 319–34.

 Studies the sequence of performers' names added by Handel to the conducting score of *Messiah*, providing new information about its early performances and especially about multiple versions. Musical examples.

501. Cuming, Geoffrey. "The Text of *Messiah*." *Music and Letters* 31 (1950): 226–30.

 Shows that the *Messiah* libretto owes as much to the Anglican Book of Common Prayer as it does to the Bible. Briefly discusses the question of responsibility for the libretto.

502. Dean, Winton. "The Dramatic Elements in Handel's Oratorios." *Proceedings of the Royal Musical Association* 79 (1952–53): 33–49.

 Introduces the theory, later fully expounded in item 503, that the oratorios should be viewed as dramas, rather than as some kind of church music. Outline of the discussion which followed the lecture is particularly revealing of vestigial Victorian attitudes.

503. _____. *Handel's Dramatic Oratorios and Masques.* London: Oxford University Press, 1959. 694p. ML 410 H13 D35.

Advocates a fresh view of the oratorios as essentially dramatic works, not the religious monuments of Victorian tradition. An invaluable compendium of source information. Highly informed discussions of background, style, and performance history. Useful appendixes, including a list of borrowings. Musical examples. Index, bibliography.

* _____. "How Should Handel's Oratorios Be Staged?" *Musical Newsletter* 1/4 (1971): 11–15.

Cited below as item 811.

* Derr, Ellwood. "Handel's Procedures for Composing with Materials from Telemann's 'Harmonischer Gottes-Dienst' in *Solomon*." *Göttinger Händel-Beiträge* 1 (1984): 116–46.

Cited above as item 336.

504. Dietz, Hanns-Bertold. *Die Chorfuge bei G.F. Händel: ein Beitrag zur Kompositionstechnik des Barock.* Tutzing: Hans Schneider, 1961. 150p. ML 410 H13 D54.

Investigates Handel's choral fugues, with special reference to influences and general tendencies of the period. The section on conventions in fugal theme-writing is particularly enlightening. Bibliography, musical examples.

* Ewerhart, Rudolf. "New Sources for Handel's *La Resurrezione*." *Music and Letters* 41 (1960): 127.

Cited above as item 296.

505. Fedossejew, Iwan. "Georg Friedrich Händel und die antike Tradition in der Musik." In *Konferenzbericht Halle (Saale) 1983*, pp. 93–99.

Suggests that, at points of majestic stasis, Handel achieves an epic effect in the oratorios that is similar to that of Homer

Oratorios

and Greek tragedies. Argument is weakened by a misunderstanding of English genres.

* Fleischhauer, Günter. "Zur Verwendung einiger Tanzrhythmen in den Chorsätzen der Oratorien G.F. Händels." In *Konferenzbericht Halle (Saale) 1980*, pp. 96–116.

Cited below as item 747.

* ———. "Zur Funktion und Bedeutung einiger Instrumentalstücke in den Oratorien G.F. Händels." In *Konferenzbericht Halle (Saale) 1981*, pp. 68–85.

Cited below as item 675.

506. Frederichs, Henning. *Das Verhältnis von Text und Musik in den Brockespassionen Keisers, Händels, Telemanns und Matthesons.* Munich: Musikverlag Emil Katzbichler, 1975. 203p. ML 3260 F8. ISBN 3-87397-108-9.

Examines the sources, literary background and style, and the music of the four settings of Brockes' Passion poem. Musical examples, tables, bibliography.

507. ———. "Zur theologischen Interpretation der Brockes-Passion von G.Fr. Händel." *Göttinger Händel-Beiträge* 1 (1984): 21–34.

Establishes that Handel's setting of Brockes' Passion text preceded Telemann's and Mattheson's. Compares the four settings, showing that Keiser's reveals the strongest affinity for the text. Handel's, which remained popular into the nineteenth century, is the least closely bound to the text.

* Fuld, James J. "The First Complete Printing of Handel's *Messiah.*" *Music and Letters* 55 (1974): 454–57.

Cited above as item 298.

* Gelles, George, "Mozart's Version of *Messiah.*" *American Choral Review* 10/1 (1968): 55–65.

Cited below as item 862.

508. Gorali, Moshe and Rivka Watson. *The Old Testament in the Works of George Frideric Handel.* Amli Studies in Music Bibliography. Haifa: Haifa Museum and Amli Library, 1982. 40p. ML 410 H13 G67 1982.

Lists Handel's works on Old Testament sources. Hebrew translation of *Esther*.

* Gudger, William D. "Handel's Last Compositions and His Borrowings from Habermann (Part 2)." *Current Musicology* 23 (1977): 28–45.

Cited above as item 338.

* _____. "A Borrowing from Kerll in *Messiah*." *Musical Times* 118 (1977): 1038–.

Cited above as item 339.

509. _____. "Skizzen und Entwürfe für den Amen-Chor in Händels *Messias*." *Händel-Jahrbuch* 26 (1980): 83–114.

Reflects on the primary issues in the study of Handel's compositional process. Examines sketches and drafts for "He was despised," "Let all the angels of God," and "Amen," showing that Handel worked on parts of *Messiah* before the legendary twenty-two days in which he wrote out the final draft. Analytical notes on the "Amen" chorus. Musical examples.

510. _____. "Sketches and Drafts for *Messiah*." *American Choral Review* 27/2–3 (1985): 31–44.

Slightly shortened English version of item 509.

511. Hall, James S. "The 12/8 Setting of 'Rejoice . . .'." *Musical Opinion* 929 (February, 1955): 277–79.

Brief discussion of Handel's original version of "Rejoice Greatly" from *Messiah*.

Oratorios

512. _____. Letter to the Editor. *Music and Letters* 37 (1956): 98–100.

Elegantly takes issue with item 542, especially on Handel's own preferred versions of "How Beautiful Are the Feet" and "Rejoice Greatly" in *Messiah*. Presents information on Handel's use of more than four soloists for *Messiah*.

513. Harris, Ellen T. "An American Offers Advice to Handel." *American Choral Review* 27/2–3 (1985): 55–62.

Examines a book of essays by James Ralph published in London in 1728 as *The Touch-Stone: or, Historical, Political, Philosophical, and Theological Essays on the Reigning Diversions of the Town*. Ralph suggested the use of Old Testament and Apocryphal stories and the increased use of chorus in opera.

* Herbage, Julian. *Messiah*. London: Max Parrish & Co. Ltd., 1948. 72p. MT 115 H133 H4.

Cited below as item 870.

514. _____. "The Oratorios." In *Handel: A Symposium*, pp. 66–131. Ed. Gerald Abraham. London: Oxford University Press, 1954. ML 410 H13 A66.

Outlines Handel's career as an oratorio composer, offering general comments on each work. Brief musical examples.

515. Hicks, Anthony. "Handel's *La resurrezione*." *Musical Times* 110 (1969): 145–48.

Offers background information and informed commentary, as well as a brief description of the sources.

516. _____. "The Late Additions to Handel's Oratorios and the Role of the Younger Smith." In *Music in Eighteenth-Century England: Essays in Memory of Charles Cudworth*, pp. 147–69. Ed. Christopher Hogwood and Richard Luckett. Cambridge: Cambridge University Press, 1983. ML 55 C85. ISBN 0–521-23525–1.

Examines the additions made to various oratorios for performances during the years 1753–59, when Handel was blind. Finds that additions not simply copied from earlier works are in a style not compatible with Handel's, and suggests convincingly that John Christopher Smith the younger may have played a role more significant than amanuensis.

517. Hudson, Frederick. "Das Concerto in *Judas Maccabaeus* identifiziert." *Händel-Jahrbuch* 20 (1974): 119–33.

   Identifies the "new concerto" for *Judas Maccabaeus* as the second of the *Concerti a due cori*. Describes the sources and outlines the evolution of the work.

518. Jacobi, Peter. *The Messiah Book: The Life and Times of G.F. Handel's Greatest Hit.* New York: St. Martin's Press, 1982. 186p. ML 410 H13 J3. ISBN 0–312–53072–2.

   Written in a breezy style, directed to amateurs. No footnotes. Part 1 contains a biography and a look at *Messiah*'s performance history. Part 2 features the libretto, with identification of the Biblical sources, and excerpts.

*   Jones, Ann E. "An Examination of Expressive Rhythm and Articulation Practices in the Baroque Period with Suggestions for Their Application to the Duet Choruses of 'Messiah'." DMA dissertation. University of Iowa, 1984. 155p.

   Cited below as item 762.

*   Kimbell, David. "Aspekte von Händels Umarbeitungen und Revisionen eigner Werke." *Händel-Jahrbuch* 23 (1977): 45–67.

   Cited above as item 340.

519. Knapp, J. Merrill. "Die drei Fassungen von Händels *Il trionfo del tempo.*" In *Konferenzbericht Halle (Saale) 1981*, pp. 86–94.

   Assisted by the recently-discovered libretto for the 1737 production of *Il trionfo del tempo*, leads the reader through the

Oratorios 163

labyrinth of Chrysander's *Trionfo* editions. Issues a reminder that the early *Il trionfo del tempo e del disinganno*, and not *La Resurrezione*, was Handel's first oratorio.

520. Larsen, Jens Peter. "*Esther* and the Origin of the Handelian Oratorio Tradition." *American Choral Review* 6/2 (1964): 1–5.

Discusses the historical position of the first version of *Esther*, especially with relation to the genres "masque" and "oratorio." Also in item 522.

521. _____. "Handels Weg zum Oratorium und sein *Messias*." In *50 Jahre Göttinger Händel-Festspiele*, pp. 21–28. Ed. Walter Meyerhoff. Kassel: Bärenreiter, 1970. ML 410 H13 M59.

Surveys the radical changes Handel brought to the oratorio genre. Identifies the special qualities of *Messiah* and *Israel in Egypt*. English version in item 522.

522. _____. "Handel Studies." *American Choral Review* 14/1 (1972): 5–48.

Special issue containing items 520, 521, 769, 770, and 822, all in English versions.

523. _____. *Handel's Messiah: Origins, Composition, Sources.* New York: Norton, 1972. 2nd edition. 337p. ML 410 H13 L2 1972. ISBN 0–393–00657–3.

Opens with a still-unsurpassed essay on the development of Handelian oratorio, with special reference to the choral style. Surveys text and music of *Messiah*, with a special section on changing versions. Ground-breaking chapter on sources, including a list of Handel manuscripts. Examples, facsimiles, bibliography, indexes.

524. _____. "Wort-Ton-Probleme in Händels *Messias*." *Händel-Jahrbuch* 21–22 (1975–76): 53–60.

Suggests that there is not a peculiar character to the arias based on Biblical prose texts. Discusses text-music relationships in *Messiah*, focusing on word-painting, affective writing, contrast and parody. Musical examples.

525. _____. "Die Stellung des *Messias* in Händels Oratorienschaffen." In *Konferenzbericht Halle (Saale) 1981*, pp. 58–67.

    Examines the unique textual and musical features of *Messiah* as an oratorio. Reflects on the essential differences between opera and Handelian oratorio.

*   _____. "Wandlungen der Auffassung von Händels *Messias*." *Göttinger Händel-Beiträge* I (1984): 7–20.

    Cited below as item 824.

526. Leopold, Silke. "'I've read my Bible well . . .' Bibeltext und Arienkomposition in Händels Messias." *Musica* 37 (1983): 504–507.

    Explores the text-music relationship in *Messiah* arias, especially in view of the prosaic qualities of the texts.

527. _____. "*Israel in Egypt*—ein mißglückter Glücksfall." *Göttinger Händel-Beiträge* I (1984): 35–50.

    Establishes that *Israel in Egypt* is a work of key importance in the development of Handel's English oratorio style. Discusses early performance history. Summarizes 1765 version in an appendix. Comments on the similarities in pictorial descriptions to passages in Rameau's *Hippolyte et Aricie* (1733) and *Les Indes galantes* (1735). Brief musical example from the latter.

528. Mann, Alfred. "Messiah: The Verbal Text." In *Festskrift Jens Peter Larsen*, pp. 181–88. Ed. Nils Schiørring, Henrik Glahn and Carsten E. Hatting. Copenhagen: Musikvidenskabeligt Institut, 1972. ML 55 L23 F5.

    Asserts that the use of "purely scriptural texts . . . predicated a shift of emphasis from the dominance of the contemplative aria to an essentially choral texture in which the solo element was interspersed in varying patterns." Discusses text choice in the English church music.

529. Meier, Heinz. *Typus und Funktion der Chorsätze in Georg Friedrich Händels Oratorien.* Neue Musikgeschichtliche Forschungen, 5. Wiesbaden: Breitkopf und Härtel, 1971. 158p. ML 410 H13 M47. ISBN 3-7651-0056-0.

Determines standard musical characteristics of settings of certain types of text in six types of choral movements.

* Myers, Robert Manson. *Handel's Messiah: A Touchstone of Taste.* New York, 1948.

Cited below as item 891.

530. Redlich, Hans F. "*Messiah*: The Struggle for a Definite Text." *Music Review* 27 (1966): 287-93.

Discusses *Messiah* editions by John Tobin and Watkins Shaw. Musical examples.

* Rinkel, Lawrence S. "The Forms of English Opera: Literary and Musical Responses to a Continental Genre." Ph.D. dissertation. Rutgers University, 1977. 249p.

Cited above as item 98.

531. Schering, Arnold. *Geschichte des Oratoriums.* Leipzig: Brietkopf & Härtel, 1911. Repr. Hildesheim: Georg Olms, 1966. 647 and XXXIXp. ML 3201 S42.

Pioneering attempt to give a broad, well-balanced picture of the history of oratorio. Chapter 4, devoted to Handel, contains a section on the English oratorio after his death. Indexes, musical, and textual supplement.

* Serwer, Howard. "Die Anfänge des Händelschen Oratoriums (*Esther* 1718)." In *Konferenzbericht Halle (Saale) 1981*, pp. 34-45.

Cited above as item 317.

532. _____. "In Praise of Handel's *Deborah.*" *American Choral Review* 27/2-3 (1985): 14-19.

A defense of *Deborah* against Winton Dean's indictment in *Handel's Dramatic Oratorios and Masques* (item 503). Suggests that eighteenth-century audiences were used to the unsavory aspects of the story, and that the libretto may be well suited to the composer's purposes. Comments on the success of Handel's borrowing techniques.

533. Shaw, Watkins. *A Textual and Historical Companion to Handel's Messiah.* London: Novello, 1965. 217 and 16p. MT 115 H133 S56.

Functions like a vast critical report for the author's edition of *Messiah*, describing sources, early performance history, and editorial practice. Musical examples, plates, index, bibliography.

534. Siegmund-Schulze, Walther. "Anthem, Ode, Oratorium. Ihre Ausprägung bei Georg Friedrich Händel." In *Konferenzbericht Halle (Saale) 1981*, pp. 5-20.

Sees the English oratorios as progressive, even revolutionary expressions. Remarks on the evolution of the oratorios. Focuses on the *Utrecht Te Deum*, the *Birthday Ode for Queen Anne*, Chandos anthems, *The Triumph of Time and Truth.*

* _____. "Antike Themen in Händels Opern und Oratorien." In *Konferenzbericht Halle (Saale) 1983*, pp. 7-25.

Cited above as item 472.

535. _____. "Händels Oratorium *Joseph und seine Brüder*—eine Wiederentdeckung." *Händel-Jahrbuch* 30 (1984): 81-93.

In an effort to "re-introduce" the neglected *Joseph and His Brothers*, the author offers a brief general commentary followed by more detailed analyses of six excerpts. Musical examples.

536. Smith, Ruth. "Intellectual Contexts of Handel's English Oratorios." In *Music in Eighteenth-century England: Es-*

says in Memory of Charles Cudworth, pp. 115–33. Ed. Christopher Hogwood and Richard Luckett. Cambridge: Cambridge University Press, 1983. ML 55 C85. ISBN 0-521-23525-1.

Identifies the distinctive qualities of Handel's oratorio librettos. Examines their literary contexts under the headings "Eighteenth-Century Biblical Commentary and Religious Debate," "The Religious Sublime," and "The National Epic."

537. Smith, William C. "*Samson*: The Earliest Editions and Handel's Use of the Dead March." *Musical Times* 79 (1938): 581–84. Repr. with a German trans. in *Händel-Jahrbuch* 3 (1957): 105–14; 172–80.

Announces the discovery of the first printed edition of *Samson* with choruses and recitatives. Points out that it contains the original Dead March only, without the added march from Saul. Describes nine early editions.

538. Smither, Howard E. *A History of the Oratorio*. 3 vols. Chapel Hill: University of North Carolina Press, 1977–87. 480, 393, 711p.

First volume deals with Baroque oratorio in Italy, Vienna, and Paris, offering a reliable section on Handel's early Italian oratorios. Volume two, which covers Baroque oratorio in Protestant Germany and England, offers three extended chapters on Handel's English oratorios, as well as a useful section on the *Brockespassion*. Volume 3 deals with later periods. This work presents an invaluable perspective on the genre. Musical examples, plates, illustrations, bibliography, index.

* Stahura, Mark W. "The Publishing Copy Text of Handel's *Samson*." *Journal of Musicology* 4 (1985): 207–16.

Cited above as item 323.

539. Stenzl, Jurg. "Über den Großaufbau und die Bedeutung von Händels *Messiah*." *Neue Zeitschrift für Musik* 135 (1974): 732–40.

Tackles the question of *Messiah*'s overall dramatic or literary structure. Shows that, while it lacks the normal dramatic structure of Handelian oratorio, the movements are arranged in a meaningful way.

540. _____. "'Where Grace, and Truth, and Love Abound?' Zu Rezeption und Geschichte von Händels Oratorium *Theodora* (1749)." In *Analysen: Beiträge zu einer Problemgeschichte des Komponierens. Festschrift für Hans Heinrich Eggebrecht zum 65. Geburtstag*, pp. 180–201. Ed. Werner Breig, Reinhold Brinkmann, Elmar Budde. Wiesbaden: Franz Steiner, 1984. ML 55 E44 A6 1984. ISBN 3-515-03662-8.

Discusses the reasons for *Theodora*'s early failures and patchy performance history, focusing at length on the libretto and to some extent on the music. Brief musical examples.

541. Stutzenberger, David R. "'Belshazzar,' an Oratorio by George Frideric Handel: An Edition, Critical Report and Performance Tape." DMA dissertation. University of Maryland, 1980. 3 vols. 1042p.

Offers a performance edition. Takes in account early manuscript sources and printed librettos. Not examined.

542. Tobin, John. "A *Messiah* Problem." *Music and Letters* 36 (1955): 357–64.

Describes the various versions of "How beautiful are the feet" from *Messiah*. Speculation on Handel's "preferred version" is weakened by the assumption that the variants were composed solely in order to improve the original.

* _____. *Handel at Work*. London: Cassell, 1964. 84p. ML 410 H13 T6.

Cited above as item 370.

543. _____. *Handel's Messiah: A Critical Account of the Manuscript Sources and Printed Editions*. London: Cassell, 1969. 279p. ML 410 H13 T63.

Evidently intended as a sort of companion to the author's edition in the HHA, it discusses the sources and versions ever so briefly. Much of the book is devoted to suggestions for performance, including extravagant ornamentation. Sketchy essays on Handel's harmonic practice and his treatment of the English language. Copious musical examples. Appendixes include tables of early sources and their contents. Bibliography, index.

544. Webb, Ralph T. "Views and Viewpoints: Handel's Oratorios as Drama." *College Music Symposium* 23/2 (1983): 122–44.

Assesses the extent to which tonality and other musical features contribute to the dramatic unity of the oratorios, especially *Saul* and *Solomon*. Calls for closer examination of the librettos as dramas. Tables.

545. Wieber, Georg-Friedrich. "Die Chorfuge in Händels Werken." Ph.D. dissertation. Johann Wolfgang Goethe-Universität, Frankfurt (Main), 1958.

Carefully explores the forms, techniques, and styles of Handel's choral fugues, giving many examples and appending a list. Selective bibliography.

546. Young, Percy. *The Oratorios of Handel*. London: Dennis Dobson Ltd., 1949. 244p. ML 410 H13 Y63.

Offers penetrating critical comment and general notes on the English oratorios, with an introductory essay on the origins of the genre. Very little on the Italian oratorios or on sources and versions. Musical examples, index.

* Zimmerman, Franklin. "Händels Parodie-Ouvertüre zu *Susanna*: Eine neue Ansicht über die Entstehungsfrage." *Händel-Jahrbuch* 24 (1978): 19–30.

Cited above as item 375.

4. Odes and Serenatas

547. Burrows, Donald. "Handel and *Alexander's Feast.*" *Musical Times* 123 (1982): 252–55.

    Describes the principal features of the revisions of 1739, 1742, and 1751. Musical examples.

* _____. "The Composition and First Performance of Handel's *Alexander's Feast.*" *Music and Letters* 64 (1983): 206–11.

    Cited above as item 289.

* Burrows, Donald. "The Sources of *Alexander's Feast.*" *Music and Letters* 66 (1985): 87–88.

    Cited above as item 290.

548. Cooper, Barry. "The Organ Parts to Handel's *Alexander's Feast.*" *Music and Letters* 59 (1978): 159–79.

    Reconstructs the complex textual history of *Alexander's Feast*. Describes in detail the contents of two organ part-books which feature fully written out organ parts.

549. Dean, Winton. "An Unrecognized Handel Singer: Carlo Arrigoni." *Musical Times* 118 (1977): 556–58.

    Straightens out a number of details about the early performance history of *Alexander's Feast*, and in particular about the participation of singer-lutenist-composer Carlo Arrigoni (1697–1744).

550. Heap, Harold E. "Festival Odes for St. Cecilia's Day in England from Their Inception to the Time of Handel." DMA dissertation. University of Illinois, 1980. 123p.

    Traces the course of St. Cecilia odes from Purcell to Handel. Not examined.

* Herbage, Julian. "The Secular Oratorios and Cantatas." In *Handel: A Symposium*, pp. 132–55. Ed. Gerald Abraham.

Odes and Serenatas   171

        London: Oxford University Press, 1954. ML 410 H13 A66.

        Cited below as item 563.

551.   Hicks, Anthony. "Handel and *Il Parnasso in festa*." *Musical Times* 112 (1971): 338–40.

        General discussion of the 1734 *festa teatrale*, with notes on its history.

*   Hollander, John. *The Untuning of the Sky: Ideas of Music in English Poetry, 1500–1700*. Princeton: Princeton University Press, 1961. 467p. ML 3849 H54.

        Cited above as item 45.

552.   Lincoln, Stoddard. "Handel's Music for Queen Anne." *Musical Quarterly* 45 (1959): 191–207.

        Offers somewhat speculative notes on Handel's entrenchment in England, followed by a penetrating discussion of the Birthday Ode for Queen Anne. Comments on the Utrecht Te Deum further establish that he must have studied English traditions with great care. A few musical examples.

553.   McGuinness, Rosamond. *English Court Odes 1660–1820*. Oxford: Clarendon Press, 1971. 249p. ML 1631 M2.

        Shows in Chapter 6 that the *Birthday Ode* has many unique features even though Handel imitated Purcell in many respects. Includes a chronological list of performances of Court Birthday and New Year odes between 1660 and 1820. Bibliography, detailed index.

554.   Müller-Blattau, Joseph. "Händels Festkantate zur 500-Jahr Feier der Stadt Elbing 1737." In *50 Jahre Göttinger Händel-Festspiele*, pp. 120–32. Ed. Walter Meyerhoff. Kassel: Bärenreiter, 1970. ML 410 H13 M59.

        Presents a letter written by J.C. Smith from the town of Elbing which implies that Handel was there in the Fall of 1737 and was involved in the preparation of *Hermann von Balcke*, a curious pasticcio using some of his arias. (Actually, the letter's authenticity is in question, and there is no reason to believe that Handel journeyed to Elbing.)

555. Myers, Robert M. *Handel, Dryden and Milton*. London: Bowes and Bowes, 1956. 158p. ML 410 H13 M96.

Discusses Handel's use of poetry by Dryden and Milton. Focuses on English critics' responses to Handel's settings. Appended are complete texts of *Alexander's Feast* (including versions set by Jeremiah Clarke and Thomas Clayton), *Song for St. Cecilia's Day* (including the version set by G.B. Draghi), *L'allegro, il penseroso, ed il moderato*, *Samson*, and the *Occasional Oratorio*. Index.

556. Ostergren, Eduardo A. "A Conductor's Study of George Frideric Handel's Ode for Saint Cecilia's Day." DMA dissertation. Indiana University, 1980. 206p.

Offers historical background on the feast and on Cecilian works of Handel and his predecessors. Analyzes the ode and discusses performance practices. Not examined.

557. Schrade, Leo. "Studien zu Händel's *Alexanderfest*." *Händel-Jahrbuch* 1933, pp. 38-114.

Outlines performance history of *Alexander's Feast* on the continent from Mozart to the time of writing. Compares Handel's setting of Dryden to Marcello's setting of the Conti translation. Discusses the genesis of Handel's work. Gives commentary on the work itself.

* Windszus, Wolfram. "Georg Friedrich Händel: 'Aci, Galatea e Polifemo,' Cantate von 1708—'Acis und Galatea,'' Masque von 1718—'Acis and Galatea,' italienisch-englische Serenata von 1732." Phil. diss. Hamburg, 1975. Published as Diss.-Druck Hamburg, 1979.

Cited below as item 580.

5. English Pastorals, Masques, Music Dramas, and Theatre Music

558. Beechey, Gwilym. "*Acis and Galatea*: Some Notes on a Handel Masterpiece." *Musical Opinion* 108 (1985): 277–29; 258–60.

    In Part I, briefly introduces the literary sources of *Acis and Galatea*. Part II contains a concise commentary on the music. Musical examples.

* Beeks, Graydon. "Handel and Music for the Earl of Carnarvon." In *Bach, Handel, Scarlatti: Tercentenary Essays*, pp. 1–20. Ed. Peter Williams. Cambridge: Cambridge University Press, 1985. ML 55 B14 1985. ISBN 0–521–25217–2.

    Cited below as item 616.

559. Best, Terence. "*Acis and Galatea*." *Musical Times* 113 (1972): 43.

    Announces in a brief letter to the editor the discovery of a document which points to 1718 as the composition date of *Acis and Galatea*.

560. Brownell, Morris R. "Ears of an Untoward Make: Pope and Handel." *Musical Quarterly* 62 (1976): 554–70.

    Attempts to explode the myth of Pope's musical insensibility. Speculates that he collaborated on the libretto of *Haman and Mordecai*, the early version of *Esther*.

561. Dean Winton. "The Choice of Hercules." *The Listener* 49 (1953): 989.

    Outlines poetic origins of Handel's "Musical Interlude." Remarks on music, both newly composed and adapted from *Alceste*.

*   _____. *Handel's Dramatic Oratorios and Masques.* London: Oxford University Press, 1959. 694p. ML 410 H13.

Cited above as item 503.

562.   _____. "Masque into Opera." *Musical Times* 108 (1967): 605–606.

Briefly places *Acis and Galatea* in the historical context of English opera and introduces the music.

563.   Herbage, Julian. "The Secular Oratorios and Cantatas." In *Handel: A Symposium*, pp. 132–55. Ed. Gerald Abraham. London: Oxford University Press, 1954. ML 410 H13 A66.

General discussion, with short musical examples, of English odes, serenatas and theater music, with *Hercules* and *Acis and Galatea*.

564.   Hicks, Anthony. "Ravishing Semele." *Musical Times* 114 (1973): 275–80.

Cranky but meticulous review of recent editions of *Semele* and the *Wedding Anthem*. Significant details on an authentic text for *Semele*.

565.   _____. "Handel's Music for *Comus*." *Musical Times* 117 (1976): 28–29.

Describes the newly identified music written by Handel for a performance of Milton's *Comus*. Musical examples.

*   Hudson, Fredrick. "The New Bedford Manuscript Part-Books of Handel's Setting of *L'allegro*." *Notes* 33 (1977): 531–52.

Cited above as item 305.

566.   Langley, Hubert. "Congreve and Handel." *The Listener* 53 (1955): 357.

Charming commentary on *Semele*.

567. Lewis, Anthony. "Some Notes on Editing Handel's *Semele*." In *Essays on Opera and English Music in Honour of Sir Jack Westrup*, pp. 79–83. Ed. F.W. Sternfeld, Nigel Fortune, and Edward Olleson. Oxford: Blackwell, 1975. ML 55 E8. ISBN 0–631–15890–1.

Justifies the decision made for a recent edition to re-insert an aria excised by Handel. Describes two other arias cut by the composer. Gives the original B section of "Where'er you walk." Musical examples.

568. Lincoln, Stoddard. "The First Setting of Congreve's *Semele*." *Music and Letters* 44 (1963): 103–17.

Discusses the 1707 setting by John Eccles. Interesting remarks on the English adaptation of Italian recitative style. Musical examples. See also the correspondence on pp. 417–19.

569. Matthews, Betty. "Unpublished Letters concerning Handel." *Music and Letters* 40 (1959): 261–68.

Presents five letters from the correspondence of the Earl of Shaftesbury written between 1736 and 1748, including a long one about Handel written by J.C. Smith in July of 1743. Unique information on the music for *Comus*. See also Winton Dean's letter to the editor, pp. 406–407.

570. Patterson, William Hugh. "'Semele': Structure in a Baroque Opera." Ph.D. dissertation. Washington University, 1982. 113p.

Treats John Eccles' setting of *Semele*, comparing it to Handel's. Not examined.

571. Price, Curtis. "Handel and the Alchemist." *Musical Times* 116 (1975): 787–88.

A recently discovered Walsh print shows that Handel's "act-music" for *The Alchemist* was extracted from his opera

Rodrigo and used in a 1710 revival of Ben Jonson's play before Handel even came to London. Background information on incidental music in general.

572. Rendall, E. "The Influence of Henry Purcell on Handel, Traced in Acis and Galatea." *Musical Times* 36 (1895): 293-96.

Entirely intuitive comparison of certain passages in *Acis and Galatea* with similar passages in *Dido and Aeneas*.

573. Rogers, Patrick. "Dating 'Acis and Galatea': A Newly Discovered Letter." *Musical Times* 114 (1973): 792.

Announces the discovery of a letter which confirms that *Acis and Galatea* was composed during the spring of 1718.

574. Siegmund-Schultze, Walther. "Die Dejanira-Szene im Oratorium *Hercules*." In *G.F. Händel: Thema mit 20 Variationen*, pp. 105-108. Halle (Saale): VEB Druck, 1965.

Demonstrates with descriptive commentary that the strength of the Dejanira scene in *Hercules* lies in its unique structure. Musical examples.

575. Solomon, Jon. "Reflections of Ovid in Semele's Mirror." *Music and Letters* 63 (1982): 226-41.

Identifies the poetic sources for several passages in *Semele*. Musical example.

576. _____. "Polyphemus's Whistle in Handel's *Acis and Galatea*." *Music and Letters* 64 (1983): 37-43.

Illuminates the textual sources for *Acis and Galatea*, explaining why Handel chose a flute for Polyphemus' aria "O Ruddier Than the Cherry." See also Anthony Hicks' letter in volume 65, pp. 231-16, and the reply pp. 321-22.

577. Squire, William Barclay. "A Lost Handel Manuscript." *Musical Times* 62 (1921): 690-92.

Describes an important source for the 1732 version of *Acis and Galatea* and for the early *Aci, Galatea e Polifemo*, which reappeared a few years before the article.

* _____. "Handel's *Semele*." *Musical Times* 66 (1925): 137–39.

Cited below as item 830.

578. Steglich, Rudolf. "Der Schlußchor von Händels *Acis und Galatea*: Analyse." *Händel-Jahrbuch* 1930, pp. 147–59.

Pedestrian commentary with examples on the final chorus of *Acis and Galatea*.

579. Trowell, Brian. "Congreve and the 1744 *Semele* Libretto." *Musical Times* 111 (1970): 993–94.

Shows that almost all of the textual additions to Congreve's 1706 libretto for Handel's setting come from other poems by Congreve. Since this method is similar to Newburgh Hamilton's in *Samson*, it seems likely that he prepared the 1744 libretto.

580. Windszus, Wolfram. "Georg Friedrich Händel: 'Aci, Galatea e Polifemo,' Cantata von 1708—'Acis und Galatea,' Masque von 1718—'Acis and Galatea,' italienisch-englische Serenata von 1732." Phil. diss. Hamburg, 1975. Published as Diss.-Druck Hamburg, 1979.

Critical report for HHA.

581. Zander, Ernst. "Der Schlußchor von Händels *Acis und Galatea*: Ergänzung." *Händel-Jahrbuch* 1930, 145–47.

Mentions nineteen bars of *Acis and Galatea*'s final chorus which were omitted in Chrysander's edition.

582. Zimmermann, Franklin B. "Georg Friedrich Händels neu entdeckte Musik aus *Comus*: 'There in blissful shade'." *Händel-Jahrbuch* 20 (1974): 109–18.

Shows that a work entitled "Serenata à 9" in the Newman Flower collection at Manchester is actually Handel's music for *Comus*. Musical examples.

6. Vocal Chamber Music

583. Baselt, Bernd. "Georg Friedrich Händel: English Songs." In *Dichtung und Musik: W. Siegmund-Schultze zum 65. Geburtstag*, pp. 5–22. Ed. Siegfried Bimberg. Halle (Saale): Martin Luther Universität Halle-Wittenberg, 1982. Wissenschaftliche Beiträge 1982/47 (G9).

Discusses "The Morning is Charming" (*Hunting Song*), "I Like the Am'rous Youth That's Free," and "Love's But the Frailty of the Mind." Complete scores appended.

584. Bill, Oswald. "Die Liebesklage der Armida. Händels Kantate HWV 105 im Spiegel Bachscher Aufführungspraxis." In *Georg Friedrich Händel. Ausstellung aus Anlaß der Händel-Festspiele des Badischen Staatstheaters Karlsruhe 1985*, pp. 25–40. Ed. Klaus Häfner and Kurt Pietschmann. Karlsruhe: Badische Landesbibliothek, 1985. ML 141 K36 H33. ISBN 3-88705-013-4.

Gives background, general description, and text with commentary of Handel's cantata *Armida abbandonata*. Describes a set of parts copied in part by J.S. Bach and C.P.E. Bach ca. 1728–31. Illustrations and color plates of the Bach copies.

585. Boyd, Malcolm. *"La solitudine*: A Handel Discovery." *Musical Times* 109 (1968): 1111–14.

Describes the incomplete autograph of the cantata entitled *La solitudine* (*L'aure grate, il fresco rio*), which Chrysander used for his edition. Announces the discovery of a copy by J.C. Smith the elder in the Cardiff Public Library of a complete work which represents a dramatic revision of the setting in the autograph. Musical example, tiny photographic reproduction.

Vocal Chamber Music 179

586. Braun, Werner. "B.H. Brockes' 'Irdisches Vergnügen in Gott' in den Vertonungen G.Ph. Telemanns und G.Fr. Händels." *Händel-Jahrbuch* 1 (1955): 42–71.

   Compares settings by Telemann and Handel (HWV 202–10) of Brockes' poetry, with emphasis on Mattheson and contemporary German criticism. The fundamental differences between the two composers' treatments lie in their approaches to aesthetic theories of imitation. Establishes that Handel's arias were composed between 1724 and 1727. Musical examples.

587. _____. "Drei deutsche Arien: Ein Jugendwerk Händels?" *Acta musicologica* 42 (1970): 248–51.

   Proves conclusively that three German arias once thought to be by Handel are actually by Johann Mattheson. These are "In deinem schönen Mund," "Endlich muß man doch entdecken," and "Ein höher Geist muß immer höher denken."

588. Bunners, Christian. "Sehen, Singen, Preisen. Zum Text und Kontext von G.Fr. Händels *Deutschen Arien*." In *Kirche-Theologie-Frömmigkeit, Festgabe für Gottfried Holtz zum 65. Geburtstag*, pp. 55–64. Berlin, 1965.

   Poses questions about the theological aspects of Handel's music, especially the German arias. Not examined.

*   Dressler, Carolyn E. "*Armida abbandonata* by George Frideric Handel: An Edition Reflecting the Performance Practice of the Baroque Era." DMA dissertation. University of Maryland, 1978. 61p.

   Cited below as item 745.

*   Ford, Walter. "Handel's Cantatas." *Proceedings of the Royal Musical Association* 58 (1931–32): 33–42.

   Cited below as item 860.

589. Geering, Arnold. "Georg Friedrich Händel's französiche Kantate." In *Musicae scientiae collectanea: Festschrift Karl Gustav Fellerer*, pp. 126–40. Ed. Heinrich Hüschen. Cologne: Arno-Volk Verlag, 1973. ML 55 F35 M8 1972.

Presents an edition of *Sans y penser*, prefaced by useful remarks on the stylistic qualities of the various movements.

* Harris, Ellen T. "The Italian in Handel." *Journal of the American Musicological Society* 33 (1980): 468–500.

  Cited above as item 389.

590. _____. "Händel in Florenz." *Händel-Jahrbuch* 27 (1981): 41–61.

    Holds that the importance of Florence as an influence on Handel has been underestimated. Examines the sources of a number of cantatas, showing that several "Roman" cantatas were actually composed in Florence and later copied for Ruspoli in Rome.

591. _____. "Handel's London Cantatas." *Göttinger Händel-Beiträge* 1 (1984): 86–102.

    Discusses twelve continuo cantatas composed or revised in England, many of which are found in a two-volume manuscript anthology in the Bodleian Library, Oxford. Describes the probable demands for such pieces, speculating on the identity of the singers for whom they were intended. Detailed analysis shows that the six alto cantatas may have been composed as a set. Concludes that the predominance of alto cantatas bespeaks a new appreciation by Handel of the alto voice. Musical examples.

592. Knapp, J. Merrill. "Zu Händels italienischen Duetten." *Göttinger Händel-Beiträge* I (1984): 51–58.

    Discusses the influence of Agostino Steffani on Handel's chamber duets. Briefly surveys his output in this genre, concentrating on the last duets, composed in 1741 and used in *Messiah*'s duet choruses. Musical examples.

593. Kniseley, S. Philip. "Händels französische Kantate." *Händel-Jahrbuch* 20 (1974): 103–108.

Vocal Chamber Music 181

Briefly reviews the history of *Sans y penser*. Argues that it is not a collection of songs, but a unified cantata, because of its tonal plan and the prevailing pastoral character of its texts.

594. Lewis, Anthony. "The Songs and Chamber Cantatas." In *Handel: A Symposium*, pp. 179-99. Ed. Gerald Abraham. London: Oxford University Press, 1954. ML 410 H13 A66.

Briefly surveys the cantatas, duets, and songs. Musical examples.

595. Mann, Alfred. "Das Kammerduett im englischen Schaffen Händels." *Göttinger Händel-Beiträge* I (1984): 59-69.

Demonstrates that the wholly individual quality of Handel's English music is due in part to the absorption of his chamber duet style, which in turn is modelled on Agostino Steffani's. Musical examples.

596. Marx, Hans Joachim. "Ein Beitrag Händels zur Accademia Ottoboniana in Rom." *Hamburger Jahrbuch für Musikwissenschaft* 1 (1974): 69-86.

Describes the two parts of Handel's autograph manuscript of the cantata *Ero e Leandro*. Speculates that Cardinal Ottoboni wrote the text. Discusses the musical style in detail. Notes that Handel borrowed from this cantata for *Agrippina*. Musical examples, photographic reproductions.

597. _____. "'Ero e Leandro': Eine unveröffentlichte Kantate G.F. Händels für Pietro Card. Ottoboni." *Bericht über den Internationalen Musikwissenschaftlichen Kongreß Berlin 1974*, pp. 303-304. Ed. H. Kühn und P. Nitsche. Kassel: Barenreiter, 1980.

Summarizes item 596.

598. _____. "Zur Kompositionsgeschichte von Händels Pastoralkantate *Apollo e Dafne*." *Göttinger Händel-Beiträge* I (1984): 70-85.

Disagreeing with item 590, argues convincingly that the *Apollo* cantata (*La terra è liberata*) was composed not for Florence, but for Hanover. Examines autographs, with details on the paper. Analyzes corrections, showing that they are connected with borrowing techniques and not with refinement *per se*. Points out that the presence of a prominent bassoon part precludes an Italian ensemble. Tables, examples, plates.

599. Mayo, John. "Handel's Italian Cantatas." Ph.D. dissertation. University of Toronto, 1977.

    The most comprehensive study of the cantatas. Describes sources, outlines known chronology, discusses musical style. Contains useful chapters on "Alternative Versions and Revisions" and "Borrowings from the Cantatas in Later Works." Tables summarize borrowings in and from the cantatas. Contends that Handel's success as an opera composer depended on compositional techniques developed in the cantatas. Bibliography.

600. _____. "Zum Vergleich des Wort-Ton-Verhältnisses in den Kantaten von Georg Friedrich Händel und Alessandro Scarlatti." In *Konferenzbericht Halle (Saale) 1978*, pp. 31–44.

    Examines Handel and Scarlatti setting of six cantata texts: *Ah che pur troppo è vero*, *Filli adorata e cara*, *Fra tante pene*, *Ne' tuoi lumi*, *Nel dolce tempo* and *Qualor l'egre pupille*. In the recitatives, the declamation is similar, but Scarlatti tends to use more varied harmonies. Scarlatti's settings feature more motto arias than Handel's. Points out that Chrysander's edition of Handel's *Nel dolce tempo* is misleading. Suggests convincingly on stylistic grounds that Handel's *Ah che pur troppo* is a very early work. Musical examples.

601. _____. "Einige Kantatenrevisionen Händels." *Händel-Jahrbuch* 27 (1981): 63–77.

    Studies the nature of the revisions in seven cantatas which exist in two versions: *E partirai, mia vita?*, *Lungi dal mio bel Nume*, *Ninfe e pastori*, *Sei pur bella*, *Sento là che ristretto*, *Le pari è la tua fè*, and *Son gelsomino*. Shows that, in each case, one version dates from the Italian period, while the other was prepared in England, most likely for instructional purposes. The later versions are unusual because they feature extremely detailed figuring of the continuo line in the composer's hand. Musical examples.

602. Mühne, Christian. "Zum Autorproblem der Kantata *Pastorella vagha bella*." *Händel-Jahrbuch* 29 (1983): 55–64.

Concludes that the cantata *Pastorella vagha bella*, although attributed to Telemann in two of its three sources, is probably by Handel. Musical examples.

* Ornstein, Doris. "On Preparing a Performing Edition of Handel's Cantata *Mi palpita il cor*." *Bach: The Quarterly Journal of the Riemenschneider Bach Institute* 10 (1979): 3–30.

Cited below as item 789.

603. Raugel, Felix. "Händels französische Lieder." In *Händel-Ehrung der Deutschen Demokratischen Republik*, pp. 115–25. Leipzig: Deutscher Verlag für Musik, 1961. ML 410 H13 H2 1959.

Shows that the texts of Handel's French songs (HWV 155) appeared in earlier French collections. Presents the music in its entirety with comments. Holds that the pieces are a study in French simplicity and naturalness.

604. Rudolph, Johanna. "Meine Seele hört im Sehen." *Händel-Jahrbuch* 7–8 (1961–62): 35–67.

Discusses the texts of Handel's *Deutsche Arien* in the context of German philosophy.

605. Schmitz, Eugen. *Geschichte der weltlichen Solokantate*. 2nd ed. Leipzig: Breitkopf und Härtel, 1955. 365p. (First published in 1914 as volume 5 of Kleine Handbücher der Musikgeschichte nach Gattungen). ML 2800 S3 1955.

Contains only a few pages on Handel's cantatas. Index.

606. Seiffert, Max. "Händels deutsche Gesänge." In *Festschrift Liliencron*, pp. 297–314. Ed. Hermann Kretzschmar. Leipzig: Breitkopf und Härtel, 1910. ML 55 F49.

Suggests that three German songs, now known not to be by Handel (item 587) are from the Halle period, in texts written by Handel himself. Speculates that the remaining nine (HWV 202–10) were composed in Hamburg in 1729 (but see item 586).

607. Serauky, Walter. "Georg Friedrich Händels italienische Kantatenwelt." In *Händel-Ehrung der Deutschen Demokratischen Republik 1959*, pp. 109–13. Leipzig: Deutsche Verlag für Musik, 1961. ML 410 H13 H21 1959.

Aptly summarizes current knowledge about the Italian cantatas, with some interesting information on their literary background.

* Steblin, Rita. "Did Handel Meet Bononcini in Rome?" *Music Review* 45 (1984): 179–93.

Cited above as item 246.

608. Steglich, Rudolf. "Ein Seitenstück zu Händels 'Largo'." *Händel-Jahrbuch* 1 (1955): 38–42.

Explains the meaning of the text to Handel's first German aria, "Künft'ger Zeiten." Discusses tempo, urging performers to consider dance types, even in vocal music.

* Timms, Colin. "Handel and Steffani: A New Handel Signature." *Musical Times* 114 (1973): 374–77.

Cited above as item 252.

* Windszus, Wolfram. "Georg Friedrich Händel: 'Aci, Galatea e Polifemo,' Cantata von 1708—'Acis und Galatea,' Masque von 1718—'Acis und Galatea,' italienisch-englische Serenata von 1732." Phil. diss. Hamburg, 1975. Published as Diss.-Druck Hamburg, 1979.

Cited above as item 580.

609. Wolff, Hellmuth Christian. "Die Lucretia-Kantaten von Benedetto Marcello und Georg Friedrich Händel." *Händel-Jahrbuch* 3 (1957): 74–88.

Comparison of settings of the Lucrezia text ("O numi eterni") by Handel and Benedetto Marcello shows that the two styles are strikingly different. Marcello exhibits close ties to Venetian opera of the later seventeenth century, and cannot be considered a composer of the so-called Neapolitan school. Notes on a curious 1951 performance in Halle.

610. Zanetti, Emilia. "A proposito di tre sconosciute cantate inglesi." *La rassegna musicale* 29 (1959): 139–42.

Discusses three curious adaptations found in a manuscript in the Biblioteca Musicale Santa Cecilia in Rome.

7. Church Music

611. Baselt, Bernd. "Händels frühe Kirchenmusik." In *Konferenzbericht Halle (Saale) 1981*, pp. 21–33.

Surveys the Latin and Italian church music, suggesting that the early *Laudate pueri* in F may have been written in Italy.

612. Beeks, Graydon F. "Handel's Chandos Anthems: The 'Extra' Movements." *Musical Times* 119 (1978): 621–23.

Argues convincingly on the basis of source information that the arias "The Lord Is Righteous" and "Happy Are the People" from Chandos anthem no. 5a *I Will Magnify Thee* are authentic. The authorship of the trio "Thou Rulest the Raging of the Sea" from no. 7 *My Song Shall Be Alway* is in doubt.

613. _____. "The Chandos Anthems and Te Deum of George Frideric Handel (1685–1759)." Ph.D. dissertation. University of California (Berkeley), 1981. 969p.

Extensive examination includes background, borrowings, versions, and style. Includes descriptive catalogue of sources. Proposes chronology, discusses compositional process. Musical examples.

614. _____. Handel's Chandos Anthems: More 'Extra' Movements." *Music and Letters* 62 (1981): 155–61.

Comments on a twenty-six-measure duet for tenor and oboe that appears at the end of the autograph of the fourth Chandos anthem (*O Sing unto the Lord*). Meticulous source study leads to the conclusion that the first instrumental movement of Anthem 11a, *Let God Arise*, should be omitted.

615. _____. "Zur Chronologie von Händels Chandos Anthems und Te Deum B-Dur." *Händel-Jahrbuch* 27 (1981): 89–105.

Proposes a revised chronology for the Chandos anthems and Te Deum based on paper studies and on analysis of performing forces. But see also item 616.

616. _____. "Handel and Music for the Earl of Carnarvon." In *Bach, Handel, Scarlatti: Tercentenary Essays*, pp. 1–20. Ed. Peter Williams. Cambridge: Cambridge University Press, 1985. ML 55 B14 1985. ISBN 0–521–25217–2.

Contains much valuable information about musical life at Cannons. Reviews the question of the chronology of the Chandos anthems, revising the results of item 615 in view of newly discovered sources and information. Discusses the sources of the cantata *Sento là che ristretto*, connections between the Concertos of Opus 3 and Cannons, and the original version of *Esther*. Speculates on the circumstances of Handel's departure from Cannons.

617. _____. "Handel's Chandos Anthems." *American Organist* 19/2 (1985): 93–96.

Offers historical background and informed commentary on the Chandos anthems. Plates.

618. Bense, Lieselotte. "Die Ausprägung der Anthem-Form bei Händel unter besonderer Berücksichtigung seiner 'Coronation Anthems'." In *Konferenzbericht Halle (Saale) 1981*, pp. 47–57.

Comments on the immense success of the Coronation anthems, especially *Zadok the Priest*. Sketches the history of the anthem, placing Handel's Coronation anthems in context.

619. Bourne, T.W. "Handel's Double *Gloria Patri*." *Monthly Musical Record* 27 (1897): 125–27.

Establishes that the double chorus *Gloria Patri* is the last movement to *Nisi Dominus*.

620. Braun, Werner. "Zur Choralkantate *Ach Herr, mich armen Sünder*." *Händel-Jahrbuch* 5 (1959): 100–106.

Reviews the history of this cantata, edited by Seiffert as by Handel but almost certainly spurious. Describes a new source discovered at Grimma. States that it cannot have been composed by Zachow and eliminates other possible composers, but leaves the attribution to Handel in doubt. Musical examples.

621. ———. "Echtheit und Datierungsfragen im vokalen Frühwerk Georg Friedrich Händels." In *Händel-Ehrung der Deutschen Demokratischen Republik 1959*, pp. 61–71. Leipzig: VEB Deutscher Verlag für Musik, 1961.

Examines the arguments surrounding the authenticity of the early vocal works, especially an Easter dialogue entitled *Triumph, ihr Christen*. Suggests that the early *Laudate pueri* in F was written during the Hamburg period.

* Burnett, Henry. "The Sacred Music of Maurice Greene (1696–1755): A Study of the Problems Confronting the Composer of English Church Music during the Early Eighteenth Century." Ph.D. dissertation. City University of New York, 1978. 566p.

Cited above as item 67.

622. Burrows, Donald J. "Handel's Peace Anthem." *Musical Times* 114 (1973): 1230–32.

Details the author's brilliant reconstruction of the "Anthem on the Peace" of 1749. Musical examples.

623. _____. "Handel and the Foundling Hospital." *Music and Letters* 58 (1977): 269–84.

Outlines Handel's relationship with the Foundling Hospital during the last ten years of his life, presenting new documentary information. Gives significant information on the text of the Foundling Hospital Anthem. Remarks on the effects of blindness on the composer.

* _____. "Handel and the 1727 Coronation." *Musical Times* 118 (1977): 469–73.

Cited above as item 186.

624. _____. "Some Misattributed Anthems." *Musical Times* 121 (1980): 521–23.

Shows how Handel's anthems have occasionally been confused with the works of other composers. Discusses two known anthems by Nicola Haym, identifies two others previously misattributed and identifies John Weldon as the composer of a fifth work. Musical examples.

625. _____. "Handel and the English Chapel Royal during the Reigns of Queen Anne and King George I." Ph.D. dissertation. Open University, 1981.

Examines Handel's association with and music for the Chapel Royal. Suggests a chronology for his Chapel Royal music of the 1720s. Includes an extended supplement and fifteen appendixes of factual background material.

626. _____. "Handel's *As Pants the Hart*." *Musical Times* 126 (1985): 113–16.

Unravels details concerning the five versions of this Chandos anthem.

627. _____. "Handel's Last English Church Music." *American Choral Review* 27/2–3 (1985): 45–54.

Discussion of the "Caroline" *Te Deum*, the *Peace Anthem*, and the *Foundling Hospital Anthem*. Anthems include borrowings from *Messiah* and the *Funeral Anthem*. Suggests that the version of the *Foundling Hospital Anthem* with solo numbers may have been composed for the official opening service of the Foundling Hospital Chapel on April 16, 1753.

628. _____. "Handel's Non-Chandos Church Music." *American Organist* 19/2 (1985): 97–101.

Offers a concise summary, with suggestions for performance. Plates.

629. Dixon, Graham. "Handel's Vesper Music—Towards a Liturgical Reconstruction." *Musical Times* 126 (1985): 393–97.

Announces the discovery of a set of manuscript eighteenth-century partbooks in Rome which includes the chant of all the antiphons and the responsory for the feast of Our Lady of Mount Carmel. Proposes a speculative model for the liturgical framework in which Handel's Roman Vespers music was performed.

630. Gille, Gottfried. "Georg Friedrich Händel: Die Kirchenmusik in seinem Leben und seinen Werk." *Der Kirchenmusiker* 36 (1985): 1–5.

Odd brief survey of the church music, virtually ignoring the important Latin church music and including notes on the oratorios. Lists performing editions.

631. Gorini, Roberto. "Un'antifona di Händel 'perduta' e 'ritrovata.' I casi delle biblioteche musicali." *Nuova rivista musicale italiana* 19 (1985): 62–74.

Announces the discovery of a copy of Handel's hitherto lost antiphon "Haec est regina virginum," composed in 1707 in Rome. Gives analytical commentary with brief musical examples. Reprints title page of the manuscript.

632. Hall, James S. "Handel among the Carmelites." *Dublin Review* 233 (1959): 121–31.

Discusses Handel's relationship with Roman Catholic dignitaries, and in particular Cardinal Colonna. Presents convincing evidence that his Latin Church music was composed for a Carmelite Festival on July 16, 1707.

633. _____. "The Problem of Handel's Latin Church Music." *Musical Times* 100 (1959): 197–200.

Attempts to sort out the Latin church music, concluding that the *Laudate pueri* in F and other miscellaneous works are "studies," while all remaining known Latin pieces were written for a Carmelite Vespers service in Rome during the summer of 1707. Speculates that *Silete venti* was composed as a gift to Cardinal Colonna in 1729.

634. Hendrie, Gerald. "Handel's 'Chandos' and Associated Anthems: An Introductory Survey." In *Bach, Handel, Scarlatti: Tercentenary Essays*, pp. 149–59. Ed. Peter Williams. Cambridge: Cambridge University Press, 1985. ML 55 B14 1985. ISBN 0–521–25217–2.

Surveys the eleven Chandos and six Chapel Royal anthems. Speculates about the origins of the *Andante* that opens "Let God Arise," suggesting unconvincingly that it might have been used as an opening for *Acis and Galatea*.

* Hicks, Anthony. "Ravishing Semele." *Musical Times* 114 (1973): 275–80.

Cited above as item 564.

635. _____. "Handel's Vespers?" *Musical Times* 126 (1985): 201.

Letter to the editor taking issue with attempts to portray Handel's Latin church music as a complete Vespers cycle.

636. Isotta, Paolo. "*Dixit Dominus Domino meo*: Struttura e semantica in Haendel e Vivaldi." *Rivista internationale di musica sacra* 2 (1981): 247–359.

Offers relentlessly methodical analyses of the *Dixit Dominus* settings of Handel and Vivaldi, with a detailed comparative summary. Provocative conclusion regarding the difference between genius and talent. Musical examples, tables, appendices.

637. Johnstone, H. Diack. "The Chandos Anthems: The Authorship of No. 12." *Musical Times* 117 (1976): 601–603.

Casts serious doubt on the authenticity of the so-called Chandos anthem "O Praise the Lord, Ye Angels of His." Suggests that it could be by Maurice Greene.

638. Jones, William R. "The Motets of Francesco Gasparini." Ph.D. dissertation. University of Southern California, 1981.

Discusses Gasparini's sixteen motets, showing how they influenced contemporaries, especially Vivaldi and Handel.

* Kümmerling, Harald. "Heinrich Bokemeyers Kopie von Händels erster Fassung des *Laudate pueri Dominum*." *Händel-Jahrbuch* 1 (1955): 102–104.

Cited above as item 313.

* Kuhn, Ronald G. "Performance Edition of a Magnificat Linked to Dionigi Erba and George Frideric Handel: Suggestions for Its Performance and Observations on Its Authorship." DMA dissertation. University of Washington, 1979. 182p.

Cited below as item 768.

639. Lam, Basil. "The Church Music." In *Handel: A Symposium*, pp. 156–78. Ed. Gerald Abraham. London: Oxford University Press, 1954. ML 410 H13 A66.

Surveys the church music, commenting on style but giving no new information. Musical examples.

* Lincoln, Stoddard. "Handel's Music for Queen Anne." *Musical Quarterly* 45 (1959): 191–207.

Cited above as item 552.

* Mann, Alfred. "Zum Concertistenprinzip bei Händel." In *Musik als Lobgesang: Festschrift für Wilhelm Ehmann*, pp. 77–82. Ed. Gerhard Mittring and Gerhard Rödding. Darmstadt: Merseburger, 1964. ML 55 E35.

Cited below as item 774.

640. Morgan, Wesley K. "Mannered Metaphor in Baroque Music." In *Essays on the Music of J.S. Bach and Other Divers Subjects: A Tribute to Gerhard Herz*, pp. 48–59. Ed. Robert L. Weaver. Louisville: University of Louisville, 1981. ML 55 H46 1981.

Psalm settings and Magnificats of the Baroque period often quote their openings at the words "sicut erat in principio" (as it was in the beginning). Outlines the history of this practice from as early as 1587. Describes its use in the three choral psalms of Handel's Roman period (HWV 232, 237, 238). Deliberates on the most appropriate general designation for such procedures, rejecting "allegory," "metaphrase," "symbol," and "icon" in favor of "metaphor."

641. Palent, Andrea. "Georg Friedrich Händels frühe Kirchenmusik: Eine Studie mit Kritischer Ausgabe der Partitur." Phil. dissertation. Martin-Luther-Universität Halle-Wittenberg, 1984.

Not examined.

642. ———. "Die italienischen und lateinischen Kirchenstücke im Gesamtschaffen von G.F. Händel." *Händel-Jahrbuch* 31 (1985): 63–78.

Ably summarizes modern information on Handel's Italian and Latin church music. The reader might use it in conjunc-

Church Music

tion with item 648, since is was prepared before the author learned of the rediscovery of *Te decus virginum*.

643. Parker-Hale, Mary Ann. "Handel's *Laudate pueri*." *American Choral Review* 24/4 (1982): 3–9.

   Examines the history and style of the D major setting of *Laudate pueri*, showing that Handel's mature choral style can be traced to the early Latin psalms. Musical examples.

644. _____. "Die frühe Fassung von Händels *Laudate pueri*: Fragen der stilistischen und chronologischen Einordnung." *Händel-Jahrbuch* 30 (1984): 11–19.

   Contends that the early F major setting of *Laudate pueri* may well have been written in Halle, as Chrysander suggested. Corrections from the autographs of both the F major and later D major settings show Handel grappling with compositional problems. Musical examples.

645. _____. "Handel's *Nisi Dominus*." *American Choral Review* 27/2–3 (1985): 7–13.

   Outlines complex source history of this early work with its elusive *Gloria Patri*. Brief stylistic analysis with examples.

646. Schering, Arnold. "Händel und der protestantische Choral." *Händel-Jahrbuch* 1928, pp. 27–40.

   Questions the authenticity of the cantata *Ach Herr, mich armen Sünder*. Discusses the four chorales in Handel's *Brockespassion*. Identifies references to chorales in the English anthems and oratorios.

647. Serauky, Walter. "Georg Friedrich Händels lateinische Kirchenmusik." *Händel-Jahrbuch* 3 (1957): 5–24.

   Stylistic commentary with examples on the Latin psalms, the motets *Salve regina* and *Filete venti* and the settings of *Alleluja, amen*.

648. Shaw, Watkins. "Handel's Vesper Music—Some MS Sources Rediscovered." *Musical Times* 126 (1985): 392–93.

Describes newly-rediscovered parts, some with corrections by Handel, for *Laudate pueri* (in D), *Haec est regina, Te decus virginum*, and *Saeviat tellus*, and a copyists' score for the *Gloria Patri* of *Nisi Dominus*. Gives history of the manuscripts, pointing out that the *Te decus* materials are the sole surviving source.

649. Siegmund-Schulze, Walther. "Handels Trauer-Anthem und Mozarts Requiem." In *G.F. Händel: Thema mit 20 Variationen*, pp. 95–104. Halle (Saale): VEB Druck, 1965.

    Gives general commentary on the background and music of Handel's Funeral Anthem and Mozart's Requiem, without offering any compelling reason to link the two.

650. Steele, John. "*Dixit Dominus*: Alessandro Scarlatti and Handel." *Studies in Music* 7 (1973): 19–27.

    Comes to the questionable conclusion that Handel knew and was directly influenced by Scarlatti's setting of *Dixit Dominus*. Detailed comparison with musical examples.

651. Stevenson, Robert. "The Eighteenth-Century Hymn Tune." *Inter-American Music Review* 2 (1979): 1–33.

    Includes a comparison of Handel's three hymn tunes with settings by J.F. Lampe. Discusses adaptations of Handel melodies for publication as hymn tunes. Musical examples.

652. Werner, Edwin. "Georg Friedrich Händels 'Trauer-Anthem' HWV 264: Eine Studie mit Kritischer Ausgabe der Partitur im Rahmen der Hallischen Händel-Ausgabe." Phil. dissertation. Martin-Luther-Universität Halle-Wittenberg, 1981.

    Not examined.

653. Wilson, J. "Handel's Tunes for Charles Welsey's Hymns: The Story Retold." *Hymn Society of Great Britain and Ireland Bulletin* 11 (1985): 32–37.

Not examined.

8. Instrumental Music

654. Bartlett, Clifford. "Handel's Solo Sonatas: A Guide to Editions." *Brio* 20 (1983): 53–57.

    Lists modern editions, assessing their usefulness to performers. Summarizes early editions. Locates all the solo sonatas in collected edition. Useful.

655. Baselt, Bernd. "Muffat and Handel: A Two-Way Exchange." *Musical Times* 120 (1979): 904–907.

    Describes a manuscript which contains copies by Muffat of two Handel prints—the *Suites de pièces* (1720) and *Six Fugues or Voluntarys for the Organ or Harpsichord* (1735). In this early example of a teaching or performance edition, Muffat added many embellishments of his own, and wrote out with precise rhythmic values many of the ornaments which were printed in small notes.

656. Best, Terence. "Handel's Keyboard Music." *Musical Times* 112 (1971): 845–48.

    Gives an excellent outline of composition and sources of the harpsichord music. The 1720 Cluer edition of *Suites de pièces pour le clavecin* represents Handel's most mature work for harpsichord, since it contains some new pieces, while later sets are made up of earlier compositions. Only a few harpsichord works were written after 1720.

657. _____. "Händels Solosonaten." *Händel-Jahrbuch* 23 (1977): 21–43.

    Slightly modified translation of item 658. Suggests that some sonatas for solo instruments should be performed with harpsichord accompaniment, and no cello or bassoon.

658. _____. "Handel's Solo Sonatas." *Music and Letters* 58 (1977): 430–38.

Describes the early editions and manuscript sources of Handel's sonatas for recorder, flute, oboe, and violin with continuo. Early editions created confusion as to the authenticity and even instrumentation. "Summary Table" is clear and informative.

659. _____. "Nachtrag zu dem Artikel 'Händel's Solosonaten.'" *Händel-Jahrbuch* 26 (1980): 121–22.

Brief addenda to item 657, including notes that the "Roger" editions of Opus 1 and 2 must now be dated 1726–32, and that the sonata Opus 1 #5 (HWV 363) was originally for oboe, and not flute. The oboe sonata Opus 1 #8 (HWV 366) can now be dated 1712–21.

660. _____. "Die Chronologie von Händels Klaviermusik." *Händel-Jahrbuch* 27 (1981): 79–87.

Summarizes information derived from recent source studies which makes possible the assignment of approximate dates to the harpsichord music for the first time. Material available in English in items 661 and 656.

661. _____. "Handel's Harpsichord Music: A Checklist." In *Music in Eighteenth-Century England: Essays in Memory of Charles Cudworth*, pp. 171–87. Ed. C. Hogwood and R. Luckett. Cambridge: Cambridge University Press, 1983. ML 55 C85 1983. ISBN 0–521–23525–1.

Discusses chronology problems, giving stylistic criteria. Especially interesting outline of distinctive features from the Hamburg period. Concise survey of publications, followed by a comprehensive annotated list of the works and their sources.

662. _____. "Further Studies on Handel's Solo Sonatas." *Händel-Jahrbuch* 30 (1984): 75–79.

Continuing research on the paper of the autographs has led to a revision of the dating of ten sonatas. Excellent summary table includes paper characteristics.

Instrumental Music 197

663. _____. "Handel's Chamber Music. Sources, Chronology and Authenticity." *Early Music* 13 (1985): 476–99.

Summarizes current knowledge, bringing together recent research by Best, Lasocki, and Flesch. Lavishly illustrated with plates, tables, and musical examples.

664. _____. "Handel's Overtures for Keyboard." *Musical Times* 126 (1985): 88–90.

Discusses the publication of the overtures to Handel's operas and oratorios in keyboard arrangements. Demonstrates that Handel had nothing to do with Walsh's first collection of 1726. Suggests that Handel probably was not involved in the large number, in Walsh's collection and in manuscript copies, which are exact transcriptions. Shows convincingly that there are twenty authentic arrangements. Examples.

665. Breig, Werner. "Bach und Händel. Konzeption des Instrumental Konzerts." In *Beilage zum Programmbuch. Bach-Tage Berlin 1978*, 1–8. Ed. Christoph Trautmann. Repr. in *Bachtage Berlin, Vorträge 1970 bis 1981*, pp. 153–64. Ed. Günther Wagner. Stuttgart: Hänssler, 1985. ML 410 B1 B25. ISBN 3–7751–0993–5.

Compares the concertos of Bach and Handel in three areas—the use of earlier compositions as models, cyclic form, and the creation of one solo keyboard concerto.

666. Burrows, Donald. "Walsh's Editions of Handel's Opera 1–5: The Texts and Their Sources." In *Music in Eighteenth Century England: Essays in Memory of Charles Cudworth*, pp. 79–102. Ed. C. Hogwood and R. Luckett. Cambridge: Cambridge University Press, 1983. ML 55 C85 1983. ISBN 0–521–23525–1.

Handel probably had nothing to do with Walsh's prints of his Opus 1 (Solos), Opus 2 (Trio Sonatas), and Opus 3 (Concertos). Detailed study of engraving styles reveals that "Roger" prints of Opus 1 and 2 are Walsh forgeries, likely produced as late as 1730–33. Publications of Opus 1–3 are full of errors and spurious movements. With the organ concertos of Opus 4, the composer began co-operating. In the Opus 5 trio sonatas, Handel adapted material from the Chandos anthems himself, but Walsh may have had a heavy hand in arranging the dance movements.

667. Chrysander, Friedrich. "Händels Instrumentalkompositionen für grosses Orchester." *Vierteljahrsschrift für Musikwissenschaft* 3 (1887): 1–25; 157–88; 451–62.

Surveys the concertos and suites for orchestra. In the last part, takes issue with William Rockstro's claim to have discovered the "Concerti a due cori." Musical examples.

668. Cooper, Barry A. "English Solo Keyboard Music of the Middle and Late Baroque." Ph.D. dissertation. University of Oxford, 1974. 517p.

Offers a chronological survey of English solo keyboard music from 1650 to 1750. Discusses Italian influence in works of Handel, Maurice Green, James Nares, and John Christopher Smith. Includes descriptive lists of extant printed sources and principal manuscripts. Not examined.

669. _____. "Keyboard Sources in Hereford." *Research Chronicle of the Royal Musical Association* 16 (1980): 135–39.

Description and inventory of the keyboard music in the manuscripts in the Hereford Cathedral Library. Mentions a keyboard arrangement of the *Rodelinda* overture and a version of the solo part of the first movement from the organ concerto Opus 4, no. 1 (HWV 289). Written-out ornamentation is illustrated in an example. Bibliography.

670. Dale, Kathleen. "The Keyboard Music." In *Handel: A Symposium*, pp. 233–47. Ed. Gerald Abraham. London: Oxford University Press, 1954. ML 410 H13 A66.

Makes a candid general evaluation of the keyboard works, which she quaintly views as piano music. Outlines works newly discovered in the twentieth century. Discussion of the music is not detailed. No musical examples.

Instrumental Music

671. Drummond, Pippa. *The German Concerto: Five Eighteenth-Century Studies.* Oxford: Oxford University Press, 1980. 402p. ML 1263 D8. ISBN 0-19-816122-0.

    Big, bold book with a comprehensive, extended chapter on Handel's concertos. Deals with sources and history, then structure and style. Useful sections on historical background for the organ concerto and on the notion of plagarism. Appendix lists borrowed and re-used material in the concertos.

672. Farley, Charles E. "The Organ Concerti of George Frideric Handel." Ph.D. dissertation. Flordia State University, 1962. 328p.

    Presents a detailed examination focusing on style, in which the movements are classified as ritornello, dance, variation, or introduction. Not examined.

673. Farmer, Henry G. "Handel's Kettledrum: The Great Kettledrums of the Royal Artillery." In *Handel's Kettledrums and Other Papers on Military Music*, pp. 85-96. London: Hinrichsen, 1950. 2nd ed. 1960. ML 1331 F167.

    Describes artillery kettledrums, with illustrations from 1702 and 1722. Reprints original documents showing Handel borrowed the drums several times starting in 1748. They may have been used in *Joshua*, *Judas Maccabaeus*, *Alexander Balus*, and the Royal Fireworks Music.

674. Fiske, Roger. "Handel's Organ Concertos: Do They Belong to Particular Oratorios?" *Organ Yearbook* 3 (1972): 14-22.

    Notes that whenever Handel dated the autograph of an organ concerto, it can be shown that Act 2 or 3 of an oratorio performed a week or two later began in the same key. Uses this evidence convincingly to suggest first performance dates for all fourteen organ concertos of Opus 4, Opus 7, and Walsh's "Second Set" (1740). The "Cuckoo and the Nightingale" concerto (HWV 295) may have been composed as an overture to *Israel in Egypt*.

675. Fleischhauer, Günter. "Zur Funktion und Bedeutung einiger Instrumentalstücke in den Oratorien G.F. Händels." *Konferenzbericht Halle (Saale) 1981*, pp. 68–85.

Demonstrates using numerous examples how Handel expanded the role of instrumental music in the oratorios, suggesting that it was used for purposes of characterization, narration, symbolic representation, and emotional intensification. Musical examples.

676. Flesch, Siegfried. "Georg Friedrich Händels Triosonaten." Ph.D. dissertation. Martin-Luther-Universität Halle-Wittenberg, 1972.

Not examined.

677. ———. "Georg Friedrich Händels Trio-Sonaten." *Händel-Jahrbuch* 18–19 (1972–73): 139–211.

Definitive study of all the trio sonatas. Clearly organized survey covering authenticity, chronology, sources, and borrowings. Musical examples.

678. Funkhouser, S.A. "An Evaluation of G.F. Handel's Use of the Oboe in His Arias: A Catalogue, by Instrument, of Handel's Arias with Instruments, and a Performing Edition Accompanied by a Performance Tape of a Handel Aria with Oboe Solo." *Missouri Journal of Research in Music Education* 4 (1977): 115–16.

Not examined.

679. Gellrich, G. "Muffat in Händels Werkstatt." *Die Musikforschung* 13 (1960): 50–51.

Identifies source of the opening of the fifth concerto (HWV 323) from Opus 6 as a minuet from Gottlieb Muffat's *Componimenti musicali per il cembalo*.

680. Gottlieb, Robert. "Französischer, italienischer und vermischter Stil in den Solosonaten Georg Friedrich Händels." *Händel-Jahrbuch* 12 (1966): 93–108.

Identifies a distinct style, a mixture of French and Italian, in German music after 1710. This new style is exemplified by the slow movements with "walking basses" in Handel's solo sonatas. Understanding the stylistic elements affects performance practice. Musical examples are extremely useful.

681. Gould, Albert O. "The Flute Sonatas of Georg Friedrich Händel: A Stylistic Analysis and Historical Study." Ed.D. dissertation. University of Illinois, 1961. 206p.

Offers a stylistic analysis of the flute sonatas, a history of the transverse flute, and comparison with contemporary flute and violin sonatas (including Corelli's Opus 5). Not examined.

682. Gudger, William D. "The Organ Concertos of G.F. Handel: A Study Based on the Primary Sources." Ph.D. dissertation. Yale University, 1973. 608p.

The first book to discuss the concertos after a profound consideration of the interrelation of primary sources. Studies Handel's compositional method by examining sketches, corrections, and borrowings. Appendix furnishes data on unpublished music.

* ———. "Handel's Last Compositions and His Borrowings from Habermann (Part I)." *Current Musicology* 22 (1976): 61–72.

Cited above as item 337.

683. ———. "Handel's Harp Concerto." *American Harp Journal* 6/3 (1978): 14–22.

Confirms that the concerto HWV 294 was originally composed in its harp version as part of *Alexander's Feast* (1736). The up-to-date style of the harp concerto, which is associated with Timotheus and his lyre, contrasts with the conservative style of the organ concerto, which represents St. Cecilia. Concludes with annotated bibliography. Appears in German in *Mitteilungsblatt der Vereinigung deutscher Harfenisten* 3,31 (1978–79): 12–20.

684. _____. "Handel's Organ Concertos in Walsh's Arrangements for Solo Keyboard." *Organ Yearbook* 10 (1979): 63–82.

A clear introduction to the textual problems of the organ concertos. Walsh issued the orchestral parts and the keyboard part for Opus 4 separately. The keyboard part was arranged so that it could be played by an unaccompanied solo player. Chrysander used Walsh's edition, giving the misleading impression that the organ always doubled during the *tutti* sections. Later collections prepared by Walsh and by J.C. Smith the younger compounded the source problems.

685. _____. "Performing the Handel Organ Concertos as Keyboard Solos: A New Edition of Walsh's Transcriptions (1738)." *Diapason* 72/12 (1981): 6–10.

Introduces the author's edition of the transcriptions. Includes performance suggestions. Musical examples.

686. Hill, Cecil. "Die Abschrift von Händels 'Wassermusik' in der Sammlung Newman Flower." *Händel-Jahrbuch* 17 (1971): 75–88.

A significant copy of the Water Music in the Newman Flower collection was not available when the new HHA edition was prepared. Can be used as a supplement to the critical report of that edition.

687. Hill, Robert. "'Der Himmel weiß, wo diese Sachen hingekommen sind': Reconstructing the Lost Keyboard Notebooks of the Young Bach and Handel." In *Bach, Handel, Scarlatti: Tercentenary Essays*, pp. 161–72. Ed. Peter Williams. Cambridge: Press Syndicate of University of Cambridge, 1985. ML 55 B14 1985. ISBN 0-521-25217-2.

Discusses a lost copybook from around 1699 described in item 125. Speculates that the book, copied under Zachow's supervision, was primarily an anthology of examples of learned counterpoint.

688. Hofmann, Klaus. "Zu Händels Fitzwilliam-Sonate in G-Dur. Eine Replik." *Tibia* 3 (1981): 391–96.

Takes issue with David Lasocki's contention (item 698) that the "Fitzwilliam" sonata in G major is spurious. But see item 699. Musical examples.

689. Horton, John. "The Chamber Music." In *Handel: A Symposium*, pp. 248–61. Ed. Gerald Abraham. London: Oxford University Press, 1954. ML 410 H13 A66.

Comments on the problems of authenticity as they stood at the time of writing. Cursory stylistic survey of the sonatas for one or two instruments with continuo.

690. Hutchings, Arthur. *The Baroque Concerto*. 2nd ed. London: Faber and Faber, 1963. 363p. ML 1263 H85.

Gives useful background information. Handel chapter (pp. 292–304) is confined to Opus 3 and 6. Elegant and erudite. Index and bibliography.

* Johnstone, H. Diack. "An Unknown Book of Organ Voluntaries." *Musical Times* 108 (1967): 1003–1007.

Cited above as item 306.

691. Kahle, Felix. *Georg Friedrich Händels Cembalosuiten*. Eisenach: H. Kahle, 1928. 217p. with music supplement. ML 410 H13 K.

Offers a stylistic analysis of the keyboard suites, with the inevitable Bach-Handel comparison. Takes into consideration Walsh's 1733 print and the early copies located in Berlin at the time of writing. Musical examples. Bibliography.

* Kimbell, David. "Aspekte von Händels Umarbeitungen und Revisionen eigener Werke." *Händel-Jahrbuch* 23 (1977): 45–67.

Cited above as item 340.

692. Kubik, Reinhold. "Zu Händels Solosonaten. Addenda zu einem Aufsatz von Terence Best." *Händel-Jahrbuch* 26 (1980): 115–19.

A Brussels manuscript contains a unique copy of a G major flute sonata attributed to Handel. Kubik has prepared an edition under Handel's name, but see item 698. The suggestion that a D major flute sonata in the manuscript was composed by Johann Sigismund Weiss, and gave Handel the inspiration for the opening of the D major violin sonata (HWV 371) was later withdrawn by the author (see item 698). A sonata by Felice de Giardini, surviving in a manuscript copy in West Berlin, has been wrongly attributed to Handel.

693. Lam, Basil. "The Orchestral Music." In *Handel: A Symposium*, pp. 200–32. Ed. Gerald Abraham. London: Oxford University Press, 1954. ML 410 H13 A66.

Seeks to champion the quality of Handel's orchestral music. Comments briefly on each of the concertos and on the *Water Music* and *Music for the Royal Fireworks*. Musical examples.

694. Lasocki, David. "A New Look at Handel's Recorder Sonatas. I: Ornamentation in the First Movement of the F major Sonata." *Recorder & Music* 6 (1978): 2–8.

Discusses an ornamented version of the movement (from HWV 369) derived from an eighteenth-century barrel organ and used by David Munrow on a 1974 recording (Argo ZRG 746). Suggests that the style of ornamentation in recorder pieces should be simpler than that used in keyboard works. Generous musical examples.

695. _____. "A New Look at Handel's Recorder Sonatas. II: The Autograph Manuscripts." *Recorder & Music* 6 (1978): 71–79.

Essentially a detailed introduction to Lasocki's edition of the recorder sonatas (HWV 377, 367a, 360, 362, 365, 369) by Faber Music in 1978. Takes into account not only the

Instrumental Music

autographs, which have now come to light for all six sonatas, but also the early copies and prints.

696. _____. "A New Look at Handel's Recorder Sonatas. III: The Roger and Walsh Prints; A New View." *Recorder & Music* 6 (1979): 130–32.

With the assistance of Terence Best and Donald Burrows (see item 666), the author concludes that the "Roger" title page on the first edition of the recorder sonatas is a fake prepared by Walsh, the real publisher. The print must have appeared between 1726 and 1732, and not "ca. 1722," the traditional date. Illustration.

697. _____. "Händels Sonaten für Holzbläser in neuem Licht." *Tibia* 5 (1980): 166–76.

Brief summary of items 694, 695, 696.

698. _____ and Terence Best. "A New Flute Sonata by Handel." *Early Music* 9 (1981): 307–11.

The recent discovery of autographs and early copies shows that only one (HWV 395a) of eleven "flute" sonatas published by Chrysander was originally intended for flute. Of the others, composed for recorder, violin and oboe, two (HWV 374 and 376) are most likely not by Handel. A flute sonata in D (HWV 378) attributed to Johann Sigismund Weiss (ca. 1690–1737) in item 692 is certainly by Handel. A flute sonata in G edited by R. Kubik is not by Handel. Addendum on the correspondence page of *Early Music* 10 (1982): 575.

699. _____. "A New Dating for Handel's Recorder Sonatas." *Recorder & Music* 8 (1985): 170–71.

Assesses the effects of recent paper studies on the dating of the recorder sonatas.

700. Levin, Lia S. "The Recorder in the Music of Purcell and Handel." Ph.D. dissertation. International College (Los Angeles), 1981. 400p.

Concludes that both composers were keenly aware of the distinct tone color and characteristics of the recorder, and did not consider them easily interchangeable with other instruments, including the transverse flute. Not examined.

701. Mohr, Wilhelm. "Händels 16. Orgelkonzert." *Händel-Jahrbuch* 12 (1966): 77–91.

 An introduction to the author's performing edition of HWV 305, published by Peters in 1967. The edition, for organ with accompaniment reduced for keyboard, is somewhat speculative.

702. Morley, Max. "The Trumpet Arias in the Oratorios of George Frederic Handel." *Journal of the International Trumpet Guild* 5 (1980): 14–19.

 Offers a description of the Baroque trumpet with comments on the technical aspects of Handel's composition for it, along with performance suggestions. Useful references, musical examples.

703. Music, David W. "Handel and the Harp." *American Harp Journal* 8/3 (1982): 6–15.

 Reviews pieces and individual numbers written specifically for harp, with special reference to *Giulio Cesare*, *Esther*, *Alexander's Feast*, *Saul*, and the Harp Concerto.

704. Newman, Joel. "Handel's Use of the Recorder." *American Recorder* 5/4 (1964): 4–9.

 Goes through Handel's works by genre, listing occurences of recorder parts. Tables.

705. Newman, William S. *The Sonata in the Baroque Era*. 4th ed. New York: Norton, 1983. 476p. ML 1156 N42 1983. ISBN 0–393–95275–4.

 In spite of a few bibliographic addenda, the Handel section (pp. 291–96) is too dated to be useful, being essentially unchanged from the 1963 first edition. General material in the first part of the book gives good background. Index, bibliography.

706. Nielsen, N.K. "Handel's Organ Concertos reconsidered." *Dansk aarbog for musikforskning* 3 (1963): 3–26.

Discusses the sources. The new organ Handel had built in 1739 was probably not a chamber organ, but a larger instrument with two manuals and pedals. The concertos after 1739 were written for this instrument, which may even have had reed stops.

707. Pauly, Paul G. *G.Fr. Händels Klavierfugen*. Saarbrücken: Universität des Saarlandes, 1961. 169p. ML 410 H13 P28.

Offers a systematic discussion of all stylistic aspects of Handel's keyboard fugues. Musical examples, bibliography.

708. Pestelli, Giorgio. "Haendel e Alessandro Scarlatti: problemi di attribuzione nel MS A7663 Cass. della biblioteca del Conservatorio 'Nicolò Paganini' di Genova." *Rivista italiana di musicologia* 7 (1972): 103–14.

Of five toccatas attributed to Handel in a Genoa manuscript, three are by A. Scarlatti and one may be by Francesco Durante. Style discussion of these and the Handel example in item 709.

709. _____. "Bach, Handel, D. Scarlatti and the Toccata of the Late Baroque." In *Bach, Handel, Scarlatti: Tercentenary Essays*, pp. 277–91. Ed. Peter Williams. Cambridge: Cambridge University Press, 1985. ML 55 B14 1985. ISBN 0–521–25217–2.

Examines an early toccata (HWV 571) from the Italian period in relation to the *perpetuum mobile* toccatas of the late Baroque. Suggests tentatively that the Roman keyboard "contest" described by Mainwaring may have been with Alessandro Scarlatti, and not Domenico.

710. Pfeiffer, Christel. "Das französische Prélude non mesuré für Cembalo: Notenbild, Interpretation, Einfluß auf Froberger, Bach, Händel." *Neue Zeitschrift für Musik* 140 (1979): 132–36.

Discusses the French unmeasured prelude, making performance suggestions and showing how the style has echoes in Handel's keyboard works. Musical examples.

711. Pollart, Gene J. "The Use and Innovations of Percussion in the Works of J.S. Bach and Handel." *Percussionist* 13/3 (1976): 75–81.

Describes eighteenth-century instruments and compares Bach's use of percussion to Handel's.

712. Pont, Graham. "Handel's Overtures for Harpsichord or Organ. An Unrecognized Genre." *Early Music* 11 (1983): 309–22.

Outlines origins of French overture and emergence of keyboard versions in the last quarter of the seventeenth century. Recent works-lists omit most of the keyboard overtures. The authenticity of some is in doubt. Recommends underdotting as well as overdotting.

713. Price, Percival. "Mr. Handel and His Carillon." *Guild of Carillonneurs in North America, Bulletin* 20/1 (1969): 20–31.

Surveys Handel's associations with the carillon and related instruments. Describes his use of "Tubalcain," or carillon-like instrument, in *Saul*, *The Triumph of Time and Truth*, and *L'allegro*, and the 1739 revival of *Acis and Galatea*. Plate.

714. Redlich, Hans F. "A New 'Oboe Concerto' by Handel." *Musical Times* 97 (1956): 409–10.

Identifies an anonymous work from Walsh's "Select Harmony. Third Collection" as a Handel concerto grosso originally published as no. 4 of Opus 3. The concerto was subsequently published in HHA IV/11, but its authenticity has been seriously called into question. See Frederick Hudson in the *Kritische Bericht* (Kassel: Bärenreiter, 1963), p. 43.

715. _____. "The Oboes in Handel's Opus 6." *Musical Times* 109 (1968): 530–31.

Shows that the function of oboes in the Opus 6 concertos, obscured by early editions, is clarified by the Aylesford copy. Refers especially to no. 5. Plate. Appears in German in *Musikforschung* 21 (1968): 221–23.

716. Sadie, Stanley. *Handel Concertos*. London: BBC, 1972. BBC Music Guides. 72p. MT 130 H2 S2. ISBN 0–563–10349–3.

Suggests that Handel's early concertos show Vivaldi's influence, and that Handel turned to the old-fashioned Corellian style in Opus 6 because of its popularity in England. Fine discussion includes Water Music and Music for the Royal Fireworks.

717. Seifas, Natalie. "Concerto grosso v tvorcestve Gendelja." Ph.D. dissertation. Leningradskij Institut Teatra, Muzyki i Kinematografii, 1975. 202p.

Investigates the concerto grosso idea, with emphasis on Handel's works in the genre. Not examined.

718. _____. "Die Concerti grossi op. 6 und ihre Stellung in Händels Gesamtwerk." *Händel-Jahrbuch* 26 (1980): 9–58.

Contains a brilliant summary of general trends in High Baroque music. Shows that the Opus 6 concertos represent a synthesis of national influences. They are closely tied to an English tradition of instrumental music. Contrary to a widespread notion, Handel does use devices and structures characteristic of Vivaldi. The Opus 6 concertos feature techniques developed in Opus 3 and the organ concertos. The solo concertos should not be seen as a separate genre. First appeared in *Fragen der Theorie und Ästhetik* 12 (Leningrad, 1973) in Russian.

* Silbiger, Alexander. "Scarlatti Borrowings in Handel's Grand Concertos." *Musical Times* 125 (1984): 93–95.

    Cited above as item 368.

719. Squire, William Barclay. "Handel's Clock Music." *Musical Quarterly* 5 (1919): 538–52.

    Presents scores of the pieces Handel composed for Charles Clay's musical clock.

720. Williams, Peter. "Händel und die englische Orgelmusik." *Händel-Jahrbuch* 12 (1966): 51–76.

    Excellent background on English organ music and the duties of church organists. Handel was only one of many influences, publishing little organ music during his lifetime. He made his impact primarily as an improvisor and soloist in concertos. List of English publications of Handel's organ music up to 1815.

721. _____. "*Figurae* in the Keyboard Works of Scarlatti, Handel and Bach: An Introduction." In *Bach, Handel, Scarlatti: Tercentenary Essays*, pp. 327–46. Ed. Peter Williams. Cambridge: Cambridge University Press, 1985. ML 55 B14 1985. ISBN 0–521–25217–2.

    Argues that, in keyboard music, *figurae* tend to lose their associative properties and become versatile devices in writing idiomatic pieces. Some *figurae* suggest their own natural articulations. Puts forward the intriguing theory that the English tradition of division-playing may have influenced Handel's manipulation of motives, as in the first movement of the organ concerto Opus 7, no. 1 (HWV 306).

* Wollenberg, Susan. "Handel and Gottlieb Muffat: A Newly-Discovered Borrowing." *Musical Times* 113 (1972): 448–49.

    Cited above as item 372.

VI

PERFORMANCE PRACTICE AND THE PERFORMANCE TRADITION

1. Performance Practice

Recent years have seen the performance practice of Baroque music come of age, but not without growing pains. The argument against Romantic-style performances has essentially been won by those who demand a more faithful adherence to the composer's intentions. However, residual conflicts over such issues as the use of authentic instruments, the transposition of castrato roles, and double-dotting still crop up on the pages of contemporary journals. In addition, the performance of Handel's music presents its own peculiar problems, like the questions of whether or not to stage English oratorios and whether or not to ornament English oratorio arias in the Italian style.

The selection of items which appears below does not contain every last article in, say, the double-dotting controversy. It includes only the most significant and germane original treatises. In general, record reviews are included only when they contain especially useful information.

The reader who wishes to consult a broader range of sources from the extensive literature on performance practice should examine *Performance Practice: A Bibliography*, by Mary Vinquist and Neal Zaslaw

(New York: Norton, 1971) and its supplement in *Current Musicology* 15 (1973): 126–36.

722. Arnold, Franck, T. *The Art of Accompaniment from a Thorough-Bass as Practised in the XVIIth and XVIIIth Centuries.* London: Oxford University Press, 1931. Repr. London: Holland Press, 1961. 918p. ML 442 A76.

Gives a detailed account of the treatment of figured bass accompaniment in treatises of the seventeenth and eighteenth centuries, followed by systematic instructions. Musical examples, indexes.

723. Bach, Carl Philipp Emanuel. *Essay on the True Art of Playing Keyboard Instruments.* Trans. and ed. William J. Mitchell. New York: W.W. Norton & Co., 1949. 449p. MT 224 B132. ISBN 0-393-09716-1.

English translation of item 724, with a useful introduction and bibliography.

724. _____. *Versuch über die wahre Art das Clavier zu spielen.* Berlin: 1753–62. Facs. ed. Lothar Hoffmann-Erbrecht. Leipzig: Breitkopf & Härtel, 1957. 360p. MT 224 B13.

Issued in two volumes, it contains systematic instructions for embellishment, continuo playing, accompaniment, and improvisation. Offers comments on general issues of mid-century practice. Musical examples. Editorial notes and index.

725. Barnett, Dene. "The Performance Practice of Acting: The Eighteenth Century. Part I: Ensemble Acting." *Theatre Research International* 2 (1977): 157–86.

Presents in translation numerous passages from treatises and other primary sources relevant to the interaction of characters with each other and the audience. Focuses on tragedy and serious opera. Plates. Refers to the author's upcoming book, which deals with acting in serious opera.

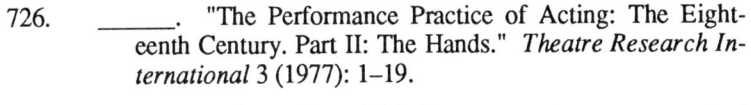

Performance Practice

726. _____. "The Performance Practice of Acting: The Eighteenth Century. Part II: The Hands." *Theatre Research International* 3 (1977): 1–19.

Continuation of item 725. Excerpts and commentary deal with the actor's use of his hands. Plates.

727. _____. "The Performance Practice of Acting: The Eighteenth Century. Part III: The Arms." *Theatre Research International* 3 (1977): 79–93.

Continuation of item 726. Describes gestures involving the arms. Plates.

728. _____. "The Performance Practice of Acting: The Eighteenth Century. Part IV: The Eyes, the Face and the Head." *Theatre Research International* 5 (1979–80): 1–36.

Eighteenth-century proscriptions and prescriptions. Many are directly related to opera. Plates.

729. _____. "The Performance Practice of Acting: The Eighteenth Century. Part V: Posture and Attitudes." *Theatre Research International* 6 (1980–81): 1–32.

Presents passages that deal with physical attitudes, right down to the position of the toes. Plates. Concludes the series begun with item 725.

*   Baselt, Bernd. "Muffat and Handel: A Two-Way Exchange." *Musical Times* 120 (1979): 904–907.

Cited above as item 655.

730. Bernstein, Walter Heinz. "Zu Fragen der Punktierung und der Continuo-Ausführung." In *Konferenzbericht Halle (Saale) 1980*, pp. 131–33.

Remarks informally on various questions of keyboard performance, especially rhythmic inequality in allemandes and the general style of continuo playing. Examples.

731. Best, Terence. "An Example of Handel Embellishment." *Musical Times* 110 (1969): 933.

Introduces an ornamented keyboard version of the aria "Sventurato, godi o core abbandonata" from *Floridante* found by the author in the British Museum (now British Library). A passage from the autograph manuscript is shown, together with Chrysander's edition of the corresponding aria excerpt.

732. Bimberg, Guido. "Handlung und Affekt in Händels Opern." In *Konferenzbericht Halle (Saale) 1980*, pp. 24–31.

Contends that the modern-day misunderstanding of the dramatic structure of Handel's operas leads to problems in performance. Especially problematic is the notion that all recitatives are concerned only with plot and all arias only with Affect.

733. _____. "Notate zu einer Dramaturgie den Händel-Opern." *Händel-Jahrbuch* 28 (1982): 35–42.

Offers general remarks on the dramatic theory of Handel's operas, then takes as examples an excerpt from the first act of *Giulio Cesare* and the aria "Verdi prati" from *Alcina*.

734. Boyden, David D. *The History of Violin Playing from Its Origins to 1761, and Its Relationship to the Violin and Violin Music*. London: Oxford University Press, 1965. 569p. ML 850 B7.

Authoritative detailed account, including four chapters on violin technique. Plates, bibliography, glossary, index.

735. Collins, Michael. "A Reconsideration of French Overdotting." *Music and Letters* 50 (1969): 111–23.

Presents overwhelming evidence, both from music and from treatises, in favor of the practice of over-dotting (or "double-dotting") in French overture style. Musical examples. See also item 748.

* Cooper, Barry. "The Organ Parts to Handel's *Alexander's Feast*." Music and Letters 59 (1978): 159–79.

Cited above as item 548.

736. Dart, Thurston, "Handel and the Continuo." *Musical Times* 106 (1965): 348-50.

   Concentrates on Handel's use of the contrasting sounds of organ and harpsichord in oratorio performances.

737. Dean, Winton. "Vocal Embellishment in a Handel Aria." In *Studies in Eighteenth-Century Music: A Tribute to Karl Geiringer*, pp. 151-59. Ed. H.C. Robbins Landon with Roger E. Chapman. London: Allen and Unwin Ltd., 1970. ML 195 L35. ISBN 0-04-780016-X.

   Discusses an embellished version in Handel's handwriting of the aria "O caro mio tesor" from *Amadigi*. Touches also on the problem of performance of dotted rhythms. Musical examples.

738. _____. "How Should Handel's Oratorios Be Staged?" *Musical Newletter* 1/4 (1971): 11-15.

   General advice on staging Handel's oratorios, with special emphasis on the treatment of the chorus.

739. _____. Ed. *G.F. Handel: Three Ornamented Arias*. Oxford: Oxford University Press, 1973. M 1505 H13. ISBN 0-19345412-2.

   An edition of three arias from *Ottone* (1723), including ornamentation surviving in Handel's hand on a Smith copy on the Bodleian library, Oxford. Fine introduction gives details of the source, speculates on the circumstances surrounding it, and comments on the ornamentaion itself. A precious source for singers of Handel's music.

*   _____. "A French Traveller's View of Handel's Operas." *Music and Letters* 55 (1974): 172-78.

   Cited above as item 429.

740. _____. "The Performance of Recitative in Late Baroque Opera." *Music and Letters* 58 (1977): 389-402.

Combines information from treatises and other primary sources, together with practical considerations, to offer suggestions on rhythm and meter style of accompaniment and appoggiaturas in secco recitatives. Reviews scholarship on the performance of cadences, concluding that the shortened cadence is most often appropriate in Handel's operas. Concludes that, when the recitatives are performed according to his principles, the dramatic and musical balance of arias and recitatives is restored, giving operas more satisfactory overall effect. Musical examples. Appears in German in *Konferenzbericht Halle (Saale) 1979*, pp. 94–103.

741. _____. "Die Aufführung von heroischen männlichen Rollen in Handel's Opern." In *Konferenzbericht Halle (Saale) 1980*, pp. 32–37.

Presents compelling musical and historical reasons for using female singers in the male operatic roles originally written for castratos. The modern practice of lowering the parts an octave and casting male singers distorts the relationship between voice and instrumental parts and obscures the subtleties of Handel's characterizations.

*   _____ and J. Merrill Knapp. *Handel's Operas 1704–1726*. Oxford: Clarendon Press, 1987. 751p. ML 410 H13 D37 1986. ISBN 0–19–315219–3.

Cited above as item 433.

742. Derr, Ellwood. "Concertante Passages in Keyboard Realizations in Handel: Some Guidelines." *Diapason* 76/9 (1985): 9–12.

Offers a detailed, informed consideration of the use of "concertino" harpsichord in "O Thou that Tellest Good Tidings to Zion" from *Messiah* and the second movement of the Ninth Concerto Grosso from Opus 6. Generous musical examples.

743. Donington, Robert. *A Performer's Guide to Baroque Music*. London: Faber and Faber, 1973. 320p. ML 457 D66. ISBN 0–571–09797–9.

Performance Practice 217

Companion volume to item 744, but intended especially for performers and teachers. Musical examples, "Reading List," index.

744. _____. *The Interpretation of Early Music : New Version.* London: Faber and Faber, 1975. 766p. ML 457 D64 1975. ISBN 0-571-04789-0.

Functions as a third edition to *The Interpretation of Early Music*, first published in 1963. Offers a comprehensive guide to performance, especially in Baroque music. Beautiful indexing and subtitles make it easy to use. Updated, with copious examples. Extensive bibliography prepared with the aid of Gloria Rose.

745. Dressler, Carolyn E. "'Armida abbandonata' by George Frideric Handel: An Edition Reflecting the Performance Practice of the Baroque Era." DMA dissertation. University of Maryland, 1978. 61 p.

Critical edition with a preface discussing various aspects of performance practice. Not examined.

746. Eisenschmidt, Joachim. *Die szenische Darstellung der Opern Händels auf der Londoner Bühne seiner Zeit.* 2 vols. Schriftenreihe des Händelhauses in Halle, Heft 5-6. Wolfenbüttel: Georg Kallmeyer Verlag, 1940-41. ML 410 H13 E3.

The first volume discusses Italian opera in London from its beginnings before Handel's arrival to the end of his operatic career. The second volume deals with non-musical issues of performance, especially acting and production style. Plates, bibliography.

747. Fleischhauer, Günter. "Zur Verwendung einiger Tanzrhythmen in den Chorsätzen der Oratorien G.F. Händels." In *Konferenzbericht Halle (Saale) 1980*, pp. 96-116.

Lists choral movements that are written in dance styles, together with theoretical descriptions of the dances themselves. Heavily documented, with musical examples and a table showing suggested tempos for Gavotte, Bourée, Sarabande, Menuet, and Gigue.

748. Fuller, David. "Dotting, the 'French Style' and Frederick Neumann's Counter-Reformation." *Early Music* 5 (1977): 517-43.

Offers a carefully reasoned response to Neumann's article "The Dotted Note and the So-called French Style" (originally published in 1965), which appeared on pp. 310-24 of the same issue. Provides an impression of the continuing heated debate on the subject of rhythmic inequality, with references to the major articles. Attacks Neumann's method of argument, suggesting that he misrepresents the facts to support his rejection of double-dotting. In an afterword, responds negatively to Neumann's article in the 1977 *Musical Quarterly*.

749. _____. "Analyzing the Performance of a Barrel Organ." *Organ Yearbook* 11 (1980): 104-15.

Fascinating account of the author's work with an English barrel organ dating from around 1800 and containing in its repertory performances of Handel's organ concertos Op. 4, nos. 2 and 5. The elaborately embellished performances, which also bore witness to a practice of rhythmic inequality, have been transcribed and edited by the author as *G.F. Handel: Two Ornamented Organ Concertos* (Hackensack N.J., 1980). See also his short article on automatic instruments in *Early Music* 11 (1983): 164-66.

750. Geminiani, Franceso. *The Art of Playing on the Violin.* London, 1751. Facs. ed. David D. Boyden. London: Oxford University Press, ca. 1951. xii, 51p. MT 262 G32.

Concise comments on the style and method of violin playing, with lengthy etudes to demonstrate. Excellent introduction evaluates Geminiani's historical position and interprets his advice. Facsimile edition reproduces informative frontispiece from the 1752 French translation.

751. Goebels, Franzpeter. "Gebundene Improvisation: Zur Ausführung der Preludes von Georg Friedrich Händel." *Musica* 39 (1985): 9-17.

Presents full realization of the preludes HWV 562 and 567, along with the scores as edited in the HHA, and commentary.

752. Gudger, William D. "Handel's Organ Concertos: A Guide to Performance Based on the Primary Sources." *Diapason* 64/10 (1973): 3-5.

Summarizes information on chronology and early sources of the organ concertos. Makes suggestions about performance. Musical example. See also letters to the editor in issues of July, 1974 and September, 1974.

* _____. "Performing the Handel Organ Concertos as Keyboard Solos: A New Edition of Walsh's Transcriptions (1738)." *Diapason* 72/12 (1981): 6-10.

Cited above as item 685.

753. _____. "Registration in the Handel Organ Concertos." *American Organist* 19/2 (1985): 71-73.

Suggests possible registrations which are historically consistent with the sort of organs Handel played in England.

754. _____. "Playing Organ Continuo in Handel's *Messiah*." *American Organist* 19/2 (1985): 91-92.

Briefly discusses the use of organ and harpsichord, making a few suggestions for the style of realization. Musical examples.

755. Hall, James S. and Martin V. "Handel's Graces." *Händel-Jahrbuch* 3 (1957): 25-43.

Describes Oxford manuscripts containing four arias ornamented in Handel's hand, all from *Ottone*. Analyzes the ornaments, with musical examples, concluding that the graces acceptable to Handel differed appreciably from those favored by other composers (notably C.P.E. Bach).

756. Hansell, Sven Hostrup. "Orchestral Practice at the Court of Cardinal Pietro Ottoboni." *Journal of the American Musicological Society* 19 (1966): 398–403.

Reports on a detailed examination of Ottoboni's account books, identifying various musicians. Finds patterns of orchestral make-up and solves problems of terminology with regard to instruments. Shows that results may be widely applicable.

757. _____. "The Cadence in 18th-Century Recitative." *Musical Quarterly* 54 (1968): 228–48.

Explains that there were two basic ways of performing the cadence, the truncated manner, most popular in Italy and in the earlier part of the century, and the delayed manner, which became widely used only later. Supports the argument with numerous quotations from treatises, musical examples and historical evidence.

758. _____. "Stage Deportment and Scenographic Design in the Italian Opera Seria of the Settecento." In *International Musicological Society: Report of the Eleventh Congress, Copenhagen 1972*, vol. 1 pp. 415–24. Ed. Henrik Glahn, Søren Sørensen and Peter Ryom. Copenhagen: Edition Wilhelm Hansen, 1974. ML 36 I6 1972. ISBN 87-7455-026-8.

Discusses the effects on operatic staging of the invention at the end of the seventeenth century of the *scena per angolo* (scene viewed at an angle), which restricted the singers to the proscenium area. Their voices could be projected well, but it encouraged them to "assume the majesty and elegance of [their] aristocratic setting with studied poses and discreet gestures."

759. Harnoncourt, Nikolaus. "Concerto grosso, Triosonate—bei Händel" and "Was ein Autograph sagt." In *Musik als Klangrede: Wege zu einem neuen Musikverständnis*, pp. 225–40. Salzburg: Residenz Verlag, 1983. ML 457 H3 1983. ISBN 3-7017-0315-9.

Offers general comments about Handel's musical language, followed by a discussion of the performance of the grand concertos, including seating arrangements of the performers and the use of a second keyboard continuo instrument for the *concertino*. Brief, general remarks on trio sonatas. Reflects on the *Jeptha* autograph, and especially on the clues to performance practice it holds.

760. Henking, Arwed. "Probleme des Rhythmus in Händels *Messias*." *Musik und Kirche* 35 (1965): 183–90.

Discusses performance problems in *Messiah*, concentrating on rhythmic practices in relation to dotted notes and triplets. Musical examples.

761. Hogwood, Christopher. "Authentic Performance and Original Instruments." In *Handel and the Fitzwilliam*, pp. 22–23. Cambridge: Fitzwilliam Museum, 1974. ML 141 C3 H3.

Comments briefly on the difference between "authentic" and "original" instruments, and on the problems associated with them, in particular harpsichord, violin and one-keyed flute.

762. Jones, Ann E. "An Examination of Expressive Rhythm and Articulation Practices in the Baroque Period with Suggestions for Their Application to the Duet Choruses of *Messiah*." DMA dissertation. University of Iowa, 1984. 155p.

Shows how study of the Italian chamber duets can be applied to the duet choruses. Not examined.

* Knapp, J. Merrill. "Handel, the Royal Academy of Music, and Its First Opera Season in London (1720)." *Musical Quarterly* 45 (1959): 145–67.

Cited above as item 444.

763. _____. "Zur Aufführungsdauer einer Händel-Oper." In *Konferenzbericht Halle (Saale) 1980*, pp. 38–41.

Urges modern day directors and conductors to be consistent with Handel's styles and practices in their efforts to avoid interminable performances of his operas. Cautions against the mutilation of da capo arias. Suggests methods for keeping the duration of operas within reasonable limits.

764. _____. "Problems with Handel Opera." *Händel-Jahrbuch* 29 (1983): 33-38.

    Extremely useful general discussion of major issues confronting present-day directors and performers of Handel's operas. Reference to the nature of Baroque opera and Italian opera in London.

765. "Kolloquium über aufführungspraktische Fragen bei Händel." *Händel-Jahrbuch* 12 (1966): 25-49.

    Focuses on performance practice of the vocal music, with commentaries by Walther Siegmund-Schulze, Konrad Sasse, Percy Young, Alfred Mann, and Ernst Meyer. Musical examples.

766. "Kolloquium: Händels Oper *Xerxes* als Inszenierungsproblem." *Händel-Jahrbuch* 20 (1974): 22-65.

    Focuses on staging problems in *Serse*, with commentary and remarks by Walther Siegmund-Schulze, Jens Peter Larsen, Reinhold Rüdiger and others.

767. Krones, Hartmut and Robert Schollum. *Vokale und allgemeine Aufführungspraxis*. Wien: Hermann Böhlaus, 1983. 292p. ML 457 K67 1983. ISBN 3-205-08371-7.

    Considers performance problems generally, including nineteenth century music. Handel's music is discussed in sections on the ornamentation of vocal music, and especially opera and oratorio, but most recent research is not always taken into account. Musical examples, indexes.

768. Kuhn, Ronald G. "Performance Edition of a Magnificat Linked to Dionigi Erba and George Frideric Handel: Suggestions for Its Performance and Observations on Its

Authorship." DMA dissertation. University of Washington, 1979. 182p.

Argues for Erba as the composer. Includes a discussion of performance techniques. Not examined.

769. Larsen, Jens Peter. "Tempoprobleme bei Händel, dargestellt am *Messias.*" In *Händel-Ehrung der Deutschen Demokratischen Republik, Konferenzberichte*, pp. 141–53. Leipzig: Deutscher Verlag für Musik, 1959. ML 410 H13 H21 1959.

Reviews contemporary evidence on the duration of Handel's oratorio performances. Includes a table summarizing metronome markings in nineteenth and early twentieth century editions of *Messiah*. English version in item 552.

770. _____. "Zur Geschichte der Messias-Aufführungstraditionen." *Händel-Jahrbuch* 13–14 (1967– 68): 13–24.

Presents a reasoned argument against elaborate ornamentation in English oratorio arias. English version in item 552.

771. Lindley, Mark. "Keyboard Technique and Articulation: Evidence for the Performance Practices of Bach, Handel and Scarlatti." In *Bach, Handel, Scarlatti: Tercentenery Essays*, pp. 207–43. Ed. Peter Williams. Cambridge: Cambridge University Press, 1985. ML 55 B14 1985. ISBN 0–521–25217–2.

Offers a series of general conclusions about keyboard technique, and especially fingering, supported by copious examples. Examines passages by Scarlatti, Bach, and Handel. Works from contemporary fingerings (in Handel's case of the Ciacone HWV 435) and documents.

772. _____. "Tecnica della tastiera e articolazione: Testimonianze della pratica esecutiva di Scarlatti, Bach, Handel." *Nuova rivista musicale italiana* 19 (1985): 20–61.

Based on item 771. 183 musical examples.

773. MacClintock, Carol. *Readings in the History of Music in Performance.* Bloomington: Indiana University Press, 1979. 432p. ML 457 R4. ISBN 0-253-14495-7.

Offers passages from contemporary works from the Middle Ages to the early nineteenth century, prefaced by short introductions and translated into English. Musical examples.

774. Mann, Alfred. "Zum Concertistenprinzip bei Händel." In *Musik als Lobgesang: Festschrift für Wilhelm Ehmann,* pp. 77–82. Ed. Gerhard Mittring and Gerhard Rödding. Darmstadt: Merseburger, 1964. ML 55 E35.

Discusses Handel's use of large and small performing groups in choral music, particularly in the Latin psalms and the Chandos anthems.

775. _____. "Zur Aufführungspraxis Händelscher Vokalmusik." *Händel-Jahrbuch* 12 (1966): 38–44.

Investigates Handel's use of chorus vs. soloists, ripieno vs. concertino, in choral works, especially *Messiah, Laudate pueri* in D, the Chandos anthems, and the Utrecht *Jubilate.* Mentions autograph annotations in the scores which provide clues to these practices.

776. _____. "The Opening of *Messiah*: A Problem of Performance Practice." *American Choral Review* 21/3 (1979): 9–13.

Discusses the over-dotting controversy. Examples.

777. _____. "Problems with Handel Oratorio." *Händel-Jahrbuch* 29 (1983): 39–41.

Transcription of a short talk dealing with the complexity of genre in the English oratorios, with remarks on its implications for performance. Mentions the performance of the trumpet parts in the chorus "Glory to God" from *Messiah.*

778. Martin, Clarence, J. "Performance Practices in Handel's Messiah." DMA dissertation. University of Cincinnati, 1968. 184p.

Not examined.

779. Mather, Betty Bang. *Interpretation of French Music from 1675 to 1775 for Woodwind and Other Performers, with Additional Comments on German and Italian Music.* New York: McGinnis & Mark, 1973. 104p. MT 80 M35.

    Easy-to-use handbook, proceeding mostly from woodwind sources but valuable to all performers of Baroque music. Concentrates on "the tasteful use of rhythmic inequality, articulation and ornamentation." Copious examples, all from primary sources. Bibliography, index.

780. McGrady, Richard. "Corelli's Violin Sonatas and the Ornamentation of Handel's Recorder Sonatas." *Recorder and Music* 3 (1971): 357–59.

    Offers analytical notes on the early ornamented version of Corelli's Opus 5 sonatas and suggests ways in which the style can be transferred to Handel's recorder sonatas. Musical examples.

781. Melkus, Eduard. "Zur Auszierung der Händel-Violinsonaten." *Das Orchester* 33 (1985): 453–68.

    Extensive discussion, with eighty short examples, of free ornamentation in the Handel violin sonatas, beginning with examples of ornamentation in Bach, Corelli, Nardini, Haydn, Hiller, Mozart, and Beethoven.

782. Meyer, Ernst Hermann. "Zur Aufführungspraxis der Händelschen Oratorien." *Konferenzbericht Halle (Saale) 1980*, pp. 68–79.

    Explores issues of performance practice in the oratorios, especially general style and performing forces, but finds time to dispute Dean's stand on the modern-day performance of castrato roles in opera (item 741). Emphasizes the importance of Handel's use primarily of English singers, not Italian, in oratorios.

783. Milhous, Judith and Robert D. Hume. "A Prompt Copy of Handel's *Radamisto*." *Musical Times* 127 (1986): 316–21.

Describes a prompter's copy of a libretto from 1720. The annotations reveal much about the original staging.

784. Montagu, Jeremy. "Handel and the Orchestra." In *Handel: A Celebration of His Life and Times*, pp. 25–28. Ed. Jacob Simon. London: National Portrait Gallery, 1985. 296p. ML 410 H13. ISBN 0–904017–68–0.

Describes the physical characteristics and sound of instruments in Handel's day, with specific reference to contemporary documents and specific London musicians.

* Morley, Max. "The Trumpet Arias in the Oratorios of George Frederic Handel." *Journal of the International Trumpet Guild* 5 (1980): 14–19.

Cited above as item 702.

785. Mozart, Leopold. *Versuch einer gründlichen Violinschule*. Augsburg: J.J. Lotter, 1756. Facs. ed. of the 3rd ed. of 1787. Hans Rudolf Jung. Leipzig: VEB Deutscher Verlag für Musik. 1968. 276, 32p. MT 262 M95.

The most widely read violin treatise of the mid-eighteenth century. It was translated into French and Dutch and was issued in three editions (1756, 1769–70, 1787) during the author's lifetime. The original work is indexed, has musical examples. The facsimile edition has helpful commentary at the end and an introduction by David Oistrach.

786. _____. *A Treatise on the Fundamental Principles of Violin Playing*. Translated by Editha Knocker. Early Music Series 6. 2nd ed. Oxford: Oxford University Press, 1951. Repr. 1985. 237p. MT 262 M9513. ISBN 0–19–318513–X.

First prepared in 1937, the translation features a translator's appendix, introduction and note to the second edition, as well as a preface by Alfred Einstein and a Note to the 1985 reprint by Alec Hyatt King.

787. Neumann, Frederick. *Ornamentation in Baroque and Post-Baroque Music, with Special Emphasis on J.S. Bach.* Princeton: Princeton University Press, 1978. 630p. MT 80 N48. ISBN 0–691–9123–4.

Concentrates on Bach but discusses a few works by Handel. Discusses ornaments by specific type, then in a chapter titled "Free Ornamentation." Useful glossary of terms and symbols, extensive bibliography, index. Musical examples.

788. _____. *Essays in Performance Practice.* Ann Arbor: UMI Research Press, 1982. Studies in Musicology, 58. 321p. ML 457 N44. ISBN 0–8357–1351–2.

An anthology of previously published essays, including the author's review of item 743 and his controversial articles on "overdotting." Musical examples, index.

789. Ornstein, Doris. "On Preparing a Performing Edition of Handel's Cantata *Mi palpita il cor.*" *Bach: The Quarterly Journal of the Riemenschneider Bach Institute* 10/3 (1979): 3–30.

Presents a performing edition of HWV 132b with an introduction and notes.

* Pfeiffer, Christel. "Das französische 'Prélude non mesuré' für Cembalo. Notenbild-Interpretation-Einfluß auf Frohberger, Bach, Handel." *Neue Zeitschrift für Musik* 140 (1979): 132–36.

Cited above as item 710.

790. Pont, Graham. "French Overtures at the Keyboard: 'How Handel Rendered the Playing of Them'." *Musicology* 6 (1980): 29–50.

Describes the eighteenth-century annotations in a print of Handel's overtures arranged for keyboard, concluding convincingly that they are of great value as the "most extensive evidence yet discovered on the rhythmic alterations of French overtures." Among the author's clearly-stated conclusions are 1) that over-dotting is customary but not obligatory and 2) that rhythmic alteration of French overtures includes *notes inégales*. Plates, illustrations.

791. _____. "Handel and Regularization: A Third Alternative." *Early Music* 13 (1985) 500-505.

Reviews the debate on over-dotting. Questions musicologists' assumption that dotting and other rhythmic figures must be "regularized" to become consistent. An appended table shows to what extent the vocal entries in arias by Handel, Rameau, and Mozart alter the rhythmic shape of their melodically similar introductions. Plates.

792. Quantz, Johann Joachim. *Versuch einer Anweisung die flute traversière zu spielen.* Berlin, 1752. Facs. ed. of the 3rd ed. of 1789. Hansl-Peter Schmitz. Kassel: Bärenreiter, 1953. 349p., 7pl. MT 342 Q2.

Widely read and important for its general comments as well as its information on flute playing. Original is indexed, facsimile edition has brief epilogue. Musical examples.

793. _____. *On Playing the Flute.* Trans. and ed. Edward R. Reilly. London: Faber and Faber, 1966. xxxix, 365p. MT 342 Q213.

Translation of item 792, with introduction and notes.

794. Rackwitz, Werner. "Über die szenische Aufführung der Oratorien Händels." In *Konferenzbericht Halle (Saale) 1980*, pp. 86-90.

Renews the debate over staging Handel's oratorios, reviewing various arguments and concluding that they represent a dramatic tradition entirely different from opera's and should not be staged.

795. Rangel-Ribeiro, Victor. *Baroque Music: A Practical Guide for the Performer.* New York: Schirmer, 1981. 306p. MT 75 R3. ISBN 0-02-871980-8.

Offers a readable composer-oriented guide for performers, without detailed documentation. The Handel chapter features a comparison of editions and recording of the Recorder Sonata Opus 1, #11 (HWV 369) and a general discussion of the violin sonatas. In addition, there is a note on the organ concertos, a discussion of the aria "Flammende Rose" and an example from the Aria in the D minor harpsichord suite (HWV 449). Musical examples, index.

796. Redder, Jutta. "Georg Friedrich Händels Violinsonate E-Dur aus der Sicht der Interpreten." In *Zur Aufführungspraxis und Interpretation der Musik von Johann Sebastian Bach und Georg Friedrich Händel. Georg Friedrich Händel: Ein Beitrag zum 300. Geburtstag*, pp. 18–21. Studien zur Aufführungspraxis und Interpretation der Musik des 18. Jahrhunderts, 26. Ed. Eitelfriedrich Thom. Blankenburg: Kultur- und Forschungsstätte Michaelstein, 1985.

Not examined.

797. Roche, Elizabeth. "Handel's Appoggiaturas: A Tradition Destroyed." *Early Music* 13 (1985): 408–10.

Chronicles an English debate during the years 1927–35 on ornamentation, and particularly appoggiaturas, explaining the views of those who called for strict rendition of the score.

798. Sadie, Julie Anne. "Handel: In Pursuit of the Viol." *Chelys* 15 (1985): 3–24.

Explores Handel use of the bass viola da gamba in the cantata *Tra le fiamme*, the oratorio *La Resurrezione* and the opera *Giulio Cesare*, discussing the reasons for his choice and the nature of his encounters with the instrument and its players. Musical examples, plates.

799. Savage, Alan A. "On Performing the Handel Recorder Sonatas, Opus One." *Recorder and Music* 6 (1978): 9–11.

Offers brief commentaries with personal suggestions for performance. Musical example, photo.

800. Schildkret, David. "'But Who May Abide' from Handel's *Messiah*: A Problem in Performance Practice." *Bulletin of National Association of Teachers of Singing* 41/5 (1985): 5-7.

Reviews evidence of the sources, recommending performance of "But Who May Abide" by a soprano (g minor or a minor) or a female alto (e minor).

801. Thom, Eitelfriedrich. "Gedanken zur Interpretation und Aufführungspraxis der Instrumentalwerke Georg Friedrich Händels am Beispiel von drei Kompositionen." In *Konferenzbericht Halle (Saale) 1980*, pp. 124-30.

Examines the problems of style and tempo in passages from the *Music for the Royal Fireworks*, the "Oboe" concerto in g minor (HWV 287) and the so-called violin concerto ("Sonata à 5" HWV 288). Refers to recent recordings.

802. _____, ed. *Zur Aufführungspraxis und Interpretation der Musik von Johann Sebastian Bach und Georg Friedrich Händel. Georg Friedrich Händel: Ein Beitrag zum 300. Geburtstag.* Studien zur Aufführungspraxis und Interpretation der Musik des 18. Jahrhundert, 26. Blankenburg: Kultur- und Forschungsstätte Michaelstein, 1985.

Not examined.

803. Tosi, Pietro Francesco. *Opinioni de' cantori antichi, e moderni; o sieno, Osservazioni sopra il canto figurato.* Bologna, 1723. 118p. Modern ed. Luigi Leonesi. Naples: Gennaro & A. Morano, 1904. 136p. MT 820 T56.

The principal source for vocal performance practice in the Italian style. Contains notes on technical methods, as well as ornamentation, etc.

804. _____. *Observations on the Florid Song; Or, Sentiments on the Ancient and Modern Singers.* Trans. J.E. Galliard. London: J. Wilcox, 1743. 184p. and 6 pl. Repr. London: William Reeves, 1926. MT 820 A2T 613.

English translation of item 803, reprinted in modern style, without editorial additions or indexes.

805. _____. *Anleitung zur Singkunst.* Trans. Johann Friedrich Agricola. Berlin: George Ludewig Winter, 1757. Facs. ed. Kurt Wichmann. Leipzig: VEB Deutscher Verlag für Musik, 1966. 239p. MT 820 A2 T615.

German translation of item 803, published in facsimile, with extensive modern notes and commentary in a separate pamphlet. Agricola's additions are of particular interest with regard to recitative.

806. Westrup, Sir Jack. "The Cadence in Baroque Recitative." In *Natalicia musicologica Knud Jeppesen*, pp. 243–52. Ed. Bjørn Hjelmborg and Søren Sørensen. Oslo: Norsk Musikforlag, 1962. ML 55 H5.

Draws attention to observations made by theorists, questioning the almost universal use of the delayed cadence in Baroque recitative and giving examples from works by Rossi, Monteverdi, Cavalli, Cesti, Scarlatti, and Handel.

807. Williams, Peter. "Interpreting One of Handel's Free Preludes for Harpsichord." *Early Music* 13 (1985) 506–13.

Offers a realization of the Prelude in d minor HWV 563, with detailed commentary. A Table lists Handel's free and chordal preludes. Musical examples.

808. Wishart, Peter. *"Messiah" Ornamented: An Ornamented Edition of the Solos from Handel's 'Messiah'.* London: Stainer and Bell, 1974. 44p. MT 80 H25 M4. ISBN 85249-318-5.

Short introduction, followed by extravagantly ornamented versions of all the solos. Only the original and decorated vocal lines and text appear.

809. Wolff, Hellmuth Christian. *Originale Gesangsimprovisationen des 16. bis 18. Jahrhunderts.* Das Musikwerk, 41. Köln: Volk, 1972.

Includes one aria from *Rinaldo* and three from *Ottone* with the embellishments of contemporary performers.

810. Wood, Bruce. "Handel's Water Music on Period Instruments." *Early Music* 13 (1985): 554–60.

    Detailed review of seven recordings on period instruments may be useful to the prospective performer.

2. Modern Performances

In the case of Handel's operas, the history of modern performances is a fascinating one. Unlike the operas of Mozart, they did not enjoy a virtually unbroken tradition of performance, but were abandoned for two centuries. In fact, when Oskar Hagen initiated the Göttingen Handel Renaissance with a production of *Rodelinda* in 1920, it was the first Handel opera to be heard since the composer's lifetime (except for short excerpts from *Almira* performed in Hamburg in 1878). Hagen, a professor of Fine Art, prepared the operas for production himself, translating the librettos into German, re-orchestrating the scores in a somewhat Wagnerian style, making numerous cuts and transposing the heroic castrato roles so they could be performed by male singers. Since 1952, when *Agrippina* was performed at Halle, productions of operas and other works have formed a significant part of the annual Handel Festival there.

In England, Handel operas are occasionally performed by the major companies, but have been most vigorously championed by smaller groups like the Handel Opera Society, which began its productions in 1955 with *Deidamia*. The Unicorn Theatre Group at Abingdon has a particularly sterling record; by 1975, it had produced fifteen operas, all first British productions since Handel's day, and including the first modern revivals of *Floridante, Giustino, Sosarme,* and *Lotario.* As Winton Dean pointed out in 1985, all the operas had at that time been staged except for *Almira* and *Silla* (item 815).

Unlike the operas, the oratorios were performed to a greater or lesser extent throughout the nineteenth century. With a new awareness of the essentially dramatic premises of these works arose a practice of staging them like operas. Encouraged by the venerable Edward J.

Dent, this practice flourished at Cambridge during the '20s and '30s, and is still alive but not prevalent today.

Selection of the following items has been made from the surprisingly large literature on the subject of modern performance. Reviews of individual productions have been omitted unless they contain a great deal of useful detail.

811. Dean, Winton. "How Should Handel's Oratorios Be Staged?" *Musical Newsletter* 1/4 (1971): 11–15.

>Briefly lists staged performances of Handel's oratorios in this century. Regards the chorus as a source of dramatic strength. Makes suggestions for the use of chorus, choice of work, cutting, etc. in stage productions.

812. _____. "Handel Today." In *Handel and the Fitzwilliam*, pp. 18–21. Cambridge: Fitzwilliam Museum, 1974. ML 141 C3 H3.

>Argues that, in spite of (or partly because of) modern revivals on Handel's operas, the true nature and scope of his genius is not fully appreciated.

813. _____. "Twenty Years of Handel Opera." *Opera* 26 (1975): 924–30.

>Reviews English opera productions since 1955, noting the successes, particularly by smaller performing societies, and making suggestions for improvements. Photographs.

814. _____. "The Recovery of Handel's Operas." In *Music in Eighteenth-Century England: Essays in Memory of Charles Cudworth*, pp. 102–14. Ed. Christopher Hogwood and Richard Luckett. Cambridge: Cambridge University Press, 1983. ML 55 C85. ISBN 0–521–23525–1.

>Authoritative discussion of the problems of modern performance, including candid remarks about specific attempts. Survey of modern productions, starting with a severely shortened *Almira* of 1878. Issues include stage practices, voice types, performance of recitatives, ornamentation, and use of authentic instruments.

Dame Janet Baker in the title role of *Giulio Cesare*. Clive Barda/London

815. _____. "Händel heute." *Musica* 38 (1984): 522–26.

Summarizes the modern revival of Handel's operas, pointing out that in the near future all of them will have been revived except for *Silla* and *Almira*. Reviews the general styles of modern productions, suggesting specific improvements.

* _____ and Knapp, J. Merrill. *Handel's Operas 1704–1726.* Oxford: Clarendon Press, 1987. 751p. ML 410 H13 D37 1986. ISBN 0–19–315219–3.

Cited above as item 433.

816. Dent, Edward J. "Handel on the Stage." *Music and Letters* 16 (1935): 174–87.

Reviews the Handel renaissance, making revealing comments about Victorian attitudes to Handel and describing twentieth-century German revivals. Makes detailed suggestions about cuts in da capo arias, orchestral practice, performance of recitatives etc.

* _____. "The Operas." In *Handel: A Symposium*, pp. 12–65. Ed. Gerald Abraham. London: Oxford University Press, 1954. ML 410 H13 A66.

Cited above as item 434.

817. Fabian, Imre and Gerhard Persché, eds. "Wege zu Händel: Beiträge zum Jubiläumsjahr." *Oper 1985: Jahrbuch der Zeitschrift "Opernwelt"*, pp. 5–41.

Presents a series of interviews and articles in journalistic style on recent Handel productions. Includes a series of photographs from stagings in the first part of 1985 of *Messiah* (particularly fascinating), *Agrippina*, and *Giulio Cesare*.

818. Hahn, Ingolf. "Problematischer Reichtum: Händels Opern auf den Bühnen unseres Landes." *Musik und Gesellschaft* 35 (1985): 67–72.

Offers an account of Handel opera production in East Germany since the early 1950s, with a pronounced political view. Plates.

819. Herbage, Julian. "Handel's *Hercules*." *Musical Times* 97 (1956): 319.

Very short review contains information on staging of oratorios and cutting of da capo arias.

820. Heuss, Alfred. "Das Semele-Problem bei Congreve und Händel." *Zeitschrift der internationalen Musikgesellschaft* 15 (1913-14): 143-56.

Describes a recent production of *Semele* in Halle, with notes on a *Jephtha* production. Commentary on *Semele*'s words and music. Brief musical examples.

821. Kersten, Wolfgang. "Überlegungen zur Darstellung der Da-Capo-Arie bei der Inszenierung von Händel-Opern." In *Konferenzbericht Halle (Saale) 1980*, pp. 42-47.

A stage director's interpretation of the aria "Nasconde l'usignole" from *Deidamia*, which he directed in 1968.

* Knapp, J. Merrill. "Editionstechnische Probleme bei Händels Opern, im Besonderen bei *Teseo*, *Poro*, *Ezio* und *Deidamia*." In *Konferenzbericht Halle (Saale) 1982*, pp. 22-32.

Cited above as item 312.

822. Larsen, Jens Peter. "Oratorium versus Oper." In *50 Jahre Göttinger Händel-Festspiele*, pp. 113-19. Ed. Walter Meyerhoff. Kassel: Bärenreiter, 1970. ML 410 H13 M59.

Argues against the modern practice of staging Handel's oratorios, suggesting that they are not merely disguised operas, but demand their own performance style. English version in item 522.

823. _____. "Handels Oratorien—szenisch oder konzertant?" *Österreichische Musikzeitschrift* 34 (1979): 339-42.

Modern Performances 237

In a discussion of the merits of staged vs. concert performances of Handel's oratorios, stresses that oratorio has its own tradition, separate from that of opera.

824. _____. "Wandlungen der Auffassung von Händels *Messias*." *Göttinger Händel-Beiträge* 1 (1984): 7-20.

Outlines performance history of *Messiah*, commenting on adaptations over the years. Clear summary relates performance style to the true nature of *Messiah*, which is neither church music nor unstaged opera. General advice to modern performers.

825. Lewin, Waldtraut. "Warum ehren wir Händel? Erinnerungen an eine Renaissance." *Musik und Gesellschaft* 35 (1985): 67-72.

Personal notes on Halle opera revivals since 1951.

826. Pietschmann, Kurt R. "Die Wiederentdeckung der Opern von Georg Friedrich Händel für das Theater des 20 Jahrhunderts." In *Georg Friedrich Händel: Ausstellung aus Anlaß der Handel-Festspiel des Badischen Staatstheaters Karlsruhe 1985*, pp. 191-266. Ed. Klaus Häfner and Kurt R. Pietschmann. Karlsruhe: Badische Landesbibliothek, 1985. ML 141 K36 H33. ISBN 3-88705-013-4.

Reproduces numerous set and costume designs and still photographs from German revivals of operas and staged oratorios in this century. Chronicles Handel opera productions in Germany, giving names of stage directors, conductors, and designers.

827. Radcliffe, Philip. "Handel Oratorio in Cambridge." In - *Handel and the Fitzwilliam*, pp. 14-17. Cambridge: Fitzwilliam Museum, 1974. ML 141 C3 H3.

Reminisces about productions of *Semele, Samson, Jephtha, The Choice of Hercules, Susanna, Saul,* and *Solomon* mounted at Cambridge from 1925-48.

828. Rüdiger, Reinhold. "Erfahrungen bei der Inszenierung von Händel-Opern." In *Konferenzbericht Halle (Saale) 1984*, pp. 133–49.

Informed account of performances of Handel's stage works early in the twentieth century. Discusses the problems of modern productions from a stage director's point of view.

* Siegmund-Schultze, Walther. "10 Jahre Händel-Pflege und Händel-Forschung." *Händel-Jahrbuch* 7–8 (1961–62): 5–33.

Cited below as item 914.

829. _____. "Händels Oper auf der modernen Bühne." *Händel-Jahrbuch* 28 (1982): 15–21.

Entirely subjective evaluation of the present state of Handel opera production.

830. Squire, William Barclay. "Handel's *Semele*." *Musical Times* 66 (1925): 127–39.

Brief general commentary and illuminating remarks on Handel revivals.

831. Stompor, Stephan. "Zu einigen neueren Aufführungen von Opern Händels." In *Konferenzbericht Halle (Saale) 1980*, pp. 48–50.

Remarks on recent Handel opera productions in Erfurt and Potsdam.

832. Wiesmann, Sigrid, ed. "Händels *Giulio Cesare*." In *Werk und Wiedergabe: Musiktheater exemplarisch interpretiert*, pp. 49–96. Bayreuth: Mühl'scher Universitätsverlag Bayreuth, 1980. ML 1700 W38. ISBN 3-921733-23-5.

Offers three articles followed by a discussion focusing on the 1978 Frankfurt production of *Giulio Cesare* by Horst Zankl (stage director) and Nikolaus Harnoncourt (musical director). Articles are a description of the background of Handel's *seria* operas by Reinhard Strohm, a discussion of problems in performance practice (especially recitative and ornamentation in da capo arias) by Martin Ruhnke and Ludwig Finscher's remarks on the production. Musical examples, plates.

833. Wolff, Hellmuth Christian. *Die Händel-Oper auf der modernen Bühne: Ein Beitrag zu Geschichte und Praxis der Opern-Bearbeitung und -Inszenierung in der Zeit von 1920 bis 1956.* Leipzig: Deutscher Verlag für Musik, 1957. 54p., 99 Plates. ML 3858 W6.

Includes a penetrating essay on twentieth-century German Handel revivals, showing how Oskar Hagen and others dealt with problems of translation and performance style. Discussions of performance practice, modern productions of operas by Baroque composers other than Handel. Plates are photographs of productions or designer's drawings, each annotated in detail.

834. _____. "*Agrippina*—1959 bis 1979." In *Konferenzbericht Halle (Saale) 1980*, pp. 51–58.

Comments on performances of *Agrippina* in Munich (1966), Zürich (1970), Altenburg (1978), Weimar (1978) and Erfurt (1978).

835. Zauft, Karin. "Probleme der deutschen Übersetzung Händelscher Libretti." In *Konferenzbericht Halle (Saale) 1982*, pp. 113–22.

Investigates problems of translating the operas into German, with special reference to *Poro*. Interesting comments on word-music relationships, but the reader's appreciation is limited because textual examples appear only in fragments.

3. The Handel Tradition: Reputation and Practice

The German word *Rezeptionsgeschichte* (literally, "reception history") denotes the study of the fate of a work or a repertoire in different times and places, critical and social attitudes towards it and its composer, its influence on other composers and, to some extent, styles of performance. Favored especially by German musicologists, *Rezeptionsgeschichte*, according to Carl Dahlhaus, is concerned with "general functional relationships between compositional models, conventional patterns of perception, aesthetic ideas, ethical norms and the roles and institutions of society" (*Foundations of Music History*. Trans J.B. Robinson, p. 67. Cambridge: Cambridge University Press, 1983).

In a particularly penetrating discussion of this field as it relates to Schumann's arrangements of Bach, Alan Lessem has suggested that "it proposes a possibly heretical alternative to the accepted view of music history as the study of artifacts which, even if historically conditioned, must, if they are to be properly understood, be cleansed of the impure accretions of time and restored to their original and authentic state" ("Schumann's Arrangements of Bach as Reception History," *The Journal of Musicological Research* 7, 1986, p. 31).

836. Anthoniecek, Theophil. *Zur Pflege Händelscher Musik in der 2. Hälfte des 18. Jahrhunderts*. Veröffentlichungen der Kommission für Musikforschung, 4. Vienna: Böhlaus, 1966. 58p. ML 410 H13 A8.

Concentrates on performances of Handel's music in Europe between 1760 and 1772. Not examined, but see the review by Edward Olleson in *Music and Letters* 48 (1967): 281.

837. Arnold, Denis. "Charity Music in Eighteenth-Century Dublin." *Galpin Society Journal* 21 (1968): 162–74.

Chronicles the achievements of Dr. Bartholomew Mosse, who continued the tradition of fund-raising concerts in Dublin from 1749 to 1773. Performances of Handel oratorios figure prominently.

* Baselt, Bernd. "Miscellanea Handeliana." In *Der Komponist und sein Adressat: Musikästhetische Beiträge zur Autor-Adressat-Relation*, pp. 60–88. Ed. Siegfried Bimberg. Wissenschaftliche Beiträge der Martin-Luther-Universität Halle-Wittemberg 1976/23, G 3. Halle: Martin-Luther-Universität, 1976.

Cited above as item 332.

838. _____. "Händel-Edition im Verständnis des 19. Jahrhunderts." In *Konferenzbericht Halle (Saale) 1984*, pp. 46–61.

Offers an account of Chrysander's complete Handel edition. Plates.

839. _____. "Thematisch-systematisches Verzeichnis der Werke Georg Friedrich Händels." *Beiträge zur Musikwissenschaft* 27 (1985): 37–47.

Summarizes the background and editorial policy of the author's new thematic catalogue (item 377).

840. _____. "Händel-Editionen zur Zeit der Wiener Klassik." In *Georg Friedrich Händel: Ausstellung aus Anlaß der Händel-Festspiele des Badischen Staatstheaters Karlsruhe 1985*, pp. 109–125. Ed. Klaus Häfner and Kurt R. Pietschmann. Karlsruhe: Badische Landesbibliothek, 1985. ML 141 K36 H33. ISBN 3-88705-013-4.

Discusses Arnold's Handel edition, giving a table of contents. Describes early German editions of Handel, offering a list of these up to 1830. Outlines early German attempts at collected editions of Handel.

841. Bernoulli, Eduard. *Quellen zum Studium Händelscher Chorwerke*. Mainz: Verlag der Kaiserin Friedrich Stiftung, 1906. 23p.

Offers a few miscellaneous observations on the conducting scores now in Hamburg. Reviews the contents of the six Supplement volumes published by Chrysander. Discusses the Serenata by Alessandro Stradella and Handel's use of it. Musical examples.

842. Beyschlag, Adolf. "Über Chrysanders Bearbeitung des Händel'schen *Messias* und über die Musikpraxis zur Zeit Händels." *Die Musik* 10 (1910–11): 143–58.

Shows that the 1902 Chrysander-Seiffert performing edition of *Messiah* is misleading in many respects. Includes a general essay on performance practice seen from the early twentieth-century perspective. Brief examples.

843. Boeringer, James. "Handel and the Moravians." *Journal of Church Music* 27 (1985): 6–9.

 Gives an impression of the Moravian community's enthusiasm for Handel's music. Describes the eighteenth-century copies of Handel's music in the Moravian archives at Bethlehem, Pennsylvania. Plates.

844. Boyd, Malcolm. "John Stanley and the Foundling Hospital." *Soundings* 5 (1975): 73–81.

 Investigates the relationship of the organist John Stanley with the Foundling Hospital. Gives details of Messiah performances there during the 1760s and 1770s.

845. Bradbury, William F. and Guild, Courtenay. *History of the Handel and Haydn Society of Boston, Massachusetts.* Vol. 2. Boston: A. Mudge, 1833–1934. Repr. New York: Da Capo Press, 1977. 185, 161p. app. ML 200.8 B72 H33 1977. ISBN 0–306–79506–X (V.2).

 Continuation of item 853.

846. Coopersmith, Jacob M. "Handelian Lacunae: A Project." *Musical Quarterly* 21 (1935): 224–29.

 Outlines an ambitious plan, never fulfilled, to complete the Handel edition, publish a thematic index, and complete Chrysander's biography.

847. Cudworth, Charles. "Fitzwilliam and Handel." In *Handel and the Fitzwilliam*, pp. 7–9. Cambridge: Fitzwilliam Museum, 1974. ML 141 C3 H3.

 Notes on Viscount Fitzwilliam's collection of Handel's music and his role in helping to inaugurate the Handel Commemoration of 1784. Also on the Barrett Lennard collection, given to the Fitzwilliam in 1902.

848. Dadelsen, Georg von. "Bach—Händel—Telemann." *Musica* 35 (1981): 29–32.

Muses on the varying *Rezeptionsgeschichten* of the three composers.

849. Darenberg, Karl H. "Georg Friedrich Händel im Spiegel Englischer Stimmen des 18. Jahrhunderts." *Händel-Jahrbuch* 7–8 (1961–62): 137–87.

Presents passages about Handel's music from English critical writings during the years 1740–1800. Useful commentary.

850. Dean, Winton. "Mattheson's arrangements of Handel's *Radamisto* for the Hamburg Opera." In *New Mattheson Studies*, pp. 169–78. Ed. George J. Buelow and H.J. Marx. Cambridge: Cambridge University Press, 1983. ML 55 M327 N5 1983. ISBN 0–521–25115–X.

Describes Mattheson's successful adaptations of *Radamisto*, including cuts, translations, transpositions of voice parts, lengthening of recitatives, etc.

851. ———. "Some Aspects of Handel Scholarship Today." *Händel-Jahrbuch* 31 (1985): 131–37.

Laments the lack of progress in Handel scholarship and reviews the author's own recent discoveries, especially with regard to the operas before 1726.

852. Decker-Hauff, Hansmartin. "Zur Händel-Rezeption in Württemberg in 1850." In *Logos musicae: Festschrift Albert Palm*, pp. 32–35. Ed. Rüdiger Görner. Wiesbaden: Franz Steiner Verlag, 1982. ML 55 P26 1982. ISBN 3–515–03535–4.

Sketches the activities of the Württemberg Handelian Wilhelm B. Dölker (1816–68).

853. Dwight, John S. and Charles C. Perkins. *History of the Handel and Haydn Society, of Boston, Massachusetts.* Vol. 1. Boston: A. Mudge, 1883–93. Repr. New York: Da Capo Press, 1977. 518p., app. ML 200.8 B7 H332. ISBN 0-306-77429-1.

Exceedingly detailed chronicle of the Society from 1815 to 1890. Reprint has a Table of Contents prepared by Judith Tick. Photographs. For volume 2, see item 845.

854. Ebling, Wolfgang. "Gervinus und die Händel-Rezeption." In *Georg Gottfried Gervinus (1805–1871) und die Musik*, pp. 20–74. Beiträge zur Musikforschung 15. Munich: Musikverlag Emil Katzbichler, 1985. ISBN 3-87397-264-6.

Examines the significant role of Gervinus, a German historian, in the founding of the German Handel Society and the collected edition. Summarizes Handel *Rezeptionsgeschichte* during the eighteenth and nineteenth centuries.

855. Edelmann, Bernd. "Händel-Aufführungen in den Akademien der Wiener Tonkünstlersozietät." *Göttinger Händel-Beiträge* I (1984): 172–99.

Reevaluates the historical importance of van Swieten's role in introducing Handel's music to late eighteenth-century Vienna. Shows that Handel's choruses were performed publicly by the Wiener Tonkünstlersozietät as early as 1778. Gives a sample program, discusses the principal participants (including Salieri) and examines surviving performance materials.

* Farncombe, Charles. "G.F. Handel Seen through Other Eyes: Testimonies and Judgements of the Composer's English Contemporaries." In *Georg Friedrich Händel. Ausstellung aus Anlaß der Händel-Festspiele des Badischen Staatstheaters Karlsruhe 1985*, pp. 41–58. Ed. Klaus Häfner and Kurt R. Pietschmann. Karlsruhe: Badische Landesbibliothek, 1985. ML 141 K36 H33. ISBN 3-88705-013-4.

Cited above as item 196.

856. Federhofer, Hellmut. "Unbekannte Kopien von Werken Händels und anderer Meister seiner Zeit." In *Festschrift Otto Erich Deutsch zum 80. Geburtstag*, pp. 51–65. Ed. Walter Gerstenberg, Jan LaRue and Wolfgang Rehm. Kassel: Bärenreiter, 1963. ML 55 D5 F4.

Lists the contents of three manuscript collections in the Diocesan archives in Graz from the 1720s, including various arias and keyboard works by Handel. In addition, there are three late eighteenth-century collections of anthem and oratorio excerpts. Interesting for the study of eighteenth-century Handel enthusiasm in Austria.

857. Fellerer, K.G. "Fortunato Santini als Sammler und Bearbeiter Händelscher Werke." *Händel-Jahrbuch* 2 (1929): 25–40.

Describes how Santini, an early nineteenth-century collector, translated and adapted Handel's works, especially sacred choral works. Musical examples.

858. _____. "Haendels *Acis und Galatea* in der Bearbeitung Mozarts (KV 566)." *Deutsches Mozartfest der deutschen Mozart-Gesellschaft 1975*, pp. 32–40. Ed. Erich Valentin. Schwetzinger: Deutsche Mozart-Gesellschaft, 1975. ML 410 M954.

Discusses Mozart's version of *Acis and Galatea*, with comments on the late eighteenth-century view of earlier music.

859. Fellinger, Imogen. "Händel in der deutschen Musikkritik des 18. Jahrhunderts." In *Georg Friedrich Händel: Ausstellung aus Anlaß der Händel-Festspiele des Badischen Staatstheaters Karlsruhe 1985*, pp. 95–108. Ed. Klaus Häfner and Kurt R. Pietschmann. Karlsruhe: Badische Landesbibliothek, 1985. ML 141 K36 H33. ISBN 3-88705-013-4.

Examines the coverage of Handel in books and articles by Mattheson, Marpurg, Scheibe, Hiller, and Reichardt.

860. Ford, Walter. "Handel's Cantatas." *Proceedings of the Royal Musical Association* 58 (1931–32): 33–42.

Period piece which is particularly illuminating on the curious *Rezeptionsgeschichte* of the cantatas.

861. Gardiner, John Eliot. "Händels Werke in historischer und in heutiger Aufführungspraxis in England." In *Bachtage Berlin: Vortzäge 1970 bis 1981*, pp. 165–74. Ed. Günther Wagner. Stuttgart: Hänssler-Verlag, 1985. ML 55 B18. ISBN 3-7751-0993-5.

Shows how twentieth-century misconceptions about Handel's music have their roots in English practices of the eighteenth and nineteenth centuries. Interesting notes on the Crystal Palace festivals during the latter part of the nineteenth century.

862. Gelles, George. "Mozart's Version of *Messiah*." *American Choral Review* 10/1 (1968): 55–65.

Points out that most editions of Mozart's arrangement are corrupt. Discusses the authentic Mozart version. Musical examples.

863. Glöckner, Andreas. "Johann Sebastian Bachs Aufführungen zeitgenössischer Passionsmusiken." *Bach-Jahrbuch* 63 (1977): 75–118.

Details Bach's copying and performance of Passion music by Keiser, Telemann, Graun, and Handel (*Brockespassion* and early disputed *Johannespassion*). Musical examples, plates, catalogue of sources.

864. Gloede, Wilhelm. "Mozart und Händel: Anmerkungen zum Bach-Händel-Jahr 1985." *Acta Mozartiana* 32 (1985): 1–7.

Comments briefly on the older composer's influence, giving examples of "Handelian" themes in Mozart.

865. Grefar-Dellin, Martin. "Händel: Fülle des Wohllauts." In *Was ist Größe? Sieben Deutsche und ein deutsches Problem*, pp. 89–108. Munich: Piper, 1985. BF 412 G64. ISBN 3-492-02941-8.

Seeks to define the greatness of Handel in a somewhat rambling survey supplemented by eighteenth-century accounts.

866. Haake, Claus. "Händel-Auffürungen durch Laienchöre." In *Georg Friedrich Händel 1685–1985: Bekenntnisse, Befunde, Berichte*, pp. 82–86. Ed. Walther Siegmund-Schultze. Haale (Saale): Georg-Friedrich-Händel-Zentrum, 1985.

Discusses modern performances by amateur choirs in the DDR. Photos.

867. Hall, Roger L. "Early Performances of Bach and Handel in America." *Journal of Church Music* 27/5 (1985): 4–7.

Describes American Handel performances of the 1780s and 1790s. Plates.

868. Hamilton, Phyllis. "Handel in the Papers of the Edinburgh Musical Society (1728–1798)." *Brio* 1/2 (1964): 19–22.

Presents documents, including a series of letters to Handel and Smith requesting scores, detailing music-making in Edinburgh in the mid-eighteenth century.

869. Harnisch, Klaus. "Telemann als Bearbeiter von Händels Oper *Riccardo I* (Hamburg 1729)." In *Die Bedeutung Georg Philipp Telemanns für die Entwicklung der europäischen Musikkultur im 18. Jahrhundert: Bericht über die Internationale Wissenschaftliche Konferenz anläßlich der Georg-Philipp-Telemann-Ehrung der DDR, Magdeburg 12. bis 18. März 1981*, pp. 114–20. Ed. Günter Fleischhauer, Wolf Hobohm, and Walther Siegmund-Schultze. Magdeburg: Zentrum für Telemann-Pflege-und-Forschung, 1983.

Examines the manuscript score of Telemann's arrangement of Handel's *Riccardo primo*, produced in Hamburg in 1729. Speculates that Handel might have used the Cluer print of 1728. Using Chrysander's questionable edition of the London original for comparison, summarizes the extensive changes, showing in brief musical examples the effect of octave transposition on heroic castrato parts.

870. Herbage, Julian. *Messiah*. London: Max Parrish & Co. Ltd., 1948. 72p. MT 115 H133 H4.

Lively and occasionally fanciful history of *Messiah* from its inception through the nineteenth century. Non-technical and essentially popular, but it provides a good summary of reception history in England. Index, plates, copious illustrations.

871. Hübler, Klaus-K. "Schönberg und Händel: Über systembedingtes Unverständnis." *Musik und Bildung* 14 (1982): 791–800.

Reflects on Schönberg's view of musical history and offers a detailed analysis of his arrangement for string quartet and orchestra of Handel's Concerto grosso Opus 6, no. 7. Musical examples.

872. Hudson, Frederick. "Die Händel-Tradition in England." *Musica* 10 (1956): 580–85.

Summarizes the essential features of the reception of Handel's music in England. Plates.

873. Johnson, Harold Earle. *Hallelujah, Amen! The Story of the Handel and Haydn Society of Boston*. Boston: Handel and Haydn Society, 1965. Repr. New York: Da Capo, 1981. XIV, 256p. ML 200.8 B72 H34 1981. ISBN 0–306–79598–1.

History of the Society affords a unique picture of Handel practice in nineteenth-century America. Appendix lists works performed by the group. Illustrations. 1981 reprint has an introduction by Richard Crawford.

874. Johnstone, H. Diack. "A Ringside Seat at the Handel Commemoration." *Musical Times* 125 (1984): 632–36.

Presents contemporary comments on the accounts of the 1784 Handel Commemoration.

875. *Katalog zu den Sammlungen des Händel-Hauses in Halle.* 7 vols. Halle: Händel-Haus, 1961–80. 331, 288, 380, 164, 292, 332, 527p. ML 136 H27 H3.

Catalogue of the Händel-Haus collection. Many items are not related to Handel. Volume 1 details the manuscripts, volumes 2, 3, and 4 include portraits and other pictures, volumes 5, 6, and 7 describe the instrument collection. Plates.

876. Koch, Annerose. "Die Bearbeitung Händelscher Opern auf der Hamburger Bühne des frühen 18. Jahrhunderts." Phil. Diss. Martin-Luther-Universität Halle-Wittenberg, 1982.

Not examined.

877. Kunze, Stefan. "Georg Friedrich Händel: Ruhm und Nachruhm." In *Karlsruher Händel-Vorträge*, pp. 5–13. Ed. Kurt R. Pietschmann and Gabriele Eikermann. Karlsruhe: Badisches Staatstheater Karlsruhe, 1985. ML 410 H13 K37.

Offers a concise, informative summary of Handel's reputation, especially in Germany, showing how he was greatly admired and even idolized until the rediscovery of Bach's St. Matthew Passion in 1829, then received less attention until the twentieth-century "Renaissance."

878. Lange, Wilgard. *Händel-Rezeption bei Felix Mendelssohn Bartholdy.* Dissertation. Martin-Luther-Universität Halle-Wittenberg, 1981.

Not examined.

879. ———. "Mendelssohns Händel-Bearbeitungen." In *Konferenzbericht Halle (Saale) 1984*, pp. 70–77.

Points out that, although Mendelssohn first encountered Handel's choral works in their reorchestrations by Mozart and Zelter, he later made considerable efforts to perform them in a more authentic manner. Examines extant organ parts written out by Mendelssohn for *Solomon* and *Israel in Egypt*. Mendelssohn's *Israel* edition stays scrupulously close to the Handel sources.

880. Larsen, Jens Peter. "Händel und Haydn." In *Konferenzbericht Halle (Saale) 1977*, pp. 25–33. Repr. *Händel-Jahrbuch* 28 (1982): 93–99.

    Assesses the effects on Haydn of hearing Handel's music performed in London, with special reference to *Israel in Egypt* and *The Creation*.

* ———. "Wandlungen der Auffassung von Händels *Messias*." *Göttinger Händel-Beiträge* 1 (1984): 7–20.

    Cited above as item 824.

881. ———. "Händel-Pflege und Händel-Bild im 20. Jahrhundert." *Österreichische Musikzeitschrift* 40 (1985): 82–88.

    Comments on modern-day Handel performances, emphasizing the author's well-known view of the distinctions between opera and oratorio performance.

882. Lebermann, Walter. "Apokryph, Plagiat, Korruptel oder Falsifikat?" *Musikforschung* 20 (1967): 413–25.

    Discusses early twentieth-century editions of spurious eighteenth-century works, including a viola concerto published as Handel in 1925. Musical examples.

* Le Huray, Peter and James Day, eds. *Music and Aesthetics in the Eighteenth and Early Nineteenth Centuries*. Cambridge: Cambridge University Press, 1981. 597p. ML 3845 M97. ISBN 0521–23426–3.

    Cited above as item 47.

883. Lenneberg, Hans. "Handel, Bach and Relative Success." *Bach: The Quarterly Journal of the Riemenschneider Bach Institute* 12/4 (1981): 22–27 and 13/2 (1982): 17–22.

   Comments on the two composers' reputations during the eighteenth century, especially as suggested by the early biographies. Takes a questionable view of Mainwaring (item 132).

884. Lynch, Robert D. "Händels *Ottone*: Telemanns Hamburger Bearbeitung." *Händel-Jahrbuch* 27 (1981): 117–39.

   Discusses Telemann's 1726 adaptation of *Ottone* for the Hamburg stage. Offers copious details on the production. Lists thirty-two Italian operas staged at the Goosemarket Theater between 1718 and 1738. Compares Handel's original setting of "Falsa imagine" with Telemann's newly composed version. Musical examples.

885. Margraf, Horst-Tanu and Max Schneider. "Die Händel-Feste in Halle." *Musica* 10 (1956): 591–98.

   Reviews the history of the modern Halle festivals with special reference to the opera productions. Photographs.

886. Marx-Weber, Magda. "Hamburger Händel-Pflege im späten 18. Jahrhundert." In *Händel und Hamburg: Ausstellung anläßlich des 300. Geburtstages von Georg Friedrich Händel*, pp. 133–40. Ed. Hans Joachim Marx. Hamburg: Karl Dieter Wagner, 1985. ML 410 H13. ISBN 3-88979-009-7.

   Describes how the Handel tradition in Hamburg, defunct since the closing of the Opera in 1738, was revived in the 1760s and 1770s.

887. Matthews, Betty. "Wesley's Finances and Handel's Hymns." *Musical Times* 114 (1973): 137–39.

   Relates how, in a time of particular turbulence in his personal life, Samuel Wesley tried to cure his financial woes by publishing Handel's hymn tunes.

888. _____. "Joah Bates: A Remarkable Amateur." *Musical Times* 126 (1985): 749–53.

Records the life and times of this eighteenth-century musical amateur, including the 1784 Handel Commemoration in which he played an important role as conductor. Illustration.

889. Miller, Miriam. "The Early Novello Octavo Editions." In *Music and Bibliography: Essays in Honour of Alec Hyatt King*, pp. 160–69. Ed. Oliver Neighbour. London: Clive Bingley Ltd., 1980. ML 55 K57 M87. ISBN 0–85157–296–0.

Reveals much about the nineteenth-century choral tradition in this brief discussion of the octavo editions which began in 1846 with *Messiah*.

890. Müller-Blattau, Joseph. "Händel und Goethe." *Händel-Jahrbuch* 1932, pp. 25–37.

Chronicles the poet's fascination with Handel.

891. Myers, Robert Manson. *Handel's Messiah: A Touchstone of Taste*. New York: MacMillan, 1948. 338p. ML 410 H13 M97.

Offers a history of Handel's years in England, as well as a chapter on the creation of *Messiah*, but the most illuminating parts of the book deal at length with *Messiah*'s reception in England and America in the late eighteenth and early nineteeth centuries. Plates, index, bibliography.

892. Palm, Albert. "Händels Nachwirkung in Frankreich." *Händel-Jahrbuch* 13–14 (1967–68): 61–82.

Examines the critical view of Handel in writings of Jérôme Joseph de Momigny, an early nineteenth-century Parisian theorist.

893. Pecman, Rudolf. "Georg Friedrich Händel in der Auffassung des Grafen Heinrich Haugwitz." In *Zur Aufführungspraxis und Interpretation der Musik von Johann Sebastian Bach*

und Georg Friedrich Händel. Georg Friedrich Händel: Ein Beitrag zum 300. Geburtstag, pp. 24–27. Ed. Eitelfriedrich Thom. Blankenburg: Kultur- und Forschungsstätte Michaelstein, 1985.

Not examined.

894. Piechocki, Werner. "Zur Geschichte des Händeldenkmals in Halle." *Händel-Jahrbuch* 31 (1985): 79–113.

 Chronicles the planning and construction of the Handel monument in Halle, offering a unique glimpse of mid-nineteenth century attitudes. Plates.

895. Porter, Cecilia Hopkins. "The New Public and the Reordering of the Musical Establishment: The Lower Rhine Music Festivals, 1818–67." *Nineteenth-Century Music* 3 (1980): 211–24.

 Documents the "restoration" of Handel's oratorios at the Festival. Tables.

896. Rackwitz, Werner. "Die Händel-Beziehungen Franz Liszts." *Händel-Jahrbuch* 7–8 (1961–62): 189–218.

 Contends that, unlike other nineteenth-century composers, Liszt and Schumann truly appreciated Handel's music. Notes on performances of Handel's oratorios and keyboard works, the 1859 German Handel celebrations, and Handel's influence on Liszt's music.

897. _____. "Zum Händel-Bild deutscher England-Reisender in der zweiten Hälfte des 18. Jahrhunderts." *Händel-Jahrbuch* 21–22 (1975–76): 109–40.

 Presents excerpts from the letters and reports of German travellers in England during the second half of the eighteenth century. Includes a fascinating description of a *Messiah* performance in Westminster Abbey.

898. _____. *Geschichte und Gegenwart der Hallischen Händel-Renaissance*. 2 vols. Schriften des Händelhauses in Halle,

1 and 2. Halle an der Saale: Händelhaus, 1977–79. 122, 131p. ML 410 H13 R12 v. 1–v. 2.

Offers an account of Handel practice in Halle, starting in 1803 with Daniel Gottlieb Türk's *Messiah* performance and finishing with the 1979 Handel Festival. Plates.

899. _____. "A.F.J. Thibauts Beiträge zur Händel-Renaissance im 19. Jahrhundert." *Händel-Jahrbuch* 26 (1980): 59–82.

Shows that the Heidelberg jurist and musical amateur A.F.J. Thibaut (1772–1840) held strong views on music, aesthetics and education which were influential in the nineteenth-century Handel Renaissance.

900. _____. "Werk und Persönlichkeit Händels im Verständnis von Musikern und Musikgelehrten des 19. Jahrhunderts." In *Konferenzbericht Halle (Saale) 1984*, pp. 8–44.

Presents quotations about Handel from Karl Marx, Goethe, Beethoven, Schubert, Chopin, Wagner, and many others. Interesting facts about Handel scholarship, especially about Gervinus and Chrysander.

901. Rätzer, Manfred. "Zur Pflege der Opern Händels an den Theatern der DDR im Zeitraum 1950–1983." In *Georg Friedrich Händel 1685–1985: Bekenntnisse, Befunde, Berichte*, pp. 64–81. Ed. Walther Siegmund-Schultze. Halle (Saale): Georg-Friedrich-Händel-Zentrum, 1985.

Includes a list of Handel operas staged in the DDR. Photos.

902. Redway, Virginia Larkin. "Handel in Colonial and Post-Colonial America." *Musical Quarterly* 21 (1935): 190–207.

Chronicles the creation of an American tradition of Handel performances. Discusses influences on the music and the appearance of Handel's music in early American publications. Plates.

The Handel Tradition

903. Robinson, Michael F. "The Decline of British Music, 1760–1800." *Studi musicali* 7 (1978): 269–84.

    Suggests that the figure of Handel was crucial to the evolution of the "great man" theory in art. Proposes that "with Handel's death something superlatively good went out of British musical composition, something that was not replaced at least for a while." Reflects on the problematic position of music in English society during the late eighteenth century.

904. Rolland, Romain. "Briefe an Félix Raugel und Aufsätze über Georg Friedrich Händel." *Händel-Jahrbuch* 9 (1963): 7–48.

    Raugel presents a series of letters written to him by Rolland during 1911–13, followed by extremely short essays on the *Water Music*, *Alexander's Feast*, *Hercules*, and *Messiah*. The materials appear in French, followed by the German translations of Dorothea Siegmund-Schultze.

905. Rudolph, Johanna. "Romain Rolland und sein Händel-Bild." *Händel-Jahrbuch* 1 (1955): 29–37.

    The epilogue to a 1944 German edition of Rolland's Handel monographs. Holds that the French scholar's most significant contribution was his understanding of the fundamental distinction between drama in opera and drama in oratorio.

906. Sadie, Stanley. "Concert Life in Eighteenth Century England." *Proceedings of the Royal Musical Association* 85 (1958–59): 17–30.

    Gives an account of concert life outside London.

907. Schneider, Frank. "Händel in Schönbergs Händen. Zur 'Konzert für Streichquartett und Orchester B-Dur in freier Umgestaltung nach dem Concerto Grosso Opus 6 Nr. 7'." *Händel-Jahrbuch* 30 (1984): 107–19.

    Documents the genesis of Schönberg's concerto on Handel's Opus 6, no. 7 and describes the work.

908. Schulze, Hans-Joachim. "Ein apokryphes Händel-Concerto in Joh. Seb. Bachs Handschrift?" *Bach-Jahrbuch* 66 (1980): 27–33.

Shows that an f minor Concerto in Bach's handwriting once thought to be a Handel work is actually the Concerto grosso Op. 1, no. 8 by Pietro Locatelli.

909. Serauky, Walter. "Bach—Händel—Telemann in ihrem musikalischen Verhältnis." *Händel-Jahrbuch* 1 (1955): 72–101.

Examines the biographical and musical relationships among the three composers, including some dubious "borrowings." Musical examples.

910. Serwer, Howard. "Händel in Bethlehem." *Händel-Jahrbuch* 27 (1981): 107–16.

Describes a series of early copies of Handel oratorios and other choral works located in the Moravian Music Foundation Archives in Bethlehem, Pennsylvania. Suggests that they may have been made in England and raises other questions about them.

911. Shaw, George Bernard. "Causerie on Handel in England." Repr. in *How to Become a Musical Critic*, pp. 272–81. Ed. Dan Laurence. London: Rupert Hart-Davis, 1960. ML 286.8 L5 S36.

Witty essay written during the early years of this century in which the author comments on Handel's exalted position in England and bemoans the use of monster choruses in performances of his oratorios.

912. Shaw, Watkins. "Handel in MT, 1844–1984." *Musical Times* 126 (1985): 85–87.

Reviews the treatment of Handel in *Musical Times*, mentioning especially important contributions and showing how the journal has reflected prevailing attitudes.

*   Shedlock, John S. "Handel's Borrowings." *Musical Times* 42 (1901): 450–52, 526–28, 596–600, 756.

Cited above as item 365.

913.   Siegmund-Schultze, Walther. "Die Musik Georg Friedrich Händels im Urteil der Deutschen Klassik." *Händel-Jahrbuch* 4 (1958): 32–70.

Presents a selection of critical comments about Handel's music, starting right after his death with Mainwaring and Mattheson, and continuing through Burney, Hawkins, Hiller, Reichardt, Herder, and Goethe. Musical examples.

914.   _____. "10 Jahre Händel-Pflege und Händel-Forschung." *Händel-Jahrbuch* 7–8 (1961–62): 5–33.

Chronicles the origins of the modern Halle Handel Festival and of the Georg-Friedrich-Händel-Gesellschaft. Summarizes the contents of the *Händel-Jahrbuch* for 1955–60. Mentions the most significant achievements of the previous decade in Händel-scholarship. Lists the major works performed at the Halle Festival during the years 1952–61.

915.   _____. "Georg Friedrich Händel als ein Wegbereiter der Wiener Klassik." *Händel-Jahrbuch* 27 (1981): 23–36.

Examines influences of Handel on the music of Gluck, Mozart, Haydn, and Beethoven. Cites one example by each composer that may have been modelled on a specific work by Handel.

916.   _____. "Händel und Brahms." *Händel-Jahrbuch* 29 (1983): 75–83.

Discusses the influence of Handel on Brahms, especially in the vocal music. Draws numerous general comparisons between the two composers.

917.   _____. "Wandlungen und Stationen. Zur wissenschaftlichen und praktischen Aneignung von Händels Werk in der DDR." *Musik und Gesellschaft* 35 (1985): 58–63.

Reviews post-war Handel practice in the DDR, both in the academic realm (where he was "freed from the falsifications of the Nazis" and "reclaimed for the German socialist heritage") and in the areas of performance. Plates.

918. _____. "Die Händel-Renaissance in der DDR." In *Georg Friedrich Händel 1685–1985: Bekenntnisse, Befunde, Berichte*, pp. 29–34. Ed. Walther Siegmund-Schultze. Halle (Saale): Georg-Friedrich-Händel-Zentrum, 1985.

General discussion of Handel practice since the early 1950s, placing it in a political context.

919. Sievers, Heinrich. "Händel und die Musik in Hannover." In *Hannoversche Musikgeschichte: Dokumente, Kritiken und Meinungen Bd. 1*, pp. 161–257. Tutzing: Hans Schneider, 1979. ML 275.8 H3 S5. ISBN 3–7952–0282–5.

Briefly reviews Handel's biographical connections with Hannover, then presents an exhaustive survey of Handel performances there from the eighteenth century until 1979. Includes a section on Handel operas in Braunschweig between 1723 and 1743. Plates.

920. Smither, Howard E. "*Messiah* and Progress in Victorian England." *Early Music* 13 (1985): 339–48.

Assesses the role played by *Messiah* in English life as reflected in the musical journals of the Victorian period, with notes on performing societies and the great festivals. Illustrations.

921. Steglich, Rudolf and Uwe Martin. "Die Göttinger Händelopern-Renaissance." *Musica* 10 (1956): 585–91.

Summarizes the history of opera productions in Göttingen during the years 1920 to 1953. Plates.

922. Stockmann, Bernhard. "Händel-Forschung in Hamburg: Friedrich Chrysander." In *Händel und Hamburg: Ausstellung anläßlich des 300. Geburtstages von Georg Friedrich Händel*, pp. 151–58. Ed. Hans Joachim Marx. Hamburg:

Karl Dieter Wagner, 1985. ML 410 H13. ISBN 3-88979-009-7.

Sketches Chrysander's career as a Handel scholar, evaluating his monumental biography and the complete works edition. Notes on the eccentric performing arrangement of *Messiah*.

923. Stompor, Stephan. "Die deutschen Aufführungen von Opern Händels in der ersten Hälfte des 18. Jahrhunderts." Ph.D. dissertation. Universität Halle, 1975. 257, 260, 89p.

Examines Handel's early German operas and chronicles the adaptations of operas for German stages in the early eighteenth century, focusing on the details of printed librettos and extant musical sources for productions in Hamburg and Braunschweig. Not examined.

924. Temperley, Nicholas. "The Limits of Authenticity: A Discussion." *Early Music* 12 (1984): 16–20.

In his part of a series of essays, the author argues, using *Messiah* as his example, that performance traditions can have their own legitimate values.

925. ———. "Handel's Influence on English Music." *Monthly Musical Record* 90 (1986): 163–74.

Shows that Handel's influence on English music during the late eighteenth and nineteenth centuries has been exaggerated. Mentions post-Handelian oratorios and concert music. Musical examples.

926. Towe, Teri Noel. "*Messiah*: Reduplication without Redundancy: Editions and Recordings Past and Present." *American Organist* 19/2 (1985): 74–90.

Presents an informative summary of *Messiah*'s treatment by editors and conductors. Includes a list of recordings. Plates.

927. Voss, Egon. "Überall die andaurende Trommete von Händels Ruhm? Eine Betrachtung über den Erfolg des *Messias*." *Neue Zeitschrift für Musik* 146/6 (1985): 5–9.

Traces the changing views of *Messiah*, starting with the eighteenth-century English reception, moving to Mozart's arrangements and finally citing an 1824 essay in which A.B. Marx sees the work as church music. Illustrations.

928. Wagner, Undine. "Konzertpodium—Museum—Forschungszentrum: Das Händel-Haus in Halle." *Musik und Gesellschaft* 35 (1985): 76–78.

Notes on the collection and programs of the Händel-Haus.

929. Walsh, T.J. "Opera in Dublin—1705–1797, the Social Scene." Ph.D. dissertation. University of Dublin, 1972.

Discusses Dublin productions of Handel works, especially during the first half of the century. Not examined.

930. Weber, William. "Intellectual Bases of the Handelian Tradition, 1759–1800." *Proceedings of the Royal Musical Association* 108 (1981–82): 100–14.

Examines the intellectual principles behind the development of a classicistic historical repertory, in which Handel's music formed a central core. Shows that these principles were embodied in the Concerts of Ancient Music.

931. Werner, Edwin. "Zur Entwicklung der Aufführungspraxis Händelscher Werke in ausgehenden 18. und im 19. Jahrhundert." In *Konferenzbericht Halle (Saale) 1984*, pp. 89–101.

Traces the increasing lack of understanding of Handelian performance practices during the late eighteenth and nineteenth centuries. Summarizes trends in nineteenth century performances of Handel's music, especially the oratorios.

932. Wolff, Christoph. "Mozart's *Messiah*: 'The Spirit of Handel' from van Swieten's Hands." In *Music and Civilization:*

Essays in Honor of Paul Henry Lang, pp. 1-14. Ed. Maria Rika Maniates, Edmond Strainchamps and Christopher Hatch. New York: Norton, 1984. ML 55 L213. ISBN 0-393-01677-3.

Examines the co-operative efforts of Mozart and Van Swieten in arranging *Messiah* for Vienna in 1789, suggesting that the latter played a more significant role than has hitherto been realized. Points out that, of all the early performances in Germany and Austria, the Viennese one of 1789 was "the least abridged and mutilated." Plates.

933. Young, Percy M. "Das Händelsche Oratorium ein Jahr nach dem Wendepunkt 1784." In *Konferenzbericht Halle (Saale) 1980*, pp. 80-85.

Describes the 1786 lenten oratorio season in London, examining the comments of a contemporary critic and noting how the groundwork was laid for the Victorian view of Handel.

934. _____. "Die englische Suche nach dem wahren Händel im 19. Jahrhundert." In *Konferenzbericht Halle (Saale) 1984*, pp. 62-69.

Begins with a brief description of the nineteenth century English view of Handel as essentially a composer of sacred choral music. Discusses nineteenth century performances of the choral music. Lively documentation.

935. _____. "Einflüße von Bach und Händel auf die Meisterwerke Edward Elgars." In *Zur Aufführungspraxis und Interpretation der Musik von Johann Sebastian Bach und Georg Friedrich Händel. Georg Friedrich Händel: Ein Beitrag zum 300. Geburstag*, pp. 27-30. Studien zu Aufführungspraxis und Interpretation der Musik des 18. Jahrhunderts, 26. Ed. Eitelfriedrich Thom. Blankenburg: Kultur- und Forschungsstätte, Michaelstein, 1985.

Not examined.

936. Zaslaw, Neal. "Handel and Leclair." *Current Musicology* 9 (1969): 183–89.

Demonstrates that Jean-Marie Leclair L'aîné must have been familiar with Handel's music.

937. Zauft, Karin. "Das Rezeptionsverhalten des 19. Jahrhunderts in seiner Auswirkung auf die Interpretation und Rezeption von Händels Opern." In *Konferenzbericht Halle (Saale) 1984*, pp. 150–56.

Examines the conflict between "authentic" and "Romantic" performance practices of Handel's operas, showing how the "Romantic" concepts were necessary and logical for the nineteenth and early twentieth century.

938. _____. "25 Händel-Opern am Landestheater Halle im Zeitraum von 34 Jahren: zu einigen Aspekten ihrer Interpretation in Vergangenheit und Gegenwart." In *Georg Friedrich Händel 1685–1985: Bekenntnisse, Befunde, Berichte*, pp. 51–63. Ed. Walther Siegmund-Schultze. Halle (Saale): Georg-Friedrich-Händel-Zentrum, 1985.

Discusses Halle opera productions. Photos.

BIBLIOGRAPHIES AND BIBLIOGRAPHIC ESSAYS

The following have been selected either for their comprehensiveness or their particular unique emphasis. Readers looking for information on particular works should consult the corresponding items in the *Händel-Handbuch* (item 377). The fifth volume of the *Handbuch*, currently in preparation, will be a bibliography.

A few books on particular genres, for example items 433 and 503, have extensive bibliographies. Keeping up with research is greatly facilitated by the use of RILM (*Répertoire internationale de littérature musicale* v. 1–, 1967–) and *The Music Index* (v. 2–, 1949–). The American Handel Society is planning a computerized Handel bibliography "as an electronic counterpart to the bibliography now in preparation in Halle" (*AHS Newsletter* I/1, April 1986, p. 4).

Abert, Anna Amalie. "Die Barockoper: Ein Bericht über die Forschung seit 1945." *Acta musicologica* 41 (1969): 154–57.

Baselt, Bernd, Siegfried Flesch, and Walther Siegmund-Schultze. "Zur Händel-Forschung: Ein Forschungsbericht 1967–1981." *Beiträge zur Musikwissenschaft* 24 (1982): 235–75.

Baselt, Bernd. "Zum Stand der Händel-Forschung: Literaturbericht 1967–81." *Beiträge zur Musikwissenschaft* 24 (1982): 238–51. (notes, pp. 268–74).

Dean, Winton. "Bibliography." In *The New Grove Handel*, pp. 167–79. New York: Norton, 1983.

Deutsch, Otto Erich. "Bibliography." In *Handel: A Documentary Biography*, pp. 863–86. London: Adam and Charles Black, 1955.

Flesch, Siegfried. "Anmerkungen zur Hallischen Händel-Ausgabe und zu einigen anderen Händel-Publikationen." *Beiträge zur Musikwissenschaft* 24 (1982): 251–65. (notes, pp. 274–75).

Hogwood, Christopher. "Select Bibliography." In *Handel*, pp. 295–98. London: Thames and Hudson, 1984.

Knapp, J. Merrill. "Zum Stand der amerikanischen Händel-Forschung." *Händel-Jahrbuch* 31 (1985): 59–60.

Koch, Annerose. "Händel-Publikationen der DDR seit 1959." In *Georg Friedrich Händel 1685–1985: Bekenntnisse, Befunde, Berichte*, pp. 94–102. Ed. Walther Siegmund-Schultze. Halle (Saale): Georg-Friedrich-Händel-Zentrum, 1985.

Mann, Alfred and J. Merrill Knapp. "The Present State of Handel Research." *Acta musicologica* 41 (1969): 4–26.

Marx, Hans-Joachim. "Bibliographie der Händel-Literatur 1979 bis 1983." *Göttinger Händel-Beiträge* 1 (1984): 201–10.

Sasse, Konrad. *Händel Bibliographie*. 2nd edition. Leipzig: VEB Deutscher Verlag für Musik, 1967.

Siegmund-Schultze, Walther. "Zur Händel-Forschung: Ein Forschungsbericht 1967–81." *Beiträge zur Musikwissenschaft* 24 (1982): 235–38. (notes, pp. 265–68).

Smith, William C. "Bibliography." In Sir Newman Flower's *George Frideric Handel: His Personality and His Times*, pp. 362–82. 3rd edition. London: Cassell & Co., 1959.

Smither, Howard E. "The Baroque Oratorio—a Report on Research since 1945." *Acta musicologica* 48 (1976): 5–76.

Taut, Kurt. "Verzeichnis des Schriftums über Georg Friedrich Händel." *Händel-Jahrbuch* 6 (1933): 1–153.

DISCOGRAPHIES

A comprehensive Handel discography, supported by the American Handel Society, has been undertaken by David Edelberg of Montreal. Readers can remain up to date by consulting current issues of the *New Schwann Record and Tape Guide*.

Allorto, R. and R. Ewerhart. "Discografia ragionata delle musiche italiane di Haendel." *L'approdo musicale* 3/12 (1960): 47–73.

Beaussant, Philippe. "Discographie des oeuvres de Haendel." In Romain Rolland's *Haendel*, pp. 295–308. Rev. ed. Paris: Éditions Albin Michel, 1975.

Dean, Winton. "Handel's Dramatic Music on Records." *Music and Letters* 39 (1958): 57–65.

Elste, Martin. "Bach-Schütz-Händel: Anmerkungen zur Geschichte ihrer Schallplatten 1888–1985." *Fono-Forum* 30 (1985): Heft 4–6.

Marx, Hans Joachim. "Händel-Diskographie I: Die Opern und Schauspielmusiken." *Göttinger Händel-Beiträge* I (1984): 211–18.

_____. "Händel-Diskographie II: Die Oratorien, Serenaden und Oden." *Göttinger Händel-Beiträge* II (1986): 267–83.

Sadie, Stanley. "The Operas of Handel." In *Opera on Record* vol. 2, pp. 26–55. Ed. Alan Blyth. London: Hutchinson, 1983. (Discography by Malcolm Walker).

Sasse, Konrad. "Verzeichnis der Schallplatten mit Werken von Georg Friedrich Händel in Deutschland für die Jahre 1952–1954." *Händel-Jahrbuch* 1 (1955): 139–49.

Schaefer, Hansjürgen. "Händel-Schallplatten." *Händel-Jahrbuch* 15–16 (1969–70): 157–63.

_____. "Händel auf Schallplatten." In *Georg Friedrich Händel 1685–1985: Bekenntnisse, Befunde, Berichte*, pp. 87–93. Ed. Walther Siegmund-Schultze. Halle (Saale): Georg-Friedrich-Händel-Zentrum, 1985.

HANDEL SOCIETIES

The American Handel Society
Department of Music
University of Maryland
College Park, Maryland
USA 20742

Georg-Friedrich-Händel-Gesellschaft
Heinrich-Schütz-Allee 33–35
3500 Kassel
Bundesrepublik Deutschland

Göttinger Händel-Gesellschaft
Hainholzweg 3/5
3400 Göttingen
Bundesrepublik Deutschland

For detailed information on Handel societies of the past, see Georg Feder, "Händelgesellschaften," *Musik in Geschichte und Gegenwart*. Vol. 5, cols. 1286–1291.

HANDEL ARCHIVE

Händel-Archiv
 Hans Joachim Marx, Director
 Musikwissenschaftliches Institut
 Universität Hamburg
 Neue Rabenstraße 13
 2000 Hamburg 36

NEWSLETTERS AND JOURNALS

Göttinger Händel-Beiträge
   v. 1–
   1984– (every two years)
   ISBN 3–7618–0779–1

Newsletter of the American Handel Society
   v. 1–
   1986– (three times yearly)
   ISSN 0888–8701

Händel-Jahrbuch
   first series v. 1–6
   1928–33
   present series v. 1–
   1955–

REVIEWS OF HALLISCHE HÄNDEL-AUSGABE EDITIONS

Series I

Vol. 1 *Alexander's Feast*
 Dean, Winton. *Music and Letters* 40 (1959): 299–301.
 Müller-Blattau, Joseph. *Die Musikforschung* 13 (1960): 379–82.

Vol. 17 *Messiah*
 Dean, Winton. *Musical Times* 108 (1967): 157–58
 Geck, Martin. *Musik und Kirche* 40 (1970): 41–43.
 Mann, Alfred. *Notes* 24 (1967–68): 337–38.
 Redlich, Hans F. "'Messiah': The Struggle for a Definite Text." *Music Review* 27 (1966): 287–93.
 Unsigned Editorial. *Music and Letters* 47 (1966): 191–97.

Vol. 31 *The Choice of Hercules* (vocal score)
 Westrup, J.A. *Music and Letters* 45 (1964): 288.

Series II

Vol. 39 *Serse*
 Raynor, Henry. *Music Review* 21 (1960): 258–59.

Series III

Vol. 1 *Dixit Dominus*
 Dean, Winton. *Musical Times* 103 (1962): 110.

Series IV

Vol. 1 *Keyboard Works I: The Eight Great Suites*
Dart, Thurston. *Music and Letters* 37 (1956): 400–403.
Smith, William C. *Notes* 13 (1955–56): 680–81.

Vol. 2 *Organ Concerti I: Op. 4, No. 1–6*
Noss, Luther. *Notes* 15 (1957–58): 145–46.
Riedel, Friedrich Wilhelm. *Musikforschung* 12 (1959): 532–33.

Vol. 3 *Eleven Sonatas for Flute and Figured Bass*
Dart, Thurston. *Music and Letters* 37 (1956): 400–403.
Smith, William C. *Notes* 13 (1955–56): 680–81.

Vol. 4 *Six Sonatas for Violin and Figured Bass*
Dart, Thurston. *Music and Letters* 37 (1956): 400–403.
Smith, William C. *Notes* 13 (1955–56): 680–81.

Vol. 5 *Keyboard Works II: Second Collection of 1733*
Crow, Rodd. *Notes* 28 (1971–72): 763–65.
Hicks, Anthony. *Musical Times* 116 (1975): 249–51.
Hoffmann-Erbrecht, Lothar. *Musikforschung* 26 (1973): 411–12.

Vol. 6 *Keyboard Works III: Individual Suites and Pieces*
Crow, Todd. *Notes* 28 (1971–72): 763–65.
Hicks, Anthony. *Musical Times* 116 (1975): 249–51.
Hoffmann-Erbrecht, Lothar. *Musikforschung* 26 (1973): 411–12.

Vol. 10/1 *Nine Sonatas for Two Violins and Basso Continuo*
Schaefer, Hansjürgen. *Musik und Gesellschaft* 22 (1972): 693.

Vol. 11 *Six Concerti Grossi, Op. 3*
Raynor, Henry. *Music Review* 22 (1961): 81–82.

Vol. 12 *Eight Concerti*
Cahn, Peter. *Musikforschung* 30 (1977): 262–63.
Crow, Todd. *Notes* 29 (1972–73): 311–14.

Vol. 14 *Twelve Concerti Grossi, Op. 6*
Rönnau, Klaus. *Musikforschung* 20 (1967): 475–79.

Vol. 17 *Keyboard Works IV: Individual Suites and Pieces 2*
Schott, Howard. *Early Music* 7 (1979): 269–73.

Supplement

Vol. 1 *Composition Lessons*
Stockmeier, Wolfgang. *Musik und Kirche* 51 (1981): 191.

INDEX OF HANDEL'S WORKS

Ach Herr, mich armen Sünder (spurious), 620, 646
Aci, Galatea e Polifemo, 249, 577, 580
Acis and Galatea, 90, 299, 314, 319, 332, 418, 558–59, 562–63, 572–73, 576–78, 581, 713, 858
Admeto, 403, 429, 469, 473
Agrippina, 248–49, 330–31, 383, 449, 486, 488, 596, 817, 834
Ah che pur troppo e vero, 600
Alceste, 76, 469, 561
The Alchemist, 571
Alcina, 382, 408, 440
Alessandro, 432
Alexander Balus, 673
Alexander's Feast, 45, 289–90, 345, 362, 364, 547–49, 555, 557, 683, 703
L'Allegro, il Penseroso ed il Moderato, 203, 299, 555, 713
Almira, 114, 204, 211, 402, 414, 456–57, 474
Amadigi, 295, 331, 425, 443, 737
Amarilli vezzosa, 403
Anthem on the Peace, 622, 627
anthems, 261, 618, 628, 634

Apollo e Dafne, 187, 329, 385, 598
Aria in d (HWV 449), 795
Arianna in Creta, 440
Ariodante, 172, 335, 382, 440
Armida abbandonata, 584, 745
Atalanta, 364, 427, 440
Athalia, 475
L'aure grate, 285

Belshazzar, 164, 311, 364, 541
Brockespassion, 184, 494, 499, 646, 863

cantatas, 15, 118, 210, 260, 389, 440, 506, 507, 590–91, 594, 599–601, 605, 607
chamber duets, 15, 592, 595
chamber music, 303, 663, 689
Chandos anthems, 534, 612–17, 626, 634, 637, 774–75
The Choice of Hercules, 469, 561, 827
church music, 71, 628, 630, 639
Ciacone (HWV 435), 771
clock music, 719
Comus, 565, 569, 582
Concerti a due cori, 667
concertos, 15, 303, 665, 667, 671, 690, 693, 717, 759

concertos, Op. 6, 368, 679, 715, 717–18, 871, 907
concertos, Op. 3, 666, 714, 717
Il Consiglio, 222
Coronation Anthems, 287, 618

Daphne, 301, 403, 414, 440, 456
Deborah, 532
Deidamia, 312, 383, 821
Delirio amoroso, 222
Dettingen Te Deum, 346
Deutsche Arien, 184, 586–88, 604, 606, 608, 795
Dixit Dominus, 249, 636, 640, 650
Donna che in ciel, 249

E partirai, mia vita, 601
Ero e Leandro, 596
Esther, 271, 317, 475, 520, 560, 616, 703
Ezio, 312, 406, 411, 475, 481

Faramondo, 479
Filli adorata e cara, 600
Floridante, 318, 731
Florindo, 300, 403, 414, 440, 456
Foundling Hospital anthem, 623, 627
Fra tante pene, 600
Funeral anthem, 316, 349–50, 627, 649, 652

Giulio Cesare, 408, 410, 415, 422, 431, 435, 445, 463, 466, 703, 798, 817, 832

Haec est regina virginum, 631, 648
harp concerto, 683, 703
Hercules, 173, 364, 469, 563, 574, 819
hymns, 651, 653

Israel in Egypt, 203, 228, 342, 527, 674, 879–80

Jephtha, 338, 363, 492, 497, 759, 820, 827
Joseph, 342, 535
Joshua, 673
Judas Maccabaeus, 364, 517, 673

keyboard music, 261, 303, 371, 656, 660–61, 668–70, 691, 707, 710, 721, 771–72, 795

Latin church music, 257, 611, 629, 632–33, 635, 641–42, 647–48, 774
Laudate pueri in D, 640, 643, 775
Laudate pueri in F, 204, 313, 611, 621, 644
Lucio Cornelio Silla, 331, 446
Lungi dal mio bel Nume, 601

Messiah, 172, 203, 261, 291, 298, 320, 334, 339, 342, 370, 374, 385, 495–96, 500, 501, 509–12, 518, 521, 523–26, 528, 530, 533, 539,

542–43, 627, 754, 760, 762, 769–70, 775–76, 778, 800, 808, 817, 824, 842, 844, 862, 870, 889, 891, 897, 920, 926–27, 932
Mi palpita il cor, 789
Muzio scevola, 271

Ne' tuoi lumi, 600
Nel dolce tempo, 600
Nero, 297, 414, 456, 474
Ninfe e pastori, 601
Nisi dominus, 328, 619, 632–33, 640, 645, 648

"Oboe" concerto in g (HWV 287), 801
Occasional Oratorio, 203, 555
Ode for St. Cecilia's Day, 45, 550, 555–56
Ode for the Birthday of Queen Anne, 126, 534, 552–53
odes, 15, 563
O numi eterni, 609
operas, 21, 108, 392, 401, 407, 408, 412, 433–34, 436–37, 440, 442, 450, 452–55, 458–62, 467, 470, 472, 474, 476, 484–85, 487, 732–33, 740–41, 746, 763–64, 812–16, 825–26, 828–29, 833, 835, 876, 901, 919, 921, 923, 937–38
opera librettos, 73, 326, 456, 477, 480
oratorios, 15, 235, 440, 472, 490–91, 502–506, 508, 513–14, 521, 529, 531, 534, 538, 544–46, 675, 738, 747, 777, 782, 794, 811, 822–23, 837
oratorio librettos, 498, 536
organ concertos, 671–72, 674, 682, 684–85, 701, 706
organ concertos, Op. 7, 337, 372
organ concertos, Op. 4, 666, 669, 684, 749, 752–53
organ music, 720
Orlando, 335, 405, 478
Ormisda, 326
Ottone, 114, 309, 428, 739, 755, 809, 884
overtures, 303; (for keyboard) 664, 712, 790

Le pari è la tua fè, 601
Il Parnasso in festa, 385, 440, 551
pasticcios, 482
Il pastor fido, 331, 418, 440
Pastorella vagha bella, 602
Poro, 312, 409, 419–21, 439, 483, 835
preludes, 710, 751, 807

Qualor l'egre pupille, 600
Qual sento io non conosciuto, 403
Qual ti riveggio o Dio, 264

Radamisto, 164, 383 438, 444, 783, 850
La resurrezione, 249, 257, 260, 296, 314, 383, 515, 798

Riccardo primo, 310, 423, 869
Rinaldo, 64, 109, 193, 318, 331, 383, 451, 471, 809
Rodelinda, 330, 431, 575
Rodrigo, 120, 248–49, 330–31, 448
Royal Fireworks Music, 384, 673, 693, 801

Saeviat tellus, 648
St. John Passion (spurious), 493, 863
Salve regina, 249
Samson, 236, 284, 323, 345, 364, 491, 537, 555, 827
Sans y penser, 589, 593, 603
Saul, 98, 203, 346, 703, 713, 827
Scipione, 330, 424
Se tu non lasci amore, 264, 324
Sei pur bella, 601
Semele, 76, 564, 556–68, 570, 575, 579, 820, 827, 830
Sento là che ristretto, 601, 616
Serse, 415, 464, 468, 766
Silete venti, 633
Siroe, 429
Six Fugues or Voluntarys, 223, 655
La Solitudine, 585
Solomon, 336, 492, 827, 879
Sonata à 5 (HVW 288), 801
sonatas, 15, 654, 657–59, 666, 680, 705
sonatas for flute and continuo, 658–59, 662–63, 681, 692, 698
sonatas for oboe and continuo, 658–59, 662–63
sonatas for recorder and continuo, 658–59, 662–63, 694–97, 699, 780, 795, 799
sonatas for violin and continuo, 658–59, 662–63, 781, 796
Son gelsamino, 591, 601
songs, 15, 322, 583, 594
Sosarme, 430
Stelle, perfide stelle, 246
Suites de pièces (1720), 164, 655–56
Susanna, 374–75, 827

Tamerlano, 431, 447
Te decus virginum, 648
Te Deum (HWV 280, "Caroline"), 627
Te Deum in A (HWV 282), 287
Teseo, 295, 312, 331, 441
Theodora, 225, 492, 540
toccata, 708–709
Tolomeo, 429
Tra le fiamme, 798
trio sonatas, 204, 666, 676–77
Il trionfo del tempo e del disinganno, 222, 260, 340, 348, 403, 519
Triumph, ihr Christen, 621
The Triumph of Time and Truth, 340, 348, 385, 497, 519, 534, 713

Utrecht Te Deum and Jubilate, 283, 534, 552, 775

Handel's Works

Venceslao, 465

Water Music, 140, 288, 321, 384, 686, 693, 810
Wedding anthem, 564

Zadok the Priest, 618

INDEX OF NAMES

Alexander the Great, 439
Angelini, Antonio, 327
Princess Anne, 214
Queen Anne, 79, 552
Albinoni, Tomaso, 26
Ariosti, Attilio, 87, 444
Arne, Thomas (senior), 90
Arne, Thomas Augustine, 103
Arnold, Samuel, 293, 302, 840
Arrigoni, Carlo, 549
Ashley-Cooper, Anthony, 225
Avison, Charles, 47, 49, 86

Bach, C.P.E., 584, 755
Bach, J.S., 220, 233, 253, 371, 393, 413, 493, 584, 691, 721, 771–72, 787, 848, 863, 867, 883, 908, 909, 935
Bates, Joah, 888
Beethoven, Ludwig van, 63, 466, 900, 915
Betterton, Thomas, 92
Blow, John, 374–75
Bokemeyer, Heinrich, 313
Bononcini, Antonio Maria, 88
Bononcini, Giovanni, 88, 191, 246, 359, 444, 464, 468
Boyce, William, 66
Brahms, Johannes, 916
Brockes, Barthold Heinrich, 110, 184, 506–507, 586

Brydges, James (Duke of Chandos) 65, 175, 247, 616
Burney, Charles, 125, 127, 913
Bussani, Francesco, 463
Buxtehude, Dietrich, 334

Campra, Andre, 415
Carissimi, Giacomo, 345, 491
Cavalli, 121, 464, 806
Cesti, Pier Antonio, 806
Chamberlayne, John, 188
Chopin, Frédéric, 900
Chrysander, Friedrich, 402, 838, 842, 900, 922
Cibber, Colley, 69
Clarke, Jeremiah, 103, 555
Clausen, Hans Dieter, 279
Clay, Charles, 719
Clayton, Thomas, 555
Cocchi, Antonio, 73
Coke, Thomas, 459–60
Colonna, Cardinal, 623–33
Congreve, William, 579
Conti, Antonio, 73, 557
Corelli, Arcangelo, 26, 257, 342, 716, 780
Corfe, James, 226
Coxe, William, 140
Cristofori, Bartolomeo, 195

281

Dalley-Scarlett, Robert, 286
De Fesch, Willem, 66
Delany, Mary, 72, 94
Denner, Balthasar, 207
Destouches, 443
Dölker, Wilhelm, 852
Draghi, G.B., 555
Dryden, John, 45, 50, 56, 62, 555, 557
Durante, Francesco, 708
Durfey, Thomas, 83

Eccles, John, 566, 568
Elgar, Edward, 935
Erba, 768

Fabricius, Johann Albert, 110
Feustking, Friedrich, 457
Fiorè, Andrea, 360
Fitzwilliam, *Viscount*, 847
Fougeroux, Pierre, 429
Franck, 114
Frederick, Prince of Wales, 81, 192, 251

Gabrieli, Giovanni, 342
Galliard, Johann Ernst, 103
Gasparini, Francesco, 25, 355, 479, 638
George I, 8, 11, 12
George II, 8, 11, 12, 70, 81, 186
George III, 8, 11, 12, 239
Gervinus, Georg Gottfried, 900
Gethin, Thomas, 185
Giardini, Felice de, 692
Gismondi, Celeste Resse ("La Celestina"), 478

Gluck, Christoph Willibald, 406, 915
Goethe, Johann Wolfgang, 890, 900
Goldoni, Carlo, 117
Granville, Bernard, 229–30, 324
Graun, Carl Heinrich, 348, 356, 489, 863
Greene, Maurice, 66, 67, 668
Grimani, Vincenzo, 248, 486

Habermann, Franz Johann, 337–38, 363, 366
Hagen, Oskar, 833, 921
Hall, James S., 311
Hamilton, Newburgh, 212, 579
Harris, James, 47, 225
Hasse, Johann Adolph, 25, 93, 420
Haugwitz, Heinrich, 893
Haussmann, Elias Gottlieb, 253
Hawkins, John, 125
Haydn, Franz Josef, 880, 915
Haym, Nicola, 428, 431, 441, 447, 463, 478, 624
Heidegger, 458, 462
Herder, J.G., 913
Hiller, Johann Adam, 859
Hogarth, William, 52
Homer, 505
Houbraken, Jacobus, 244
Hübner, Johann, 110
Hudson, Thomas, 207

Jennens, Charles, 126, 203, 528
Johnson, Samuel, 128

Names

Jonson, Ben, 571
Juvarra, Filippo, 435

Keiser, Reinhard, 114, 335, 352–54, 402, 450, 494, 506–507, 863
Kerll, Johann Casper, 339
Krieger, Johann Phillipp, 350
Kusser, Johann Sigismund, 114
Kyte, Francis, 244

La Coste, Louis, 415
La Motte, Antoine, 425, 443
Lampe, John Frederic, 90, 102, 103, 651
Leclair, Jean-Marie, 936
Legrenzi, Giovanni, 121, 360
Leo, Leonardo, 451
Linke, D., 294
Liszt, Franz, 896
Locke, Matthew, 83
Lotti, Antonio, 356

Maffei, Scipione, 73
Mainwaring, John, 125, 130, 239
Mancini, Francesco, 465
Marcello, Benedetto, 193, 557, 609
Marpurg, Friedrich Wilhelm, 859
Marx, Adolph Bernhard, 927
Marx, Karl, 900
Mattheson, Johann, 30, 135, 183, 211, 223, 450, 493–94, 506–507, 587, 850, 859
Mauro, O., 404

Medici, Ferdinard, 194–95, 248
Medici, Gian Gastone, 248
Mendelssohn, Felix, 878–79
Metastasio, Pietro, 406, 420, 475, 481, 483
Minato, Nicolo, 468
Milton, John, 56, 98, 555, 565
Monteverdi, Claudio, 806
Mosse, Bartholomen, 837
Mozart, Wolfgang, 63, 415, 557, 649, 791, 858, 862, 864, 879, 915, 927, 932
Muffat, Gottlieb, 372, 655, 679

Nardini, 781
Nares, John, 668
Noris, Matteo, 430

Orlandini, Giuseppe, 360
Ottoboni, Antonio, 435
Ottoboni, Pietro, 435, 596, 756

Palladio, Andrea, 41
Pallavicini, Carlo, 121, 488
Pallavicino, S.B., 428
Pampani, Gaetano, 465
Pamphilj, Benedetto, 222
Pancieri, 457
Perti, Giacomo Antonio, 195
Philips, Ambrose, 126
Piovene, Agostino, 447
Pollarolo, Carlo Francesco, 121, 465
Pope, Alexander, 50, 56, 100, 228, 560
Porpora, Nicola, 25, 99
Porta, Giovanni, 355

Purcell, Daniel, 103
Purcell, Henry, 83, 373–74, 376, 386, 399, 550, 553, 572

Quinault, Philippe, 441

Racine, 475
Ralph, James, 513
Rameau, Jean Philippe, 342, 527, 791
Reichardt, 913
Rich, John, 68
Richey, Michael, 110
Robinson, Anastasia, 87
Rolland, Romain, 904–905
Rolli, Paolo, 37, 73, 87, 101, 424, 430
Ronish, Martha, 271
Rossi, Giacomo, 425
Rossi, Luigi, 806
Roubiliac, Louis, 205
Ruspoli, 590

Salvi, Antonio, 248
Santini, Fortunato, 857
Sarro, Domenico, 360
Sartorio, Antonio, 121, 463
Scarlatti, Alessandro, 116, 194, 257, 327, 357–58, 389, 600, 650, 708–709, 806
Scarlatti, Domenico, 257, 368, 709, 721, 771–72
Schaum, J.O.H., 265, 840
Scheibe, Johann, 859
Schönberg, Arnold, 871, 907
Schubert, Franz, 900
Schütz, Heinrich, 349

Shaftesbury, Earl of, 56, 569
Silvani, Francesco, 448
Simpson, Redmond, 221
Smith, J.C.(elder), 140, 201, 202, 294, 430, 554, 569, 585
Smith, J.C. (younger), 103, 125, 140, 218, 516, 668
Smollett, Tobias, 50
Snow, Valentine, 245
Stampiglia, 468
Stanley, John, 844
Steffani, Agostino, 248, 252, 360, 592, 595
Stradella, Alessandro, 347, 841
Swiney, Owen, 77

Tacitus, 438
Taylor, John, 206, 233
Taylor, Sedley, 361
Telemann, Georg Philipp, 114, 213, 333, 336, 351, 364, 450, 494, 506–507, 586, 848, 863, 869, 884, 909
Theile, Johann, 114
Thibault, A.F.J., 899
Torelli, Giuseppe, 26
Turk, Daniel Gottlieb, 898
Tyers, Jonathan, 205

Urio, Francesco, 346

Van Swieten, Gottfried, 855, 932
Vignati, Giuseppe, 360
Vinci, Leonardo, 25, 420
Vivaldi, Antonio, 26, 636, 716, 718

Wagner, Richard, 900
Walsh, John, 664, 666, 696
Waltz, Gustavus, 241
Weiss, Johann Sigismund, 692, 698
Weldon, John, 624
Wesley, Samuel, 887
Whatman, James, 304

Zachow, Friedrich Wilhelm, 106, 113, 254, 620
Zelter, Carl Friedrich, 879
Zeno, Apostolo, 465
Ziani, Marc Antonio, 121, 448

INDEX OF AUTHORS

Abraham, Gerald, 15, 142, 381
Alexandre-Debray, Janine, 143
Allen, Burt, 490
Andrieux, Maurice, 1
Anthoniecek, Theophil, 836
Ardry, Roger, 491
Arlt, Jerry Ann, 492
Arnold, Frank, 722, 837
Artz, Frederick, 27
Avery, Emmett, 89
Avison, Charles, 47, 49

Bach, C.P.E., 723–24
Baker, C.H. Collins, 65
Baker, Muriel I., 65
Barber, Elinore, 283
Barnett, Dene, 725–29
Bartlett, Clifford, 654
Bartlett, Ian, 66
Baselt, Bernd, 331–33, 377, 382, 401–404, 493, 583, 611, 655, 838–40
Bate, Walter Jackson, 28
Becker, Heinz, 180, 383, 494
Beechey, Gwilyn, 284, 558
Beeks, Graydon, 495, 612–17
Bell, A. Craig, 181, 378
Bennett, Joseph, 334
Bense, Lieselotte, 618
Benson, J. Allanson, 496
Benzoni, Gino, 115

Bernoulli, Eduard, 841
Bernstein, Walter, 730
Best, Terence, 559, 656–64, 731
Beyschlag, Adolf, 842
Bianconi, Lorenzo, 405
Bill, Oswald, 584
Bimberg, Guido, 406–12, 732–33
Blandford, W.F.H., 384
Blunt, Anthony, 29
Boeringer, James, 843
Boetticher, Wolfgang, 497
Bourne, T.W., 619
Boyd, Malcolm, 285, 585, 844
Boyden, David, 734
Bradbury, William, 845
Brainard, Paul, 413
Braun, Werner, 16, 182–84, 414, 586–87, 620–21
Bredenfoerder, Elisabeth, 498
Brieg, Werner, 665
Britsch, Edwin, 499
Brown, Leslie, 415
Brown, Patricia, 286
Brownell, Morris, 560
Browning, J.D., 128
Buelow, George, 30–32
Bukofzer, Manfred, 17
Bunners, Christian, 588
Burnett, Henry, 67

Burney, Charles, 123–24
Burrows, Donald, 144, 185–87, 271, 287–91, 416, 500, 547, 622–28, 666
Burt, Nathaniel, 33

Carswell, John, 2
Castriota, Alessandra, 385
Celletti, Rodolfo, 417
Chapman, Clive, 68
Chisholm, Duncan, 418
Chrysander, Friedrich, 145, 188, 667
Cibber, Colly, 69
Clausen, Hans Dieter, 258
Collins, Michael, 735
Cooper, Barry, 548, 668–69
Coopersmith, J.M., 189, 292–93, 846
Coxe, William, 125
Cudworth, Charles, 190, 847
Cuming, Geoffrey, 501
Cummings, Graham, 419–21

Dadelsen, Georg von, 848
Dahlhaus, Carl, 18
Dale, Kathleen, 670
Dammann, Rolf, 34
Darenberg, Karlheinz, 35, 849
Dart, Thurston, 191, 736
Daub, Peggy, 70, 192
Day, James, 47
Dean, Winton, 126, 147, 294–95, 335, 422–23, 502–503, 549, 561–62, 737–41, 811–15, 850–51
Dearnley, Christopher, 71

Decker-Hauff, Hansmartin, 852
Delany, Mary, 72
Della Seta, Fabrizio, 193
Dent, Edward, 116, 148, 386, 434, 816
Derr, Ellwood, 336, 742
Deutsch, Otto Erich, 149
Dietz, Hanns-Berthold, 504
Dixon, Graham, 629
Dobrée, Bonamy, 36
Donington, Robert, 743–44
Dorris, George, 73
Downes, John, 74
Dressler, Carolyn, 745
Drummond, Pippa, 671
Duck, Leonard, 259
Dwight, John, 853

Ebling, Wolfgang, 854
Eckardt, Hans, 104
Edelmann, Bernd, 855
Eisenschmidt, Joachim, 746
Elkin, Robert, 75
Erdmannsdörffer, Bernhard, 4
Eschenburg, Johann J., 124
Ewerhart, Rudolf, 260, 296

Fabbri, Mario, 194–95
Fabian, Imre, 817
Farley, Charles, 672
Farmer, Henry, 673
Farncombe, Charles, 196
Fassini, Serto, 37
Fauchier-Magnan, Adrien, 5
Federhofer, Hellmut, 856
Fedossejew, Iwan, 505
Fellerer, K.G., 857–58

Authors

Fellinger, Imogen, 859
Fellowes, Edmund, H., 261
Ferrero, Mercedes, 435
Feustking, Friedrich, 297
Finscher, Ludwig, 832
Fiske, Roger, 76, 674
Fleischhauer, Günter, 197, 675, 747
Flemming, Willi, 105
Flesch, Siegfried, 146, 377, 676–77
Flower, Newman, 150
Flummerfelt, Joseph, 106
Ford, Walter, 860
Fortune, Nigel, 21
Foss, Michael, 38
Frederichs, Henning, 506–507
Fuld, James, 298
Fuller, David, 387, 748–49
Fuller-Maitland, J.A., 19, 262
Funkhouser, S.A., 678

Gardiner, John Eliot, 861
Gay, Peter, 39
Geering, Arnold, 589
Gelles, George, 862
Gellrich, G., 679
Geminiani, Francesco, 750
Gibson, Elizabeth, 77
Gille, Gottfried, 630
Glöckner, Andreas, 863
Gloede, Wilhelm, 864
Goebels, Franzpeter, 751
Goldoni, Carlo, 117
Gooch, Byran, 78
Gorali, Moshe, 508
Gorini, Roberto, 631

Gottlieb, Robert, 680
Gould, Albert, 681
Grant, Kerry, 127
Greenacombe, John, 198
Grefar-Dellin, Martin, 865
Gregg, Edward, 79
Gress, Johannes, 199
Grout, Donald Jay, 436
Gudger, William, 337–39, 509–10, 682–85, 752–54
Guild, Courtenay, 845
Gwacharija, Washa, 437–39

Haake, Claus, 866
Häfner, Klaus, 200
Hagstrum, Jean, 40
Hahn, Ingolf, 818
Hall, James S., 201–202, 299, 511–12, 632–33, 755
Hall, Martin, 755
Hall, Roger, 867
Halsband, Robert, 128
Halton, Ragnhild, 80
Hamilton, Phyliis, 868
Hansell, Sven, 756–58
Harnisch, Klaus, 869
Harnoncourt, Nikolaus, 759
Harris, Ellen, 388–89, 440, 513, 590–91
Harris, James, 47, 132
Harris, John, 41
Hawkins, John, 129
Hazard, Paul, 42, 43
Heap, Harold, 550
Heawood, Edward, 272
Hempel, Eberhard, 44
Hendrie, Gerald, 634

289

Henking, Arwed, 760
Herbage, Julian, 514, 563, 819, 870
Herder, J.G., 139
Heriot, Angus, 20
Hervey, John, 81
Heuss, Alfred, 820
Hicks, Anthony, 203–204, 273–74, 379, 515–16, 551, 564–65, 635
Highfill, Philip, 82
Hill, Cecil, 686
Hill, Robert, 687
Hiller, Johann Adam, 139
Hinsch, Hinrich, 300–301
Hirsch, Paul, 302
Hodgkinson, Terence, 205
Hoffmann, Hans, 153
Hofmann, Klaus, 688
Hogwood, Christopher, 154, 761
Holborn, Hajo, 6
Hollander, John, 45
Hopkinson, Cecil, 303
Horton, John, 689
Hübler, Klaus, 871
Hudson, Frederick, 275–76, 304–305, 517, 872
Hume, Robert, 83, 84, 91, 459–62, 783
Hutchings, Arthur, 690

Illing, Robert, 307–308
Isotta, Paolo, 636

Jaacks, Gisela, 107
Jackson, David, 206
Jacobi, Peter, 518
Jensen, H. James, 46
Johnson, Harold, 873
Johnstone, H. Diack, 306, 637, 874
Jones, Ann, 762
Jones, William, 638
Jung, Hermann, 390

Kahle, Felix, 691
Keates, Jonathan, 155
Kenny, Shirley, 85
Kerslake, John, 207
Kersten, Wolfgang, 821
Keynes, Milo, 208–209
Kimbell, David, 340, 441–43
King, Alec Hyatt, 277
Kinnear, Betty, 307–308
Kinsky, Georg, 264
Kirkendale, Ursula, 210
Kivy, Peter, 130
Knapp, J. Merrill, 85, 177, 211, 309–12, 433, 444–49, 519, 592, 763–64
Kniseley, S. Philip, 593
Koch, Annerose, 876
Koller, Heide, 450
Krause, Peter, 265
Krones, Hartmut, 767
Kubik, Reinhold, 451, 692
Kümmerling, Harald, 313
Kuhn, Ronald, 768
Kunze, Stefan, 452–53, 877

Labie, Jean-François, 156
Lam, Basil, 639, 693
Landon, H.C. Robbins, 157

Authors

Lang, Paul Henry, 158–59
Lange, Wilgard, 878–79
Langley, Hubert, 566
Larsen, Jens Peter, 278–79, 341, 520–25, 766, 769–70, 822–24, 880–81
Larsson, Roger, 86
LaRue, Jan, 280–81
Lasocki, David, 694–99
Leavis, Ralph, 342
Le Huray, Peter, 47
Leichtentritt, Hugo, 160, 391
Lenneberg, Hans, 314, 883
Leopold, Silke, 454, 526–27
Levin, Lia, 700
Lewin, Waldtraut, 825
Lewis, Anthony, 21, 392, 567, 594
Libin, Laurence, 314
Lincoln, Stoddard, 552, 568
Lindemann, Frayda, 393
Lindgren, Lowell, 22, 87–88
Lindley, Mark, 771–72
Lipking, Lawrence, 48
Lippman, Edward, 49
Loewenberg, Alfred, 455
Longaker, Mark, 131
Lonsdale, Roger, 50
Lord, Phillip, 90
Lowenthal, Ruth, 212
Lutz, Martin, 343
Lynch, Robert, 456–57, 884

MacClintock, Carol, 773
Maertens, Willi, 213
Mainwaring, John, 132–34
Mann, A.H., 262

Mann, Alfred, 51, 135, 214–21, 315, 344, 528, 595, 765, 774–77
Margraf, Horst-Tanu, 885
Martin, Clarence, 778
Martin, Uwe, 921
Marx, Hans Joachim, 108, 161, 222–24, 597–98
Marx-Weber, Magda, 886
Massenkeil, Günther, 345
Mather, Betty, 779
Matheson, Johann, 136, 139
Matthews, Betty, 225–27, 569, 887–88
Mayo, John, 599–601
McCarthy, Margaret, 228
McGrady, Richard, 780
McGuiness, Rosamund, 553
McLean, Hugh, 229–30
Meier, Heinz, 529
Melkus, Eduard, 781
Meyer, Ernst, 765, 782
Meyer, Reinhart, 109
Milhous, Judith, 91, 92, 458–62, 783
Miller, Miriam, 889
Millner, Frederick, 93
Mohr, Wilhelm, 701
Monson, Craig, 463
Montagu, Jeremy, 23, 784
Morelli, G., 231
Morgan, Wesley, 640
Morley, Max, 702
Moser, H.J., 232
Mozart, Leopold, 785–86
Mühne, Christian, 602
Müller-Blattau, Joseph, 162–63, 554, 890

Mueller von Asow, Erich, 164–65
Mueller von Asow, Hedwig, 165
Music, David, 703
Myers, Robert M., 94, 555, 891

Nalbach, Daniel, 95
Neumann, Frederick, 787–88
Neville, Don, 266
Newman, Joel, 704
Newman, William, 705
Nicoll, Allardyce, 96
Nicolson, Harold, 137
Nielson, N.K., 706

Ober, William, 233
Ornstein, Doris, 789
Ostergren, Eduardo, 556
Osthoff, Wolfgang, 464
Owen, John, 7

Palent, Andrea, 641–42
Palisca, Claude, 24
Palm, Albert, 892
Parker-Hale, Mary Ann, 643–45
Patterson, William, 570
Paulson, Ronald, 52
Pauly, Paul, 707
Pecman, Rudolf, 166, 465–66, 893
Perkins, Charles, 853
Perschë, Gerhard, 817
Pestelli, Giorgio, 708–709
Pfeiffer, Christel, 710
Picker, Martin, 316

Piechocki, Werner, 894
Pietschmann, Kurt, 826
Plumb, John, 8
Poladian, Sirvart, 467
Pollart, Gene, 711
Pont, Graham, 712, 790–91
Ponter, Cecilia, 895
Powers, Harold, 468
Price, Curtis, 97, 571, 485
Price, Percival, 713
Price, Robert, 132
Prout, Ebenezer, 346–48

Quantz, Johann Joachim, 792–93
Quazza, Guido, 9

Rackwitz, Werner, 234, 469, 794, 896–900
Radcliffe, Philip, 827
Ratzer, Manfred, 901
Rangel-Ribeiro, Victor, 795
Rathje, Jürgen, 110
Raugel, Felix, 603
Raynor, Henry, 53
Redder, Jutta, 796
Redlich, Hans, 530, 714–15
Redway, Virginia, 902
Reich, Herbert, 349–50
Reichardt, Johann, 138
Rendall, E., 572
Ringer, Alexander, 235
Rinkel, Lawrence, 98
Roberts, John, 351–60
Robinson, Michael, 99, 903
Robinson, Percy, 361–62
Roche, Elizabeth, 797

Authors

Rockstro, William, 167
Rogers, Patrick, 100, 573
Rogerson, Brewster, 54
Rolland, Romain, 168, 904
Ronish, Martha, 267
Roscoe, Christopher, 236
Rose, Gloria, 118
Rudolph, Johanna, 169, 604, 905
Rüdiger, Reinhold, 766, 828
Ruhnke, Martin, 832

Sadie, Julie Anne, 798
Sadie, Stanley, 716, 906
Sasse, Konrad, 237, 470, 765
Savage, Alan, 799
Schere, Barrymore, 471
Schering, Arnold, 531, 646
Schickling, Dieter, 238
Schildkret, David, 800
Schmitz, Eugen, 605
Schneider, Frank, 907
Schneider, Max, 885
Schoelcher, Victor, 170
Schollum, Robert, 767
Scholz, Rudolf, 394
Schrade, Leo, 557
Schubart, C.F.D., 139
Schulze, Hans-Joachim, 908
Schumann, Reinhold, 10
Scott, Arthur, 11
Scouten, Arthur, 89
Segel, Harold, 55
Seifas, Natalie, 717–18
Seiffert, Max, 363–64, 606
Serauky, Walter, 111, 171, 397, 607, 647, 909

Serwer, Howard, 317, 532, 910
Shaw, George Bernard, 911
Shaw, Watkins, 533, 648, 912
Shedlock, John, 365–66
Siegmund-Schultze, Dorothea, 56
Siegmund-Schultze, Walther, 139, 172–74, 367, 395–97, 472, 534–35, 574, 649, 765–66, 829, 913–18
Sievers, Heinrich, 919
Silbiger, Alexander, 368
Simon, Jacob, 175
Sinclair-Stevenson, Christopher, 12
Sittard, Josef, 112
Smith, Ruth, 536
Smith, William C., 140, 150, 176, 239–44, 268, 282, 318–21, 380, 473, 537
Smither, Howard, 538, 920
Solomon, Jon, 575–76
Sorenson, Scott, 245
Squire, William Barclay, 269, 322, 577, 719, 830
Stahura, Mark, 323
Stauffer, Donald, 141
Steblin, Rita, 246
Steele, John, 650
Stefani, Gino, 119
Steglich, Rudolf, 578, 608, 921
Stenzl, Jurg, 539–40
Stevenson, Robert, 651
Stockmann, Bernhard, 922
Stompor, Stephan, 474, 831, 923
Streatfeild, Richard, 101, 177, 247, 324

Strohm, Reinhard, 25, 248–49, 475–84, 832
Stutzenberger, David, 541
Summerson, John, 57
Szonntagh, Eugene, 250

Talbot, Michael, 26, 325
Tapié, Victor-Lucien, 58
Taylor, Carole, 251
Taylor, Sedley, 369
Telle, Karina, 398
Temperley, Nicholas, 924–25
Thom, Eitelfriedrich, 801–802
Thomas, Gunter, 113
Timms, Colin, 252, 326
Tobin, John, 370, 542–43
Tosi, Pietro, 803–805
Towe, Teri Noel, 926
Trowell, Brian, 485, 579
Turberville, A.S., 13

Vaussard, Maurice, 14
Voss, Egon, 927
Vlad, Roman, 253

Wagner, Undine, 928
Walker, Arthur, 270
Walsh, T.J., 929
Watanabe, Keiichiro, 327–29
Watson, Rivka, 508
Weaver, Norma, 120
Weaver, Robert, 120
Webb, Ralph, 544
Weber, William, 930
Weinstock, Herbert, 178
Werner, Edwin, 652, 931
Westrup, Jack, 21, 806

Wieber, Georg-Friedrich, 545
Wiesmann, Sigrid, 832
Williams, John G., 399
Williams, Peter, 254, 371, 720–21, 807
Wilson, J. 653
Windszus, Wolfram, 580
Wishart, Peter, 808
Wittenkower, Rudolf, 59
Wolff, Christoph, 932
Wolff, Hellmuth Christian, 21, 60, 102, 114, 121, 486–89, 609, 809, 833–34
Wollenberg, Susan, 372
Wood, Bruce, 810

Young, Percy, 61, 62, 103, 125, 179, 255–56, 546, 765, 933–35

Zander, Ernst, 581
Zanetti, Emilia, 257, 610
Zanetti, Roberto, 122
Zankl, Horst, 832
Zaslaw, Neal, 936
Zauft, Karin, 63, 835, 937–38
Zgorzelecki, Andrzej, 400
Zimmerman, Franklin, 373–76, 582
Zobeley, Fritz, 330
Zottos, Ian P., 64